S0-ABU-881

Don't Get Taken!

Also by Steven Mitchell Sack:

THE SALESPERSON'S LEGAL GUIDE (co-author)

DON'T GET TAKEN!

A Preventive Legal Guide to Protect Your Home, Family, Money, and Job

Steven Mitchell Sack

Member of the New York Bar

McGraw-Hill Book Company

New York St. Louis San Francisco Bogotá Guatemala
Hamburg Lisbon Madrid Mexico Montreal Panama Paris
San Juan São Paulo Tokyo Toronto

The author has used fictitious names and dates throughout this book. Any similarity to actual persons, places, or events is purely coincidental.

Copyright © 1985 by Steven Mitchell Sack

All rights reserved. Printed in the United States of America. Except as permitted under the Copyright Act of 1976, no part of this publication may be reproduced or distributed in any form or by any means, or stored in a data base or retrieval system, without the prior written permission of the publisher.

2 3 4 5 6 7 8 9 D O C D O C 8 7 6 5

ISBN 0-07-054398-4

LIBRARY OF CONGRESS CATALOGING IN PUBLICATION DATA

Sack, Steven Mitchell,
Don't get taken!
Includes index.
1. Law—United States—Popular works. I. Title.
KF387.S225   1985   349.73   84-956
ISBN 0-07-054398-4   347.3

Book design by Virginia M. Soulé

To my parents, Judith and Bernard,
who taught me that knowledge is power.

Author's Note

The information in this book is the author's attempt to reduce complex and confusing law into practical business and personal strategies. These strategies are meant to serve as helpful guidelines—points to focus upon—when entering a particular situation or transaction. They are not intended as legal advice per se, because laws often vary considerably throughout the fifty states, and the law can only be interpreted properly after analyzing a person's particular facts and needs. Thus, if you have any questions regarding the applicability of any of the information in this book, consult a lawyer, accountant, or other professional.

In addition, *Don't Get Taken!* is sold with the understanding that the publisher is not engaged in rendering legal, accounting, or other professional service. If legal advice or other expert assistance is required, the services of a competent professional should be sought.

Acknowledgments

I would like to thank the following individuals for assisting me in the preparation of this book.

First, I express my gratitude to my literary agent, Julia Coopersmith, for her capable vision and guidance.

In addition, I offer my warmest appreciation to friend and fellow attorney, Stanley M. Spiegler, who reviewed portions of the manuscript and taught me more about the practice of law than he could ever realize.

Special thanks are also directed to the following attorneys who have counseled and suggested changes in the manuscript relative to their particular expertise: Julius Kamhi, Jack Hirsch, Alan Feingertz, Martin Fogel, James Eagen, Alan Lashley, and Neil Shayne. Accolades are also given to Carole Roland for her capable secretarial skills, paralegal Heather White for her competent research assistance, and to my editor, Ken Stuart, for his faith and encouragement.

The New York City Department of Consumer Affairs is cited for the helpful suggestions on avoiding contractor abuses, as well as the United States Government Printing Office for its useful information in fighting mail fraud and enforcing the safety rights of workers (OSHA).

I would also like to extend my gratitude to Barbara Bernstein, Director of the Nassau County chapter of the New York Civil Liberties Union, for permitting me to incorporate excerpts from the excellent *Civil Liberties at Work* handbook, and Regina Carlson, Executive Director for New Jersey GASP, Inc., for enabling me to include helpful strategies for employees who wish to work in a smoke-free environment which are contained in several GASP publications. Thanks are also given to Donald Waldron for his comments about employment agency abuses; to the Bureau of Wholesale Sales Representatives for its information on how to buy a used car properly; to Robert Coulson, president of the American Arbitration Association, for his assistance and materials contained in the arbitration chapter; to the accounting and consulting firm of Coopers & Lybrand for their information about how long you should save your business and personal records; to Time Inc. for its chart on taxpayer odds of an audit; to the Bureau of Wholesale Representatives for information on used-car abuses; and to Julius Blumberg, Inc., legal publisher, for permitting me to reprint their general release form.

Finally, once again, I wish to express my appreciation and gratitude to my father, whose insight and encouragement helped make this book a reality.

Contents

Acknowledgments   ix

How to Use This Book   xv

Part I: Strategies to Protect Your Job   1

Chapter 1. All about Your Job   3

Introduction • How to Be Hired Properly • Checklist of Key
Negotiating Points • Summary of Steps to Take to Be Hired
Properly • Enforcing Your On-the-Job Rights • How to Pro-
tect Your Rights • How to Enforce Your Rights • Health and
Safety in the Workplace • On-the-Job Injuries and Workers'
Compensation • Working in a Smoke-Free Environment •
Protecting Valuable Ideas • Summary of Steps to Take while
Working for Your Employer • Asserting Your Post-Termina-
tion Rights • What to Do when You Are Fired • Negotiating
Points to Maximize Post-Termination Benefits • Additional
Points to Remember when You Are Fired • How to Resign
Properly • Summary of Steps to Take after You Resign or Are
Fired

Part II: Strategies to Protect Your Money   119

Chapter 2. You and the IRS   121

Introduction • How a Dispute Arises • How Returns Are Selected for Audit • What Are Your Chances of an IRS Audit? •
What to Do if You Are Notified of an Audit • Your Rights to
an Appeal • What Is the Best Appeals Route? • Summary of
Tax Rules to Save Money and Reduce Tax Audits (Auto Use,
Business Gifts, Parties, Travel Expenses, Convention Expenses and Business Seminars, Business Meals and Entertainment Expenses) • How Long Should You Save Your Records?

Chapter 3. Avoiding Phony Business and Investment
          Schemes   143

Introduction • Abusive Tax Shelters • Investment and Business Opportunity Frauds • Avoiding Franchise Abuses • Land Fraud and Other Real Estate Ripoffs • Avoiding Problems with Real Estate Brokers • Home Improvement and Building Contractor Abuses • What You Should Know about Mail Fraud • Used-Car Abuses • Avoiding Car Repair Abuses • Employment Agency, Search Firm, and Career Counseling Abuses

Chapter 4. Protecting Yourself when Purchasing a
          Computer for Your Business or Home   193

Introduction • Avoiding Exploitation before Making Your Purchase • Specific Negotiating Points to Consider (Software, Hardware, Service Bureau Contracts) • How to Avoid Problems before They Occur

**Part III: Strategies to Protect Your Family and
          Home   207**

Chapter 5. All about Accidents   209

Introduction • How to Prove Injuries • Checklist of Recoverable Damages • Proving Liability • Shopping-Related Accidents • Injuries from Faulty Products • What to Do in an Auto Accident • Accidents at Home • On-the-Job Accidents • Common Carrier Accidents • Final Words on the Subject of Accidents

Chapter 6. How to Get the Most from Your Lawyer   232

Introduction • Determining when You Need a Lawyer • Finding a Lawyer • The Initial Interview • Should You Hire the Lawyer You Have Met? • Confirming Your Arrangement • Additional Points about Fees • Documenting Legal Fees • Other Items to Clarify at the Interview • Problems Encountered after You Hire the Lawyer • Should You Change Your Lawyer? • Should You Appeal a Case? • Summary of Steps to Use Your Lawyer Effectively

Chapter 7. Making Small Claims Court Work for
You   259

Introduction • Who May Be Sued? • Do You Have a Valid
Claim? • Where to Sue • What Can You Sue For? • Starting
the Lawsuit • The Defendant's Response • Your Duties as
the Moving Party • Preparing for Trial • The Trial • Obtaining Judgment • Some Minor Procedural Points • Strategies if
You Are Sued in Small Claims Court • Strategies to Help You
Win Your Case (Automobile Accident Negligence Cases, Consumer Product Purchase Cases, Improper Work, Labor, and
Service Cases, Wrongful Taking and Bailment Cases, Insurance Policy Cases, Goods Sold and Delivered Cases, Loan
Cases, Assault and Battery Cases) • Summary of Steps to Increase Your Success in Small Claims Court

Chapter 8. All about Arbitration   286

Introduction • How to Obtain Arbitration • Summary of
Steps Leading to the Hearing • The Hearing • How to Increase Your Chances of Success in Arbitration • What to Do
after Obtaining a Judgment • A Word about Mediation

Chapter 9. Avoiding Collection Agency Harassment   304

Introduction • When Does the Law Apply? • What Collectors
Cannot Do • Collection Agency Efforts to Find You • What to
Do when You Are Contacted • Getting the Collection Agency
off of Your Back • How to Remedy Abuses • Summary of
Steps to Limit Collection Abuse

Glossary   318

Bibliography   328

Index   331

How to Use This Book

This book was written to save you money and aggravation.

Like most Americans, you probably know very little about the way the law affects your life. But, without this knowledge, there is a good chance you will be exploited, particularly in business and financial matters. As a practicing lawyer, I *see* the mistakes people make. Individuals rush into deals without investigating potential employers or business partners. They purchase computers, automobiles, real estate, even tax shelters, without understanding the fine print. Even worse, they fail to take simple steps to protect their job security and earnings.

The consequences of these acts are often very costly. However, unnecessary problems can be avoided if you know what to do. One of the most frustrating aspects of practicing law is telling a client he waited too long before deciding to sue, or that a case could have been worth a great deal of money if the right moves had been made. In fact, millions of dollars are lost each year by individuals who have valid claims, but who fail to take appropriate action.

That is the purpose behind *Don't Get Taken!* Since we live in a litigious world, it is essential to know how to protect your job, money, family, and home.

I learned this even before I was admitted to practice law. My grandmother fell in a supermarket and broke her hip. She told bystanders she was okay because she was embar-

xvi   Don't Get Taken!

rassed to ask for help. Despite her injuries, she managed to hobble out of the store and cross the street to her apartment before collapsing on her bed. At the trial, the store owner's lawyer argued that her hip could have been broken any time she was not in the store. My grandmother had little choice but to accept a settlement possibly ten times smaller than she might have obtained had she requested an ambulance to take her directly to a hospital.

That is the kind of aggravation I want you to avoid.

The following pages contain practical strategies for many of the personal business decisions you will make throughout your life. Whatever your background, education, and experience, this information will help detect problems *before* they occur, and make you aware of the legal consequences of your acts. If litigation becomes necessary, your chances of success and value of a claim will increase substantially because you will recognize potential exploitation and know what to do about it.

These guidelines were written to give you the edge. For example, in addition to knowing the key terms to discuss during employment negotiations, you will learn the proper steps to take if you resign or are fired from your job. I've included strategies to protect you when investing in tax shelters, business deals, franchises, real estate, business or personal computers, and numerous other items. You will learn how to hire a real estate broker, career counselor, and building contractor. In addition, since the subject of taxes is an area of vital concern, I wanted you to know how to reduce the odds of being audited by the IRS. The guidelines in the tax chapter will tell you what to do if you receive an audit notice, how to conduct yourself at the examination, and whether or not to file an appeal, besides offering ways to increase business deductions and tax savings.

It is easy to use this book. *Don't Get Taken!* is divided into three sections: strategies to protect your job, strategies to protect your money, and strategies to protect your home and family. These topics were chosen because they are important areas where Americans are frequently misinformed.

The majority of the text is written in a checklist format and I have included numerous lists of questions to ask and letters to send to protect your rights. In addition, I have provided a brief table of contents at the beginning of each chapter. This will enable you to locate a particular topic of interest quickly. The glossary at the end of the book, as well as a summary of important points at the end of each chapter, will help you understand the meaning of all legal terms and concepts and apply them properly.

Although the book was not meant to replace a lawyer, it will help you understand when you have a problem that requires a lawyer's assistance. You will learn how to eliminate potential misunderstandings with your lawyer after you hire one. In addition, the information will tell you how to make a lawyer work effectively on your behalf, besides suggesting courses of action to take before consulting a lawyer. These strategies may prove invaluable to your lawyer once one has been retained.

Of course, there are times when it is possible to obtain satisfaction on your own. *Don't Get Taken!* will tell you how to accomplish this. For example, you will learn what to do when you or a family member is involved in an auto accident. These steps will minimize civil and criminal exposure and increase the value of personal injury and property claims. Want to stop collection agency harassment? The material will tell you how. The information will inform you what to do when an employer asks you to take a lie detector test, and how to win a case or successfully defend yourself in Small Claims Court or arbitration.

It doesn't matter whether you have been intimidated or discouraged by the legal process, or disappointed by other "how to" legal books in the past. All I ask is that you keep an open mind because this book will be a very valuable resource.

The public shares a popular misconception that lawyers only represent people who are in trouble. This isn't so. Lawyers have been providing successful clients with information on *how to stay out of trouble* ever since the profession began.

That is what preventive law is all about. Just as business-people keep lawyers on retainer to obtain ongoing advice, you, too, will now have this information.

I have provided you with all the practical information my clients receive, at a fraction of the cost. Thus, keep this guide in an accessible place. Refer to it to avoid problems *before* they arise. Read the applicable sections before negotiating the terms of your new job or filing your tax return for example; it's that simple.

The benefits of applying this information can be significant. The following true story demonstrates why.

A client recently heard me lecture in Las Vegas to the members of his business association. The man introduced himself after I finished speaking. He told me that he had recently been fired from his job, and based on something he heard me say, believed he had been treated unfairly. After investigating the facts, I determined the man had been fired illegally and was owed a substantial amount of commissions and post-termination benefits from his former company.

Within two weeks I obtained a check in the amount of $42,000 on his behalf. To this day, the client cannot believe the size of the settlement, nor the speed in which it was obtained.

The experience of this individual is not unique. People throughout the United States can obtain similar recompense, provided their eyes are open. That is the concept of preventive law, and *Don't Get Taken!* Remember, if you don't know you are being exploited, you can't fight back!

I

Strategies to Protect Your Job

1

All about Your Job

- Introduction   4
- How to Be Hired Properly   5
- Checklist of Key Negotiating Points   6
- Summary of Steps to Take to Be Hired Properly   6
- Enforcing Your On-the-Job Rights   34
- How to Protect Your Rights   36
- How to Enforce Your Rights   62
- Health and Safety in the Workplace   68
- On-the-Job Injuries and Workers' Compensation   86
- Working in a Smoke-Free Environment   87
- Protecting Valuable Ideas   91
- Summary of Steps to Take while Working for Your Employer   94
- Asserting Your Post-Termination Rights   95
- What to Do when You Are Fired   98
- Negotiating Points to Maximize Post-Termination Benefits   103
- Additional Points to Remember when You Are Fired   107
- How to Resign Properly   112
- Summary of Steps to Take after You Resign or Are Fired   116

Introduction

The law previously favored employers when it came to resolving employment disputes. People could be fired at whim without cause or notice and their bosses had little fear of legal reprisal.

This is changing. New rulings have given the worker greater rights under the law. For example, federal and state statutes have recently been passed which grant some employees access to their personnel records, permit them to be represented when accused of disciplinary violations, and protect them in many other ways. Both men and women are receiving protection from on-the-job discrimination, sex harassment, unfair discharge, and mandatory lie detector tests.

This chapter will tell you what you need to know about your employment rights. No matter what type of job you have, whether you are a full-time employee, part-time worker, member of a union, independent salesperson, consultant, or tenured individual, you will learn:

- How to be hired properly
- Steps to take if you resign or are fired
- How to increase severance compensation and other benefits
- How to reduce the odds you will be fired unfairly
- How to enforce your on-the-job rights

- How to protect yourself from on-the-job sex harassment, discrimination, and invasions of privacy
- How to reduce the chances you will be sued by a former employer
- Steps to take to maximize a claim if you decide to sue your boss

(NOTE: It is estimated that more than 70 million Americans work without written contracts and basic job security. Unlike unionized employees who work under collective bargaining agreements [which often establish grievance procedures and protect members from unfair dismissals], the average worker must fend for himself.)

The following information was written specifically for people who lack employment protection. However, the application of many of these strategies depends upon your bargaining power, negotiating skill, and individual circumstances. For example, experienced workers with successful track records often command more secure jobs than first-time novices. Thus, adapt this information to suit your particular needs.

How to Be Hired Properly

The hiring phase is probably the most significant aspect of the employment relationship. By being hired properly, you can increase your job security, compensation package, and other benefits.

Many people don't know how to accomplish this. They accept work without clearly defining the terms of their employment. Others forget to ask for a written contract. They shake hands with their new employer and assume that everything will go smoothly. When misunderstandings develop, they learn that their naiveté has placed them at a significant legal disadvantage.

Checklist of Key Negotiating Points

This section will tell you how to be hired properly. You will learn why it is best to obtain a written contract and how to protect yourself in the event you don't receive one. A detailed checklist of negotiating points is provided so you will remember the items to discuss with a potential employer. You will also become familiar with points to avoid including in your contract.

Summary of Steps to Take to Be Hired Properly

First Step: Investigate
Your Potential Employer

Wise applicants investigate potential employers before accepting employment. This includes learning about a business's reputation, financial status, credit rating, and how it treats its employees. For example, if you are being hired to replace someone in an important position, find out the name of the person you are replacing and why the individual is no longer there. If possible, speak to the person. You could learn information that may affect your final decision (e.g., that the person resigned because of a failure to receive promised raises).

You can also investigate an employer's credit rating to discover if the business is having financial difficulties. This is because your goal should be to accept long-term employment and substantial benefits (e.g., stock options or pensions) from a company that will still be in existence when you retire.

Financial information is often obtained by contacting a credit reporting agency or bank. The following are significant items worth investigating:

    a. Whether the employer conducts business as a corporation, Subchapter S corporation, partnership, or sole proprietorship

b. The name of the principal shareholder(s) or partners

c. With whom does the employer maintain banking relations? For how long? What is the average balance on deposit? Does the employer have a line of credit? If so, for how much?

d. Number of employees

e. When was the last financial statement issued? Was it a certified statement? What did it show?

f. Location and kinds of real property and other assets owned by the employer

g. Does the employer have a history of litigation? Are there any outstanding encumbrances or liens?

h. Has the business been sold recently? Did the new owners assume the liabilities, or just purchase the assets?

This information is generally accessible to any individual who wishes to obtain it; ask for it when appropriate.

Second Step: Investigate the Status of the Person Hiring You

Employers sometimes argue in court that a former employee was hired by someone who did not have the authority to offer employment, negotiate compensation, and bind the company. *Avoid this.* Always investigate the title and position of the person hiring you to be sure the person has such authority.

Third Step: Beware of Illegal Employment Inquiries

The art of selecting the right person for the job is a matter of concern for employers and personnel managers.

However, some employers ask illegal questions on employment applications or during hiring interviews. For example,
inquiries pertaining to previous arrest records or drug use
are illegal because employers are supposed to consider applicants as they presently exist—not as they were in the
past.

Female applicants are often the target of discriminatory
questions. Some employers ask questions about child care
(e.g., who will look after your child?) to female applicants
and not males. In addition, other employers avoid liability
by asking potential applicants to sign documents called *waivers*. After a waiver is signed, the employer can delve into
forbidden topics, including an applicant's credit rating, medical history, and arrest record.

The following strategies will tell you what to do if you
are the victim of illegal employment inquiries.

1. *Know the law.* It is important to understand what employers can and cannot ask in order to protect yourself.

It is legal for employers to pose questions which test
your motivation, maturity, willingness to accept instruction,
interest in the job, ability to communicate, and personality.
The following questions are examples of the kinds of questions that can be asked:

- What are some of the responsibilities you had in pre-
  vious jobs?
- What skills and traits do you have that suit the needs
  of our company?
- What attracted you about the position?
- Name some of your outside interests
- How would you describe your relationship to those
  with whom you work?
- How would you describe your relationship to those
  with whom you live?

However, inquiries made into an applicant's race, color, age, sex, religion, and national origin which further discriminatory purposes are illegal.

The following chart illustrates many interview questions that are illegal under federal Equal Employment Opportunity Commission guidelines and state regulations.

SUBJECT	LEGAL	ILLEGAL
Age	Are you between 18 and 65 years of age? If not, state your age.	How old are you? What is your date of birth? Why did you decide to seek employment at your age?
Color		What is your skin coloring?
National Origin		What is your ancestry? What is your mother's native language? What is your spouse's nationality? What is your maiden name?
Citizenship	Are you a citizen of the U.S.? If not, do you intend to become one?	Of what country are you a citizen? Are your parents or spouse naturalized or native-born citizens? When did they acquire citizenship? Are you a native-born citizen?
Language	Do you speak a foreign language? If so, which one?	What is your native tongue? How did you acquire the ability to read, write, and speak a foreign language?
Relatives	Names of relatives already employed by this company.	Names, addresses, age, and other pertinent information concerning your spouse, children, or relatives not employed by the company. What type of work does your mother/father do?

SUBJECT	LEGAL	ILLEGAL
Marital Status	What is your marital status?	If married, where does your spouse work? What does your spouse do? When do you plan to marry? Do you plan on having children? Who will care for the children while you work? What is your spouse's health insurance coverage? How much does your spouse earn? What are your views on ERA? Are you a feminist? Do you advocate the use of birth control or family planning?
Disability	Do you have any impairments that interfere with your ability to work in this job? Would you submit to a company physical or provide a doctor's certificate of health after this interview?	Do you have a disability? Have you ever been treated for any of the following diseases? Have you ever been compensated for injuries? How much time have you lost because of illness in the past two years?
Arrest Record	Have you ever been convicted of a crime? Do you have a valid driver's license?	Have you ever been arrested? Have you ever pleaded guilty to a crime?
Organizations	List all organizations in which your membership is relevant to this job.	List all clubs, societies, and lodges to which you belong.
Religion		What is your religion? Are you available to work on the Sabbath? What religious holidays do you observe?

Although the preceding chart is a guideline of legal and illegal questions, the specific nature of the job may determine whether a particular question is illegal. For example, additional questions can be asked for jobs that are security sensitive, or that require employees to do difficult work.

Arrests

Generally, it is illegal for employers to ask about past arrests. This is because a substantial amount are often overcome by acquittal, withdrawal of charges, or by overturning the conviction. Thus, if asked by an employer if you were ever arrested, answer "no" if the arrest did not lead to a conviction. This will protect your rights. However, if you apply for military or civil service with the federal government, you must state the truth. Be aware of this.

Convictions

Generally, it is illegal to be asked information regarding a conviction that occurred more than seven years ago. You can be asked questions about a recent conviction, but *cannot* be refused a job unless the employer can show a direct relationship between the conviction and the job sought or that you currently pose an unreasonable risk to society. In addition, it may also be illegal to be denied employment or fired from a job as a result of current participation in a drug or alcohol treatment program, especially if enrollment does not interfere with your ability to do the job.

Medical Questions

Although it may be illegal to ask you to fill out a medical history form, an employer can ask you to submit to a pre-employment physical. This is permissible provided *all* applicants are requested to take physicals as the last part of the screening process.

Company doctors sometimes ask discriminatory questions during the examination; employers cannot deny employment on the basis of such illegal questions.

Credit Reports

Employers can conduct a credit check if this serves a legitimate business purpose. However, the Fair Credit Reporting Act restricts employers from using consumer reports for hiring or employment decisions. If the employer orders a detailed report, you must be told that the report is being ordered, together with the name and address of the credit agency that is supplying it. If you are denied a job on the basis of information supplied in the report, you can go to the agency and investigate the accuracy of the report.

Applicants for federal jobs have even greater protection. The federal Privacy Act requires most agencies to furnish applicants with the following information:

1. The authority on which the request for information is based

2. The purpose for which the elicited answer is to be used

3. Whether the applicant is obligated to answer the question

4. Who the information may be released to

5. The effect on the applicant, if any, for refusing to provide any or all of the information requested

Aggrieved individuals are permitted to sue the agency in federal court for alleged violations, and damages are recoverable when an agency misrepresents or illegally uses requested information for a different purpose.

1. *Post-employment inquiries.* An employer may ask your age or marital status after you start working in order to compute pension benefits. However, answers to such questions

cannot be used in promotion, transfer, or firing decisions, and must be asked of all employees within the organization.

2. *Check the law in your state.* Various state laws are very strict in prohibiting certain kinds of questions. Some states, including Arizona, California, Delaware, Hawaii, Kansas, Maine, Michigan, Missouri, New Hampshire, New Jersey, New York, Ohio, Rhode Island, Utah, Washington, and West Virginia have detailed guidelines on pre-employment inquiries. Be sure to investigate the laws in your state when appropriate.

3. *Avoid giving answers to discriminatory questions.* Avoid giving answers to discriminatory questions whenever you are being interviewed for a job. Sometimes you may have no choice if you want to be hired for the position. However, there are ways of handling illegal questions. For example, you can ask the interviewer to explain the significance of a discriminatory question and choose not to answer it on the basis of irrelevance.

4. *Contact an appropriate agency to protect your rights.* If you believe you were denied a job after answering an illegal question, contact an appropriate agency to protect your rights. This includes a regional office of the Civil Liberties Union, Human Rights Commission, or Equal Employment Opportunity Commission.

It is best to send a letter similar to the following to document your claim:

(Date)

Director
Appropriate Agency
Anywhere, U.S.A.

Re: Formal Protest against ABC Employer
for Illegal Hiring Practices

To Whom It May Concern:

Please treat this letter as a formal complaint against ABC employer, located at (address).

On (date), I was interviewed by (name of employee) for the position of (state). The interview took place at (location).

During this interview, I believe I was asked a variety of illegal questions. The following is a recollection of the specific questions asked (name them):

Although I answered some of the questions, I chose not to answer others on the basis of irrelevance.

After the interview, I was told by (name) that the company never hired anyone who refused to answer these questions. Although extremely qualified, I was denied the job.

I believe I was the victim of illegal and discriminatory hiring practices. Under the laws of this state, I understand your agency has the authority to investigate these charges and institute legal proceedings against the above-named, if appropriate.

Therefore, kindly investigate this matter on my behalf. You can reach me at (address), and (telephone number) if you require any additional information or assistance.

Thank you for your cooperation in this matter.

Sincerely,

(Send certified mail, return receipt requested.)

Wait a few days after sending this letter, then contact the agency to determine the appropriate course of action to take.

5. *Consult a lawyer.* Speak to a lawyer if you believe you were denied or fired from a job after being asked illegal questions. You may learn that it is worthwhile to file a private lawsuit or formal complaint with the Equal Employment Opportunity Commission on the basis of race or sex discrimination. Some states award damages and attorney fees to successful litigants. In any event, pursue your rights immediately to preserve your claim.

Fourth Step: Avoid Being Victimized by Job Misrepresentation

Many applicants are exposed to phony advertisements promising substantial income for part-time work, or offering employment with unlimited earning potential. Typical ads look like this:

BE YOUR OWN BOSS by working at home. No experience necessary. Over $500 per week possible.

You have probably seen such ads for jobs that are too good to be true. Unfortunately, most people learn that the ads are misleading only *after* they have been exploited. The following story is a typical example.

A person interested in a sales career is attracted by an ad. The ad states that a company is looking for an aggressive individual to sell its product. Experience is not necessary because the company uses national advertising and a dedicated staff to assist its employees. The ad promises substantial income immediately to job applicants.

The individual contacts the company and travels at his own expense to meet the potential employer. There he discovers the catch: it is necessary to buy $5,000 worth of product in order to sell it!

This is one example of a common illegal employment scheme. The strategies you are about to read will help you avoid becoming a victim of job misrepresentation.

1. *Be wary of guaranteed earnings claims.* Employees have the right to know the facts when told that their earnings are guaranteed. For example, are you told you will make $XXX because this is what other employees make? If so, ask the employer to authenticate his claim. The Federal Trade Commission (FTC) considers such statements to be an unfair and deceptive trade practice if you are promised an amount that exceeds the average net earnings of other employees.

2. *Know what assistance you will receive.* Some employers misrepresent the amount and quality of assistance to be rendered. Protect yourself by speaking to the people who will supposedly assist you. You may discover that exaggerated claims have been made.

3. *Beware of job offers that make you buy before you work.* This is the catch in many employment schemes—*watch for it!*

4. *Beware of work-at-home employment ads.* Many work-at-home ads are illegal. A 1979 study by the Council of Better Business Bureaus examined one kind of work-at-home ad— envelope stuffing—to determine if it was misleading. The ads guaranteed earnings up to $1,000 per week to stuff envelopes. The practice works like a pyramid scheme because the envelopes are stuffed with literature urging additional people to stuff envelopes. The council concluded that people were spending more money to purchase introductory mailing lists than could possibly be earned back.

5. *Investigate your employer before accepting employment.* Ask potential employers for bank and credit references. Avoid being hired by telephone. In addition, try to obtain a written employment contract and negotiate it properly.

6. *Protect your rights if you are exploited.* If you have been victimized by an employment scheme or work-at-home advertisement, do the following immediately:

a. Call the regional office of the Federal Trade Commission. The FTC may intercede on your behalf. After the FTC investigates an alleged violation, it can impose a cease-and-desist order to stop continued illegal practices.

b. Inform your employer you are taking action. Tell him/her you will file a complaint with the FTC if you are not reimbursed for your losses. Many employers are reluctant to tangle with the FTC and are inclined to settle matters amicably.

c. Contact your local Better Business Bureau (BBB). The BBB cannot impose sanctions like the FTC, but it can pressure a business to correct complaints. The BBB maintains a national list of individuals who are accused of engaging in misleading advertising and improper business practices. You can obtain this information by asking for it.

d. Contact the Postal Service. The Postal Service can intercede by asking employers to voluntarily halt illegal practices. It can also issue federal court orders which prevent businesses from receiving mail. In many cases, this has been successful in stopping illegal acts.

e. Speak to a lawyer or the Legal Aid Service. Some states have laws to protect victims of misleading trade practices and employment schemes. Statutes such as the Uniform Deceptive Trade Practices Act may have been passed in your state. These laws allow a person to be represented by the State Attorney General's Office (which can sue for damages and equitable relief on your behalf).

You may also recover damages in a private lawsuit on the grounds of *fraud*. Thus, be sure to take appropriate action to protect your rights.

Fifth Step: Discuss Key
Employment Terms

Never accept employment until you have clarified your compensation arrangement and benefits package. The reason is you risk being exploited by agreeing to work on a trial basis without discussing essential terms. The law says that even if you do an excellent job, you cannot make an employer hire you full-time or give you the benefits you think you deserve. Thus, no matter what type of job you accept, it is critical to discuss all the terms and conditions of employment *before* you agree to work. The following is a detailed list of important points to consider:

**Checklist of Key
Negotiating Points**

a. Date employment is to begin

b. Length of employment. Are you employed for a definite term (e.g., one year), or are you employed at will? If employed for a definite term, is the contract renewable after the expiration of the original period? Can one or both parties terminate employment prior to the expiration of the term? If so, how much notice (if any) must be given before the termination is effective?

c. Your title

d. Employment duties. Must you report to a superior?

e. Number of required working hours, sick days, holidays and vacations. If you do not use sick days and holidays, can they be taken the following year, are they lost, or will you be paid for them?

f. Employment status. Are you considered an employee or independent contractor? As an independent contractor, you are required to pay social security, withholding taxes and unemployment insurance as a matter of law

g. What is your base salary? When is it payable? Specify all deductions from your paycheck

h. Are expenses reimbursable? What, when, how, and to what extent?

i. Are bonuses given? How are they calculated and when are they paid? Are prorated bonuses given if you are fired or resign prior to the natural expiration of your contract?

j. Are commissions paid? If so, specify how they are earned. Is the commission a gross or net amount? If net, be sure you know what deductions are included

k. What are your fringe benefits? These can include use of an automobile, free parking, car insurance, gasoline allowances, death benefits, prepaid legal services, medical, dental, and hospitalization costs, life insurance, company credit cards, Keyman insurance, stock options, pension, and profit-sharing plans. Be sure you know all the ramifications of your benefit package (e.g., when does your pension or profit-sharing plan vest?)

l. Possibility of job advancement. Are periodic raises given? What is the procedure for merit raises?

m. What happens in the event that you become disabled? Define the meanings of temporary disability and permanent disability

n. Is a physical examination necessary?

o. Will relocation be required? If so, specify who will pay for it, and the manner of reimbursement

p. Can you have side ventures in a noncompeting business, or must you work exclusively on a full-time basis?

q. Are you prohibited from working for a competitor after your employment ends? If so, for how long, and where?

r. Who owns inventions and processes created by you during employment?

s. How will formal notices be communicated by one party to the other?

t. Can the contract be assigned?

u. Will disputes be resolved by litigation or binding arbitration? Can the prevailing party recover attorneys' fees and court costs from the losing party?

To perform your job better and reduce misunderstandings, it is also wise to inquire about the employer's policies regarding:

- Time clock regulations
- Rest periods
- Absences
- Safety and accident prevention
- Authorized use of telephones
- Reporting complaints

Sixth Step: Ask for a Written Contract

After agreeing on key employment terms, ask your employer to put them in writing. By doing so, you will be protected in the following ways:

1. *Potential misunderstandings will be reduced.* Oral terms are often interpreted differently by employers and employ-

ees. Inserting them in a written contract may eliminate confusion and ambiguities for both parties.

2. *It is easier to prove the terms of your employment.* A handshake only confirms that you accepted employment; it does not prove what was contracted for. This is another advantage of a written agreement. Once it is signed, the law presumes the parties incorporated their intentions into the contract. The instrument "speaks for itself" and courts will not hear testimony about understandings or discussions before the contract was signed unless the information is necessary to interpret ambiguous terms or establish particular trade customs.

3. *Your rights may be increased.* Clauses in written contracts can give you negotiating strength. For example, some employment contracts say that terms cannot be changed without the written consent of both parties. If such a clause was included in your contract and an employer attempted to reduce your salary or other benefits, this could not be done without your written approval.

Written contracts also protect employees who are fired in a manner prohibited by the contract. The following is an example of a situation that could occur:

Judith received a two-year written contract to work as a fashion designer. Her contract stated that it would be automatically renewed for an additional year if notice of termination canceling the contract was not sent by September 1st of the second year. Judith was fired on December 5th of the second year and sued for damages. The court ruled that she was entitled to additional compensation because she was terminated *improperly* (i.e., the employer failed to cancel the contract by September 1st of the second year).

(NOTE: The law requires Judith to look for another job in a similar field. This is called *mitigation of damages.* If Judith obtains a new job at a higher salary, chances are she will not be able to collect anything from her former employer.)

4. *You decrease the chances of being fired unfairly.* Working on a handshake is a risky proposition. In most states, the law says that if you are hired without a written contract *you are hired at will.* This means that you can be fired any time for any reason without advance notice! Although this is unfair, it's the law. Thousands of Americans without written contracts are suddenly fired each year and some have little success in recovering damages.

Remember, if you don't have a written contract, you are presumed to be working at will and can be fired without cause. It makes little difference if you have been working for the same company for a long time; you may have no legal recourse if you are suddenly fired. (NOTE: The law is rapidly changing in favor of employees in this area. You can protect yourself by reviewing the strategies contained in the section "What to Do if You Are Fired").

Seventh Step: Avoid Signing Contracts Containing Restrictive Covenants

If you are able to obtain a written employment contract, read it carefully before you sign it. Avoid signing contracts which contain restrictive covenants (also called covenants not to compete).

Restrictive covenants can prohibit an employee from doing many things. This includes:

1. Forming a competing venture or working for a competitor

2. Soliciting former customers or employees
3. Using the knowledge acquired on the job in future endeavors

The following clauses were taken from actual employment contracts to illustrate examples of restrictive covenants:

1. "The employee shall work exclusively for the employer on a full-time basis and will devote all of her working time, attention, and efforts to the employer's business."

2. "For a period of two (2) years after his termination of employment, the employee will not render any services, directly or indirectly, to any competing organization located in the states of New York, New Jersey, and Connecticut."

3. "The employee agrees that all designs she develops or conceives during her employment will be the sole and exclusive property of the employer, and that she will execute all documents requested by the employer to evidence its ownership thereof."

4. "The employee will not communicate or disclose any written or oral confidential information concerning the affairs of the Company or its affiliates."

For years, courts have struggled to balance the conflicting policy considerations of restrictive covenants. Some clauses are viewed as being unfair because they limit a person's ability to earn a living. However, courts also recognize the legitimate interest of an employer to safeguard his business from deliberate commercial piracy.

There are no hard and fast rules regarding the enforceability of restrictive covenants. Each court analyzes the facts on a case-by-case basis. Usually, such provisions are upheld only when they are *reasonable* in time and geographic area and are necessary to protect legitimate interests of an employer. The following case illustrates these principles:

> An employee signed a written contract which provided he would sell electrical fixtures in New York and Connecticut. The agreement contained a restrictive covenant which prohibited him from selling electrical fixtures for a competitor in those states up to three years after he resigned or was fired.
>
> The employee resigned from his job. Eight months later, the company instituted a lawsuit when it learned he was selling similar products for a competitor. *The company lost the case.* The court refused to enforce the restrictive covenant because the three-year restriction was unfair in length. The court also stated that the list of customers solicited by the employee was not confidential, and thus did not require protection.

The following points summarize what you should remember about restrictive covenants:

1. You can be prohibited from working for a competitor only if you sign a contract which contains a restrictive covenant
2. You may be subjecting yourself to a lawsuit if you sign a contract which contains such a clause
3. Consult a lawyer before signing an employment contract which contains a restrictive covenant

Explore your options if an employer threatens to sue you to enforce a restrictive convenant. You may find that the employer will *not* be successful in the event of a lawsuit, so don't be intimidated by such threats until you have spoken to a qualified lawyer.

Eighth Step: Execute
Your Contract Properly

Whenever you obtain an employment contract or any business document, read it carefully. Question all ambiguous and confusing language. Consult a lawyer if you do not understand the meaning of any terms. Contracts prepared by employers usually contain clauses which work to your disadvantage. Thus, review the agreement thoroughly.

If you are satisfied with the terms in the agreement, be sure it is signed by a bonafide representative who has the authority to bind the employer to important terms. Include the date and initial all changes. If the contract refers to a schedule or additional terms contained in another document, attach the document to the contract so it won't be misplaced. Obtain a signed copy of the executed agreement for your files; keep it in a safe place where you store other valuable documents.

Ninth Step: Clarify
Bonuses and Advances

Many employees fail to understand their rights regarding bonuses and advances—two areas where they are frequently exploited. Some people diligently work all year in the expectation of receiving a large bonus at year's end, and become disappointed when they don't receive it. This causes undue hardship because they were anticipating using the extra money to pay bills or go on vacation. Other employees unnecessarily return advances which exceed their earnings. The following information may eliminate unhappy surprises that sometimes occur in these areas:

Bonuses

A bonus is an additional sum of money paid to an employee in excess of his regular wage. There are two kinds of bonuses—bonuses enforceable by contract and gratuitous bonuses—and they differ in several respects. For example, in order to receive a bonus enforceable by contract, the following elements must be present:

1. A specific promise is made by the employer to pay a bonus

2. A method is agreed upon which the parties use to calculate the amount of bonus

3. The employee performs *additional* work, labor, services, or promises to refrain from doing something he is not obligated to do (e.g., to continue working and not resign for an additional year)

When all of these factors are present, an employee has an excellent chance of recovering a specified bonus from an employer if he is not paid.

However, the law treats gratuitous bonuses differently. If an employer controls the timing, amount, and whether or not to pay a bonus at all, or states that the money is paid in appreciation for continuous, efficient, or satisfactory service, the employee probably does not have a valid claim in the event a bonus is not paid.

Take the following steps to protect your rights if you expect to receive a bonus:

1. *Clarify how and when the bonus will be computed* (e.g., when sales exceed a certain level, on profits of the business, etc.). You may have difficulty enforcing an employer's promise to pay without such clarification. In addition, be certain you know what happens if you are fired or resign prior to the time you are to receive the bonus (e.g., will a pro-rata bonus be given?).

2. *Get it in writing.* Oral promises to pay bonuses are not always enforceable. Thus, confirm your understanding in writing to avoid this.

3. *Will you perform additional services?* Promises to pay a bonus for work, labor, or services already completed at the time the promise was made may not be valid, so be aware of this.

4. *Assert your rights.* Speak to your boss immediately if you fail to receive a bonus that was paid in the past. If you receive a lesser amount and the bonus is linked to a formula which is verifiable from the employer's records (e.g., bonuses linked to profits), you may have the right to view the company's books and records for this purpose. However, it may be necessary to consult a lawyer if the employer does not allow you to inspect its records.

Advances

People who work on a salary plus commission or straight-commission basis often receive an advance (sometimes called a draw). Advances are given to employees and independent contractors in many industries and are typically deducted from commissions as they are earned.

Workers sometimes leave their employment while the advance exceeds commission earnings. Some employers attempt to collect the excess by threatening to sue. Many employees, not knowing their rights, agree to return the difference. *This may be unnecessary.*

In most states, the law treats excess advance as *additional salary.* This means that if you do not agree to repay excess advances (e.g., by signing a written contract or acknowledging the debt in front of witnesses), the employer may be unable to collect the difference. Thus, you can protect yourself in this area if you:

1. *Avoid personal liability by contract.* An employer will have difficulty recovering money if an employment contract states that the worker is not personally liable for excess advances. The following clause illustrates such a provision in an employment contract:

The Employer shall advance Employee $XXX per week to cover Employee's travel and incidental expenses. This amount is to be charged against and deducted from any commissions to be paid. This amount shall not be a personal charge and there shall be no liability upon the Employee to refund any excess of advances over commissions.

2. *Avoid acknowledging the debt.* Employers often claim that the advance was a loan, and not additional salary. You can minimize this argument by refusing to discuss the matter with company personnel. In addition, avoid signing loan agreements, promissory notes, financial statements, or other documents which indicate personal indebtedness.

3. *Protect your rights.* If the employer states the advance was a loan, send a certified letter refuting this. If the advance was paid by check with the word "loan" written on the face of the check, cross out the word "loan" and initial it. These measures illustrate the kind of action you can take to document your protest.

Tenth Step: Remember that
No Job Lasts Forever

Some employers promise lifetime employment, yet fire employees without notice. They do this knowing that in many states, including California, employment relationships beyond a definite number of years are not valid. Other states do not enforce employment agreements exceeding one year unless they are in writing.

Lifetime contracts are difficult to obtain; many are not legally valid. For example, even the Board of Directors of a corporation may not have the legal authority to grant such a contract.

Thus, if you are employed pursuant to an oral "lifetime" contract, be aware that your job is probably not as secure as you think. Consult a lawyer if you are negotiating to receive such an agreement.

Eleventh Step: Protect Yourself If You Cannot Obtain a Written Contract

Some employers refuse to give written contracts. There are several steps to take when this happens to you.

1. *Ask for a fixed employment term.* One way to protect yourself is to ask for a fixed employment term. When you are hired for a definite term (e.g., one year), the law says you cannot be fired at the boss's whim—you can only be fired *for cause.*

The following are examples of cause which justify job terminations:

- Habitual lateness
- Prolonged absence from work
- Intoxication
- Disrespect or unprofessional conduct
- Disobedience of company work rules, regulations, and policies
- Exceeding authority
- Negligence or neglect of duty
- Dishonesty or unfaithfulness (e.g., making secret profits, stealing, misusing trade secrets, customer lists, and other confidential information)

Your chances of recovering damages in a lawsuit increase greatly when you are hired for a definite term. The reason is that employers must demonstrate that a worker's actions gave them cause to fire him; many have difficulty doing this. However, employees who do not have a written contract or other documentation often have trouble proving they were hired for a definite term. Some lawyers claim that their client's compensation arrangement (e.g., an annual bonus or yearly raise) proves he was hired for a definite term, but this argument is not always successful. Thus, it is best to confirm employment of a definite term in writing. This also satisfies the legal requirement that employment agreements exceeding one year must be in writing to be enforceable.

2. *Send a letter.* Another way to protect yourself is to write a letter after you are hired. Letter agreements may help prove your agreement, provided they are written accurately and refer to important terms.

Letter agreements should be sent whenever you cannot obtain a written contract. Ask your employer to return a signed copy where applicable and be sure to write the letter accurately because courts interpret ambiguous terms against the person who writes the letter.

The following are examples of simple letter agreements. Note that they are sent by certified mail, return receipt requested. This is essential to prove delivery. The letters also state that the employee will receive an immediate reply if any of the terms are ambiguous or incorrect. This obliges the employer to act. Such a clause benefits the employee because, in the event of a lawsuit, the employer's failure to respond may be construed as an acceptance of the terms in the letter agreement.

Sample Employee Letter Agreement

(Date)

Name of Corporate Officer
Title
ABC Corporation
Anywhere, U.S.A.

Dear (Name):

Per our discussion, it is agreed that I shall be employed by ABC as a computer analyst for an initial term of two (2) years commencing January 1, 1984. As compensation for services, I will receive a salary of thirty thousand dollars ($30,000) per annum payable in equal bimonthly installments on the first (1st) and fifteenth (15th) day of each month during the employment term.

In addition to my base salary, I will receive an annual bonus of ten thousand dollars ($10,000) payable in equal quarterly installments, and the company will promptly reimburse me for all reasonable business expenses incurred upon presentation of appropriate vouchers and records.

This bonus will be given as compensation for additional services to be rendered. Upon termination of this agreement for any reason, I shall be entitled to receive my bonus and salary for the remaining period of the quarter in which my termination occurs.

If any of the terms in this letter are not correct, please advise me accordingly in writing. Otherwise, this letter shall set forth our understanding of this matter.

I look forward to working for ABC.

Sincerely,

(Send certified mail, return receipt requested.)

**Sample Independent Sales
Representative Letter Agreement**

(Date)

Name of Corporate Officer
Title
Company Name
Anywhere, USA

Re: Employment Agreement

Dear (Name):

This letter will confirm the terms of my employment as an exclusive sales representative for your company.

I agree to represent the company in the states of Florida, Georgia, and South Carolina for a minimum period of one year commencing from the date of this letter.

The above-named territory will be covered exclusively by me with no other sales reps covering this territory. There will be no house accounts in the territory.

I will receive a commission of ten percent (10%) of the gross invoice for all accepted orders in my exclusive territory regardless of whether the orders are sent by me, received by the company through the mail, or taken at the company's place of business without my assistance.

There will be no deductions from my commission for credits or returns. Commission checks together with commission statements will be sent on the tenth (10th) day of the month following the month my orders are accepted.

I will be considered an independent contractor and will be responsible to pay all applicable social security, withholding and other employment taxes.

This contract will be automatically renewed for successive one-year terms so long as my yearly gross volume of accepted orders exceeds that of the previous year.

If any of the terms of this letter are ambiguous or incorrect, please advise me in writing. Otherwise, this letter shall set forth our understanding of this matter.

I look forward to working with you.

Sincerely,

(Send certified mail, return receipt requested.)

Twelfth Step: Recognize
Other Conditions of Employment

In some states, employers can fingerprint and photograph applicants as a condition of employment. In addition, the federal government may require you to be fingerprinted if you apply for a civil service job. However, you cannot be denied a job if you refuse to be fingerprinted and the law in your state prohibits this. Thus, investigate your state law when applicable.

You may also be required to live in the village or county where you work. So-called "residence" statutes have been declared constitutional by the United States Supreme Court. Thus, you may have to agree to live within a certain geographic territory as a condition of employment. This is particularly true if you accept a civil service job.

Summary of Steps to Take
to Be Hired Properly

1. Avoid oral promises
2. Investigate the employer before you agree to go to work:

    a. What is the financial status and credit rating of the company?

    b. Is the person hiring you authorized by the company?

    c. Does the company have a high rate of employee turnover?

3. Avoid being hired by the telephone

4. Avoid job misrepresentation claims

5. Discuss key employment terms before accepting the job

6. Negotiate employment with a definite term to reduce unfair terminations. Obligate the company to send written notice of termination before the effective termination date.

7. Obtain a written contract:

    a. Be sure to initial all changes, erasures, etc.

    b. Avoid including a restrictive covenant in the contract

    c. Save a copy of the signed agreement for your files

8. Send the employer a certified letter confirming the accepted terms if you cannot obtain a written contract

9. Consult a lawyer if the employer submits a complicated employment agreement for your signature

10. Write down all promises about job security that are made to you at the hiring interview. (The reason for this will be discussed later in the chapter.)

Enforcing Your On-the-Job Rights

Being properly hired is only the first step in the employment relationship. The second step is knowing how to enforce your on-the-job rights in the event that problems develop. Recent changes in the law are protecting workers throughout the United States from illegal invasions of privacy, employment discrimination, and dangerous working conditions. The following material will explore many of these areas in greater detail.

Privacy Rights of Employees

Most people are unaware that their privacy rights extend to the workplace. These rights are frequently violated by executives, security personnel, private investigators, and informers. The law allows employees to recover damages under a variety of legal theories when people act improperly.

This section will tell you what an employer can and cannot do on the job. The information will help you recognize abuses involving lie detector tests, searches of personal property, surveillance, questioning, interviewing, and access to personal records. It will also tell you what to do after such abuses occur.

1. *Lie detector tests.* Employers are resorting to polygraph and other truth detecting tests to verify statements on job applications, reduce employee theft, and detect if an employee is drinking on the job. The extent to which the tests reduce employee crime or detect dishonesty is difficult to measure. However, the tests are viewed by some as violating a person's fundamental rights—including rights in regard to free speech, privacy, self-incrimination, and the right to be free from illegal search and seizure. Many employees and prospective employees are outraged by the kinds of questions asked (e.g., did you go to your high school prom?, are you in debt?, when was the last time you visited your doctor?, etc.). In addition, such questions are often illegal.

Lie detector tests are causing serious problems for employees throughout the United States. It is estimated that millions of such tests are being given each year, and the number is increasing all the time. However, as the use of these tests grows, so does the size of verdicts received by innocent victims. For example, one employee was recently awarded $250,000 after being fired for failing a polygraph test. His lawyer proved that the polygraph company failed to interpret the results properly. Another man was dismissed from a retail store for failing a polygraph test. The employee proved his company *defamed* him (i.e., harmed his reputation) by firing him under circumstances strongly implying he was guilty of theft. The man received $150,000 for his troubles.

There are presently no federal laws governing the use of employee lie detector tests. The regulation of such tests is left to the states. As a result, the amount of fines, penalties, and licensing requirements varies considerably. Some states have laws prohibiting the use of lie detectors in all employment stituations. Others allow the test, but prohibit voice print identification and stress tests. A few states permit testing to prospective employees, but not employees. Others authorize testing in all situations, provided a licensed operator administers the test.

The following chart lists current testing laws on a state-by-state basis. The date inside the parentheses indicates the most recent version of the law in each state. (Source: *The National Law Journal*, January 24, 1983.)

How to Protect Your Rights

Read the following strategies when you are fired or denied a job as a result of a polygraph or other truth detecting test.

1. *Know the law.* It is currently illegal in nineteen states for employers to give lie detector tests. Other states are considering enacting similar legislation. You can learn whether your state prohibits such tests by calling the Attorney General's Office or consulting the chart.

ARE TRUTH DETECTING
TESTS PROHIBITED?

STATE	ARE TRUTH DETECTING TESTS PROHIBITED?	EXCEPTIONS	PENALTIES
Alabama	No		
Alaska—Stat. §23.10.037 (1972)	Yes—all tests	State and local law enforcement agencies may test employees	Up to $1,000 fine and/or one-year imprisonment
Arizona	No	Lie detector operators must be licensed	
Arkansas	No		
California—Lab. Code §432.2 (1981)	Yes—all tests	State and local law enforcement agencies may test employees	Misdemeanor
Colorado	No		
Connecticut—Gen. Stat. Sec 31-51g (1978)	Yes—all tests	*Prospective employees can be tested;* state and local law enforcement agencies may test employees	$250–$1,000 fine for each violation
Delaware—Del. Case Ann. Title 19 §704 (1979)	Yes—all tests	State and local law enforcement agencies may test employees	Up to $500 fine and/or 90 days imprisonment

STATE	ARE TRUTH DETECTING TESTS PROHIBITED?	EXCEPTIONS	PENALTIES
District Of Columbia—D.C. Law 2-154 (1979)	Yes—all tests	State and local law enforcement agencies may test employees	$500 fine and/or 30 days imprisonment; civil liability for unwarranted invasion of privacy
Florida	No	Lie detector operators must be licensed	
Georgia	No	Lie detector operators must be licensed	
Hawaii—Rev. Stat. §378-21-22 (1976)	Yes—but only lie detector tests	*Prospective employees can be tested*	$1,000 fine and/or one-year imprisonment
Idaho—Code Sec. §44-903-904 (1977)	Yes—but only lie detector tests	State and local law enforcement agencies may test employees	Misdemeanor
Illinois	No	Lie detector operators must be licensed (must have a college degree, six-month apprenticeship, and pass a state exam)	
Indiana	No		

State		Exemptions	Penalty
Iowa	No		
Kansas	No		
Kentucky	No	Lie detector operators must be at least 18, have studied polygraphy, and been in business for two years	
Louisiana	No		
Maine—Ann. tit. 32 §7166 (1980)	Yes—but only lie detector tests	State and local law enforcement agencies may test employees	Class D crime
Maryland—Ann. Article 100 §95 (1978)	Yes—all tests	State and local law enforcement agencies may test employees	Fine up to $100; misdemeanor
Massachusetts—Gen. Laws Ann. Ch. 149, Sec. 19b (1976)	Yes—but only lie detector tests	State and local law enforcement agencies may test employees	Fine up to $200
Michigan—Act 44, Pub. Acts of 1982	Yes—all tests		Misdemeanor; fine up to $1,000 and/or 90 days imprisonment
Minnesota—Stat. Ann. §181.75-77 (1981)	Yes—all tests		Misdemeanor; also a misdemeanor to disclose results to unauthorized parties; possi-

STATE	ARE TRUTH DETECTING TESTS PROHIBITED?	EXCEPTIONS	PENALTIES
Minnesota (cont.)			bility of injunctive relief and damages
Mississippi	No		
Missouri	No		
Montana—Rev. Codes Ann. §41-119, 120 (1977)	Yes—but only lie detector tests	State and local law enforcement agencies may test employees	Misdemeanor
Nebraska—Rev. Stat. §81-1932 (1980)	Yes—all tests	State and local law enforcement agencies may test employees; nondiscriminatory exams taken voluntarily are not subject to the law	Class II Misdemeanor
Nevada	No		
New Hampshire	No		
New Jersey—Stat. Ann. §2A:170-90.1 (1971)	Yes—but only lie detector tests	*Prospective employees can be tested*	Fine up to $1,000 and/or imprisonment not exceeding one year
New Mexico	No		

State	Permitted	Notes	Penalty
New York—Lab. Law §735 (1980)	Yes—but only psychological stress evaluators		Class B Misdemeanor upon first conviction; Class A Misdemeanor for subsequent convictions
North Carolina	No		
North Dakota	No		
Ohio	No		
Oklahoma	No		
Oregon—Rev. Stat. 659.225,227 (1979)	Yes—but only lie detector tests	The test can be given if taken voluntarily or taken by a witness in a civil or criminal trial or by a law enforcement officer during a criminal investigation	Fine not more than $500 and/or imprisonment up to one year
Pennsylvania—Cons. Stat. Ann. §7321 (1973)	Yes—but only lie detector tests	Public law enforcement agencies may test employees	Second-Degree Misdemeanor
Rhode Island—Gen. Laws §28-6.1-1-2 (1979)	Yes—all tests	State and local law enforcement agencies may test employees	Fine up to $200
South Carolina	No	Lie detector operators are regulated	

STATE	ARE TRUTH DETECTING TESTS PROHIBITED?	EXCEPTIONS	PENALTIES
South Dakota	No		
Tennessee	No		
Texas	No		
Utah	No		
Vermont	No		
Virginia	No		
Washington—Rev. Code §49.44, 120,130 (1981)	Yes—but only lie detector tests	State and local law enforcement agencies may test employees	Gross Misdemeanor
West Virginia	No		
Wisconsin—Stat. Ann. §111.326 (1980)	Yes—all tests		Misdemeanor
Wyoming	No		

If you belong to a union, re-read your collective bargaining agreement. Some agreements forbid employers from administering truth detector tests. Discuss the matter with a representative at a local union office if your collective bargaining agreement is silent on this point. Union shops can exert considerable pressure on employers to eliminate this practice.

2. *Be careful what you sign.* Some employers ask people to sign *waivers* before taking a test. Waivers should be avoided because you can surrender many of your rights by signing them. For example, you may relinquish:

a. The right to claim you were coerced into taking the test

b. The right to stop an employer or test administrator from disclosing the results to third parties (e.g., law enforcement personnel and credit reporting bureaus)

c. The right to make the test administrator release the results to you

d. The right to sue the employer and test administrator for civil damages

Some judges refuse to enforce waivers on the ground they are unconscionable; others uphold their validity. Thus, avoid signing them if possible. Try to delete any clause which absolves the employer and test administrator from liability if you must sign a waiver.

3. *Ask for the test results.* Truth detecting test results are prone to incorrect interpretation and error. Some scores fluctuate markedly depending upon the person administering the test. This is why you should always examine your score after you are fired or denied a job.

The following letter illustrates one way to effectuate this:

(Your name)
(Address)
(Date)

(Name of Employer)
(Address)

Re: Formal Demand of My Test Results

Dear (Name):

On (date) I agreed to take a (type of test) per your request. After taking the test, I was informed by (name of person) (explain how; e.g., by person, in writing) that I was (fired, denied a job, etc.).

This action has caused considerable hardship to me. Accordingly, please supply me with the following information:

1. Whether I passed or failed the test.
2. The specific questions I was asked and the specific answers I gave to each question.
3. What you considered a passing score.
4. My score for each question and my total score.
5. The names of all persons who have seen my score and/or presently have access to it.

In addition, I hereby request a copy of all written materials in your possession regarding the test. Under our state's Fair Debt Credit Reporting Act, I have the right to inspect the contents of my personnel file and make copies. If you do not comply with my request, I will take the necessary steps to effectuate same.

If I do not hear from you immediately, I shall be contacting my lawyer and the Attorney General's Office.

Thank you for your cooperation in this matter.

Sincerely,

(Send certified mail, return receipt requested.)

Although several states permit employers to refuse furnishing test results to job applicants, other states permit employees and applicants to review personnel files containing such records. Thus, always ask for your test results. You lose nothing if your employer fails to respond and you can gain valuable information if the employer cooperates.

4. *Talk to the examiner when taking the test.* This may help you learn information which may be useful if you decide to pursue a claim. For example, try to discover:

- The operator's name
- The name of his company
- How long he has administered such tests
- Whether the operator is licensed
- How the test is scored
- Who has access to the test results

5. *Take the exam in private.* There should be only two people present at the test, you and the administrator.

6. *Remember the questions you were asked.* By doing so, you may be able to prove that the questions were discriminatory.

7. *Contact a lawyer or appropriate agency if you are fired or denied a job after taking a truth detector test.* You may have a valid cause of action against the employer and/or polygraph operator on the grounds of negligence, wrongful discharge, intentional infliction of emotional distress, and defamation. Six-figure awards have recently been awarded to victims in this area.

Damages may also be recovered on other legal grounds. For example, when several minority applicants were denied jobs because they failed a pre-employment polygraph, one lawyer successfully argued that the test was not job-related and that it unfairly penalized his minority clients. The testing was stopped and the applicants were treated as though they passed the test.

If your lawyer determines that discriminatory questions were asked during the test, you can file a complaint with the Equal Employment Opportunity Commission (EEOC) to recover damages on the basis of sex or race discrimination.

(NOTE: See Part 3 of this section for further information.)

Contact your state's Attorney General's Office for details. Most Attorney Generals' offices have a Civil Rights Bureau which handles complaints about truth detector tests. According to a spokesperson at the New York Civil Rights Bureau, hundreds of lie detector complaints are received each year, and the Bureau sometimes institutes lawsuits on behalf of claimants.

(AN ADDITIONAL POINT: In many states, if you are fired for refusing to take a lie detector test, or for failing one, you will not lose your unemployment benefits if you are otherwise eligible. Thus, always appeal any denial of unemployment benefits if your employer contests the claim.)

Searches, Interrogations, and Access to Records

Employers faced with growing security problems are resorting to stricter security measures to protect company facilities, property, and employees. Although such measures accomplish their objectives, employee's rights are often violated in the process.

Searches

Employers use a variety of techniques after suspecting a worker of misconduct. These include:

1. Searching the employee's office, locker, or home without his knowledge or consent

2. Requesting the employee to open his briefcase or package upon leaving a company facility and

3. Conducting a "pat-down" search of his person

Although each case is decided on its own facts, the law generally states that office searches are permissible if an employer has reasonable basis for suspecting the employee of wrongdoing and the search is contained to *nonpersonal* areas of his office. The reason is that the office and documents relevant to company business are property of the employer and can be searched anytime.

However, clearly visible personal items *cannot* be searched and employers cannot conduct a search if there is no reasonable ground for suspicion. In addition, employers cannot conduct nonconsensual searches of your home; by doing so, they may be liable for trespass.

Legitimate searches of an employee's briefcase, locker, or packages depends upon whether the employee had a reasonable expectation of privacy. Some employers establish policies to make their employees' privacy expectations seem unreasonable. For example, they post signs reminding employees that personal property is subject to search. In addition, they distribute memos stating that surveillance measures are taken on a regular basis, and prepare employee handbooks saying that personal property should not be kept in company lockers because they are frequently opened and searched. Such measures may reduce claims of illegal privacy invasions. However, the practices must be imposed on *all* employees. For example, searching only the lockers of black employees may be illegal.

The expectation of privacy is greatest when a pat-down or other search of the employee is conducted. Knowledgeable employers are reluctant to conduct personal searches because they know the dangers involved; any number of wrong moves can lead to liability, particularly when threats, coercion, or physical abuse is involved.

In one recent case, security guards detained and searched an auto worker leaving a plant because he was suspected of stealing auto parts. According to testimony given at the trial, the guards yelled at the employee in addition to shoving him. The employee sued the company for defamation, assault, and false arrest, and was awarded $25,000.

If you believe that you are the victim of an employer's search, ask yourself the following questions:

- Were similar searches conducted before?
- Were you notified that the employer reserved the right to search? If so, how?
- What was the object of the search? Was it reasonable?
- Was personal or company property confiscated?
- What did you do during the search? Who conducted the search? What were you told? By whom?
- Did you refuse to cooperate?
- Did the search have an offensive impact? Were you grabbed, jostled, or held? Where you coerced, threatened physically, or mentally abused in order to cooperate?
- Were you held against your will? Were you so intimidated by the experience that you were afraid to leave?
- Were you chosen at random with others, or were only you searched in front of others? If so, were you stigmatized by the suspicion of wrongdoing?

If you answered yes to the last three questions, speak to a lawyer immediately to protect your rights. You may have a strong case, especially if you were fired, placed on probation, suspended, or given an official reprimand after the search.

Interrogations

Employers can question employees in an effort to discover illegal acts. However, workers have rights during these interviews. Suppose you are summoned into your supervisor's office. Several company executives and the supervisor are present. You are told that someone has been stealing company property and that you are going to be asked some questions. In this situation, you may have:

- The right to receive an explanation regarding the purpose of the interrogation (e.g., are you a suspect?)
- The right to insist on the presence of a representative at the interview if you believe it may result in disciplinary action
- The right to limit the questions to relevant matters
- The right to refuse to sign any written statements
- The right to remain silent
- The right to speak to your lawyer before you speak
- The right to leave the room at any time

You may be fired if you fail to cooperate. However, do not hesitate to assert any of your rights when necessary. If you are falsely accused of misconduct in front of others, or are threatened into answering questions at the interrogation, you may have a good cause for defamation or false imprisonment.

This regularly happens. In one recent case, a checkout clerk was accused of failing to ring up merchandise purchases. The employee was interrogated by security personnel and told to accompany them to another location for additional questioning. At the trial, the company proved that the woman failed to ring up purchases. However, a jury awarded the employee $27,500 on the grounds of false imprisonment, because the woman was never told she could leave the interrogation at any time.

Access to Records

Many employees covered under collective bargaining agreements have the right to view their records and be informed of information used in making adverse decisions. In addition, some states have passed laws which allow employees in the private sector to view their personal records and correct incomplete or inaccurate information. Other state laws require employers to seek approval before employee records can be collected, distributed, or destroyed.

In the absence of these laws, employees generally do *not* have the right to view their personal records (especially medical records, security records, and promotional schedules maintained by the employer). That is why you should investigate the law in your state when appropriate.

It may also be illegal to distribute personal information without an employee's consent. For example, the circulation of confidential memoranda within a company has given rise to many lawsuits, particularly when the employer did not take adequate precautions to determine whether derogatory information was accurate. Recently, a terminated employee sued his former boss on the basis of defamation. Letters describing the employee's poor job performance were distributed and read by several executives. The employee was awarded $90,000 after proving that company officials distributed the letters, knowing they were false.

Thus, you may have a valid lawsuit if harmful memos, letters, or other documents are distributed without your consent. The same is true if false, derogatory comments are orally made to third parties.

Wiretapping and Eavesdropping

Wiretapping and eavesdropping are generally prohibited by law. Employees have the right to be told before it occurs that their phone conversation, interview, or interrogation is being taped. In addition, company lawyers have the ethical responsibility of obtaining the consent of all parties prior to recording a conversation. Consult the law in your state, if applicable.

Rights to Unionize

The National Labor Relations Act allows employees to unionize and bargain collectively. Employers are prohibited from interfering with the exercise of these rights; they cannot penalize workers (e.g., by firing, layoffs, or demotion) who participate in such activities. In addition, an employer cannot question job applicants about their union sympathies or past activities in order to screen potential "troublemakers." Nor are they permitted to ask employees about their personal feelings toward unions.

The law also protects employees who band together to protest wages, hours, or working conditions. For example, if six nonunion employees complain about inadequate air conditioning or a smoke-filled working environment, it is likely that the employer would be prohibited from firing them as a result of this. Contact your union, regional Labor Relations Board, or Department of Labor if you believe your rights have been violated.

(AN ADDITIONAL POINT: Although you cannot be forced to join a union in order to get a job, you may be required to pay periodic dues if you work in a "union shop." In a union shop, workers and the employer are governed by a collective bargaining agreement, and agency shop fees are used to pay for the expenses incurred in administering the collective bargaining agreement. Federal employees work in an "open shop." They are *not* subject to pay fees if they choose not to join the union but are still entitled to the benefits of the union contract and union representation!)

Employment Discrimination

Employment discrimination is illegal. Thousands of people are enforcing their rights under the federal Equal Employment Opportunity Law and other statutes. More than 130,000 formal complaints are currently filed with the EEOC—one of the agencies responsible for enforcing the law, and approximately 5,000 discrimination lawsuits are tried in court each year. The remainder are either settled informally out of court, or dismissed for lack of proof.

Federal and state laws prohibit employers from discriminating against employees or potential employees on the basis of:

- Age
- Race, color, creed, religion, or national origin
- Sex or marital status
- Disability or physical handicap

Discrimination can occur during any number of the following employment stages:

- Recruiting, interviewing, and hiring
- Promotion, training, transfer, and assignment
- Discipline, layoffs, and discharge procedures

Also, an illegal act can be committed by any member of an employer's staff, from the president down to the supervisor and receptionist!

This section will help you identify when you have been the victim of employment discrimination. You will discover what practices are illegal, and learn how to file a timely complaint, prove your charges, and collect damages for your claim.

Recognizing Age Discrimination

Older Americans are currently finding it difficult to compete with younger workers and obtain employment. Some individuals are enforcing their rights under the Age Discrimination in Employment Act. This federal law forbids discrimination in all stages of employment for people between forty and seventy years of age. In fact, more than 11,000 age discrimination cases were filed with the Equal Employment Opportunity Commission in 1982 alone, up from 8,000 in 1980, and 6,000 in 1979.

Under the law, employers can:

- *Fire* older workers for inadequate job performance and good cause (e.g., tardiness, intoxication, etc.)
- *Entice* older workers into early retirement by offering additional benefits (e.g., bigger pensions, extended health insurance, substantial bonuses, etc.), which are voluntarily accepted
- *Lay off* older workers, provided younger employees are similarly treated
- *Discriminate* against older applicants when successful job performance absolutely requires that a younger person must be hired for the job (e.g., a flight controller)

However, the law forbids private employers, labor unions, state and local government agencies, and employment agencies from:

- *Denying* an older applicant a job on the basis of age
- *Imposing* compulsory retirement before age seventy
- *Coercing* older employees into retirement by threatening termination
- *Firing* older employees because of age
- *Denying* promotions, transfers, or assignments because of age
- *Penalizing* older workers with reduced privileges, employment opportunity, and compensation because of age

Various state laws also give older workers essentially the same protection.

Damages are recoverable provided it is demonstrated that a person received unfair treatment primarily because of age. Usually a pattern of discriminatory hiring and firing practices must be proved in order to be successful. The following true case illustrates this:

> A fifty-seven-year-old marketing director was recently fired. The man filed a complaint with the Equal Employment Opportunity Board in his state. The company defended the charges by arguing that the executive was but one of seventy unfortunate employees axed to save the company money. The company claimed there was no discrimination because the executive was hired when he was fifty-four years old.
>
> The company lost the case. EEOC investigators discovered that although seventy people had been fired, sixty-five new employees were hired in the following year, and only four of those employees were over the age of fifty. The executive was reinstated and awarded $48,000 in back pay, retroactive seniority, and fringe benefits.

Strategies to Help Prove
Age Discrimination

Statements, conduct and other clues may help you prove you are the victim of age discrimination. For example, beware of the following when applying for a job:

- Statements made to you by the employer that you are "overqualified"
- Requests for physical examinations that seem unnecessary and not job-related
- Being told you were rejected from a job because you lacked formal education credits, even though you are highly qualified

If you suspect you were denied a job on the basis of age, demand an explanation. Contact the EEOC if you are not satisfied with the answers given. The EEOC will conduct a formal investigation on your behalf after a complaint is filed. After discussing your case with a compliance officer, your identity will be kept confidential until you decide to file charges.

If you believe you were fired because of your age, ask yourself the following questions:

- Did you request a transfer to another position before you were fired? Was it refused? If so, were similar requests granted to younger workers?
- How were you terminated? Were you given false reasons for the termination? Did you consent to such action or send a certified letter protesting the discharge?
- Were you replaced by a younger worker? Were younger workers merely laid off, and not fired?

Positive answers to questions like these may prove that you were fired as a result of age discrimination.

Your case can be strengthened if fellow employees were also victimized. For example, 143 persons were recently forced to retire prematurely from an insurance company at the age of sixty-two. The large number of employees made it difficult for the company to overcome charges of age discrimination and workers collectively received more than $6 million in back wages.

In another case, a company denied training to two older employees and then fired them. The company claimed the men were unskilled and not qualified to continue employment. The workers filed timely claims and recovered $79,200 in lost wages, benefits, and legal fees.

These cases demonstrate the effectiveness of proving age discrimination through collective abuses. Thus, speak to other employees if you suspect you have been victimized; you may discover facts to help your case.

Sex Discrimination

The significant number of large settlements in sex discrimination cases is causing major concern to employers. For example, a U.S. District Court judge recently ordered a major airline to pay its 3,343 current and former stewardesses $52.5 million in damages. The airline violated the Equal Pay Act by giving male cabin attendants better pay, benefits, and working conditions than their female counterparts. At the trial, it was proved that males received more money for the same job, were given single rooms in hotels for overnight layovers (women had to double up), and were not disciplined equally after violating company "appearance" rules (e.g., stewardesses were suspended without pay if their weight was more than five pounds above company standards; men were not).

In another lawsuit, a major southern university was recently ordered to pay 117 women an award of $1.3 million. A Federal Court Special Master ruled that the school paid less to women on the faculty than men in comparable jobs.

However, unequal pay for equal work is not the only form of sex discrimination. The law requires similar employment policies, standards, and practices for males and females. Equal treatment is imposed in a variety of areas, including hiring, placement, job promotion, working conditions, lay-offs, and discharge. For example, it is discriminatory for an employer to:

- *Refuse* to hire women with preschool-age children while hiring men with children

- *Require* females to resign from jobs upon marriage when there is no similar requirement for males

- *Include* spouses of male employees in benefits plans while denying the same benefits to spouses of female employees

- *Restrict* certain jobs to men without offering a reasonable opportunity for women to demonstrate their ability to perform the same job adequately (e.g., firefighting)

- *Refuse* to hire, train, assign, or promote pregnant or married women, or women of child-bearing age, merely on the basis of sex

- *Deny* unemployment benefits, seniority, or lay-off credit to pregnant women, or deny granting a leave of absence for pregnancy irrespective of whether or not it is granted for illness

- Institute compulsory retirement plans with lower retirement ages for women than men

Another prohibited form of sex discrimination is sex harassment. Unwelcome sexual advances, requests for sexual favors, and verbal or physical conduct of a sexual nature constitutes sex harassment when:

1. The person must submit to such activity in order to be hired
2. The person's consent or refusal is used in making an employment decision (e.g., to offer a raise or promotion
3. Such conduct unreasonably interferes with the person's work performance or creates an intimidating, hostile, or offensive working environment (e.g., humiliating comments are repeatedly stated to the complainant)

Sex harassment cases are on the rise in a variety of nontraditional areas. For example, if you are passed over for a promotion or denied benefits in favor of an employee who has submitted to sexual advances, you too are the victim of sex harassment! You should also know that the harassment can occur from anyone—not just fellow employees or the boss. For example, sexual harassment was found in one case when female employees were required to wear revealing uniforms and suffer derogatory comments from passersby. In addition, claims of sex harassment are not only limited to women. One recent case received nationwide coverage. A jury awarded $196,500 in damages to a man who claimed his supervisor demoted him because he refused her sexual advances. According to court testimony, the employee and his supervisor met one night in a hotel room, but the employee refused to continue the relationship. The man proved he was demoted and passed over for a promotion as a result.

How to Prove Sex Harassment

In order to prove sex harassment, you must take steps to document your claim. For example, if you are being teased on the job, it is wise to complain to a supervisor *in writing*. Judges, arbitrators, and Equal Employment Opportunity Special Masters are more willing to award damages for sex harassment when a formal complaint was made requesting the offensive conduct to stop and the request was ignored. By sending a letter similar to the following, you may be able to prove a repetitive pattern of conduct and demonstrate that the offensive acts were not condoned.

(Date)

Mr. (Name)
Supervisor
QRS Company
(Address)

Re: Complaint of Sex Harassment

Dear (Name):

While working for the company, I have been the victim of a series of offensive acts which I believe constitute sex harassment.

On (date), I (describe what occurred, and by whom). I immediately (describe your reaction), and felt that such conduct should stop.

However, on (date), another incident occurred when (describe what occurred and by whom).

I find such behavior intimidating and repugnant. In fact, (describe the physical and emotional impact on you), causing me to be less efficient on the job.

Unless such conduct ceases immediately, I shall be faced with no alternative but to contact the Equal Employment Opportunity Commission to enforce my rights.

I do not wish to take such a drastic measure. All I want to do is perform my job in a professional environment.

Thank you for your cooperation in this matter.

Sincerely,

(Send certified mail, return receipt requested.)

(NOTE: Be sure to save a copy of such a letter for your files.)

You should also discuss the incident(s) with other employees to discover if they too have been the victims of similar abuse.

Remember, one of the elements of proof required in a sexual harassment case is that the employer knew or should have known of the offensive conduct and failed to take corrective action. Thus, be sure to complain in writing to management to document your claim.

Race Discrimination

The Civil Rights and Equal Employment Opportunity Acts protect minority workers from discriminatory practices. People who:

- Are denied a job on the basis of race
- Are fired because of race
- Are denied a transfer or job promotion on the basis of race
- Experience unfair prerequisites for employment which have a discriminatory impact (e.g., asking a black applicant at the hiring interview if he has an arrest record or poor credit background). This is impermissible un-

less a valid business purpose justifies the information sought

- Experience unfair prerequisites for promotion which have a discriminatory impact (e.g., devising a test which blacks are more likely to fail than whites)

are the victims of race discrimination.

If you believe you have been denied an employment opportunity on the basis of race, contact your local EEOC office immediately for assistance.

Handicap Discrimination

Most states prohibit discrimination as a result of physical handicaps. It is illegal to deny employment if a handicapped person is capable of performing the job in question. Decisions not to hire an applicant because of physical defects or a medical condition are scrutinized closely. The Rehabilitation Act of 1973, enforced by the Department of Labor, prohibits prospective job applicants from being denied employment merely because they have a history of physical or mental impairment which has been cured. In addition, federal law requires employers who receive federal aid to recruit, hire, and promote qualified handicapped persons. It is also illegal for an employer to claim that hiring a disabled person would increase insurance costs.

Religious Discrimination

The Equal Employment Opportunity Commission has promulgated guidelines with respect to religious discrimination. Employers have an obligation to make reasonable accommodations to the religious needs of employees and prospective employees. An employer must give time off for the sabbath or holy day observance, except in an emergency. In such event, the employer may give the leave without pay, may require equivalent time to be made up, or may allow the employee to charge the time against any other leave with pay except sick pay. However, these protections may not apply to employees in certain health and safety occupations or to any employee whose presence is essential on any given day. It also does not apply to private employers who can prove that an employee's absence would cause severe business hardship.

How to Enforce Your Rights

Recognizing discrimination is only part of the battle; proper steps must also be taken to enforce your rights. The law entitles victims of discrimination to recover a variety of damages. This includes reinstatement, job hiring, receiving wage adjustments, back pay and double back pay, receiving promotions, recovering legal fees, filing costs and punitive damages, or instituting an affirmative action program on behalf of fellow employees.

It is necessary to file a formal complaint with the Equal Employment Opportunity Commission or other appropriate agency to start the ball rolling. This is the most important step. No one can stop you from filing a complaint; the law forbids employers from threatening reprisals or retaliation (e.g., loss of a promotion) when action is taken.

The following facts must be included in the complaint:

- Your name
- The names, business address, and business telephone numbers of all persons who committed and/or participated in the discriminatory act(s)
- Specific events, dates, and facts to support why the act(s) were discriminatory (e.g., statistics, whether other employees or individuals were discriminated

against, and, if so, the person(s) victimized, and by whom).

On the following page is an example of a complaint filed with the EEOC alleging race discrimination. Note that the complaint must be signed and sworn by the complainant.

It is not necessary for the complaint to be lengthy or elaborate. The main purpose is to allege sufficient facts which trigger an EEOC investigation. That is the advantage of filing a complaint with the EEOC—charges of discrimination are initiated and investigated at no cost to you. If the complaint seems plausible, the EEOC will develop the claim on your behalf.

There is one loophole in the law. *Small employers* (defined as having fifteen or less employees) *are exempt from sanctions* under federal laws. Thus, if you are victimized by a "small employer," you cannot file a complaint with the EEOC or other federal agencies to recover damages. However, you may have ample recourse under state laws. For example, you can commence a private lawsuit in state court and allege damages for *assault and battery, invasion of privacy,* or *infliction of emotional distress*. Victims often recover damages for actual economic loss, emotional distress and punitive damages under these laws.

Once a formal complaint is received, the EEOC assigns it a number. A copy of the complaint, together with a request for a written response, is then sent to the employer. The employer must respond to the charges within several weeks. After charges and countercharges have been examined by an EEOC investigator, the employer is invited to attend a no-fault conference to negotiate an informal settlement. Approximately 40 percent of all complaints are disposed this way.

The conference is conducted by an experienced EEOC representative. Considerable pressure is placed on the employer to offer a money settlement (e.g., back pay) or some other form of restitution because it is understood that the

(PLEASE PRINT OR TYPE)

APPROVED BY GAO B—180541 (RO510) Expires 1-31-81	CHARGE OF DISCRIMINATION IMPORTANT: This form is affected by the Privacy Act of 1974; see Privacy Act Statement on reverse before completing it.	CHARGE NUMBER(S) (AGENCY USE ONLY) ☐ EEOC

Equal Employment Opportunity Commission

NAME (Indicate Mr., Ms. or Mrs.) EVAN SMITH	HOME TELEPHONE NUMBER (Include area code)
STREET ADDRESS Anyplace, U.S.A.	
CITY, STATE, AND ZIP CODE	COUNTY

NAMED IS THE EMPLOYER, LABOR ORGANIZATION, EMPLOYMENT AGENCY, APPRENTICESHIP COMMITTEE, STATE OR LOCAL GOVERNMENT AGENCY WHO DISCRIMINATED AGAINST ME. (If more than one list below).

NAME E F G Corp.	TELEPHONE NUMBER (Include area code) 555-1234
STREET ADDRESS Anyplace, U.S.A.	CITY, STATE, AND ZIP CODE
NAME	TELEPHONE NUMBER (Include area code)
STREET ADDRESS	CITY, STATE, AND ZIP CODE

CAUSE OF DISCRIMINATION BASED ON MY (Check appropriate box(es))

☒ RACE   ☐ COLOR   ☐ SEX   ☐ RELIGION   ☐ NATIONAL ORIGIN   ☐ OTHER (Specify)

DATE MOST RECENT OR CONTINUING DISCRIMINATION TOOK PLACE (Month, day, and year)

THE PARTICULARS ARE:

I am black. On November 12, 1984 I was notified by (name), my supervisor at EFG Corp., that I was fired. I asked (name) to tell me why I was fired; he said it was because I called in sick six times in the past year. I know of several white employees who called in sick more than six times the past year and who were not fired.

I will advise the agency if I change my address or telephone number and I will cooperate fully with it in the processing of my charge in accordance with its procedures.

I declare under penalty of perjury that the foregoing is true and correct.

DATE: 12/10/84   CHARGING PARTY (Signature) Evan Smith

EEOC FORM 5A MAR. 79   PREVIOUS EDITIONS OF ALL EEOC FORM 5'S ARE OBSOLETE AND MUST NOT BE USED

CHARGE FILE COPY

EEOC will conduct a formal investigation if a settlement is not reached, and an employer's business records, employment applications, inter-office memos, and pay records may be examined in detail by EEOC investigators if a settlement is not made.

If your case cannot be settled at the conference, several options are available:

1. The EEOC may refer the matter to an appropriate state or local human rights agency for action

2. The EEOC or Department of Justice may commence a lawsuit for you and/or others similarly situated (i.e., a class action lawsuit)

3. You can hire a lawyer and sue the employer privately

The advantage of suing an employer privately is that you may receive a quicker settlement. However, private lawsuits cost money and can be expensive. That is why it is best to contact the nearest district office of the EEOC before formulating your strategy. The following chart lists the nearest office in your region.

EEOC District and Area Offices

District offices (DO) are full-service units, handling all charge processing and all compliance and litigation enforcement functions. Area offices (AO) generally handle charge intake and initial investigations, with some of them also performing various compliance and litigation activities.

ALBUQUERQUE, AO
505 Marquette, NW, Suite 1515
Albuquerque, New Mexico 87101
(505) 766-2061

ATLANTA, DO
75 Piedmont Ave., NE,
10th floor
Atlanta, Georgia 30303
(404) 221-4566

BALTIMORE, DO
711 West 40th St., Suite 210
Baltimore, Maryland 21211
(301) 962-3932

BIRMINGHAM, DO
2121 Eighth Ave., North
Birmingham, Alabama 35203
(205) 254-1166

BOSTON, AO
150 Causeway St., Suite 1000
Boston, Massachusetts 02114
(617) 223-4535

BUFFALO, AO
One West Genessee St., Rm. 320
Buffalo, New York 14202
(716) 846-4441

CHARLOTTE, DO
1301 East Morehead
Charlotte, North Carolina 28204
(704) 371-6437

CHICAGO, DO
536 South Clark St., Rm. 234
Chicago, Illinois 60605
(312) 353-2713

CINCINNATI, AO
550 Main St., Rm. 7019
Cincinnati, Ohio 45202
(513) 684-2379

CLEVELAND, DO
1365 Ontario St., Rm. 602
Cleveland, Ohio 44114
(216) 522-7425

DALLAS, DO
1900 Pacific, 13th floor
Dallas, Texas 75201
(214) 767-4607

DAYTON, AO
200 West Second St., Rm. 608
Dayton, Ohio 45402
(513) 225-2753

DENVER, DO
1513 Stout St., 6th floor
Denver, Colorado 80202
(303) 837-2771

DETROIT, DO
660 Woodward Ave., Suite 600
Detroit, Michigan 48226
(313) 226-7636

EL PASO, AO
2211 East Missouri, Rm. E-235
El Paso, Texas 79903
(915) 543-7596

FRESNO, AO
1313 P St., Suite 103
Fresno, California 93721
(209) 487-5793

GREENSBORO, AO
324 West Market St., Rm. 132
Greensboro, North Carolina 27402
(919) 378-5174

GREENVILLE, AO
7 North Laurens St., Suite 507
Greenville, South Carolina 29602
(803) 233-1791

HOUSTON, DO
2320 LaBranch, Rm. 1101
Houston, Texas 77004
(713) 226-5561

INDIANAPOLIS, DO
46 East Ohio St., Rm. 456
Indianapolis, Indiana 46204
(317) 269-7212

JACKSON, AO
100 West Capitol St., Suite 721
Jackson, Missouri 39201
(601) 960-4537

KANSAS CITY, AO
1150 Grand, lst floor
Kansas City, Missouri 64106
(816) 374-5773

LITTLE ROCK, AO
700 West Capitol
Little Rock, Arkansas 72201
(501) 378-5901

LOS ANGELES, DO
3255 Wilshire Blvd., 9th floor
Los Angeles, California 90010
(213) 688-3400

LOUISVILLE, AO
600 Jefferson St.
Louisville, Kentucky 40202
(502) 582-6082

MEMPHIS, DO
1407 Union Ave., Suite 502
Memphis, Tennessee 38104
(901) 521-2617

MIAMI, DO
300 Biscayne Blvd. Way, Suite
414
Miami, Florida 33131
(305) 350-4491

MILWAUKEE, DO
342 North Water St., Rm. 612
Milwaukee, Wisconsin 53202
(414) 291-1111

MINNEAPOLIS, AO
12 South Sixth St.
Minneapolis, Minnesota 55402
(612) 725-6101

NASHVILLE, AO
404 James Robertson Pky., Suite
1822
Nashville, Tennessee 37219
(615) 251-5820

NEWARK, AO
744 Broad St., Rm. 502
Newark, New Jersey 07102
(201) 645-6383

NEW ORLEANS, DO
600 South St.
New Orleans, Louisiana 70130
(504) 589-3842

NEW YORK, DO
90 Church St., Rm. 1301
New York, New York 10007
(212) 264-7161

NORFOLK, AO
200 Granby Mall, Rm. 412
Norfolk, Virginia 23510
(804) 441-3470

OAKLAND, AO
1515 Clay St., Rm. 640
Oakland, California 94612
(415) 273-7588

OKLAHOMA CITY, AO
50 Penn Pl., Suite 1430
Oklahoma City, Oklahoma
73118
(405) 231-4912

PHILADELPHIA, DO
127 North Fourth St., Suite 200
Philadelphia, Pennsylvania
19106
(215) 597-7784

PHOENIX, DO
210 North Cental Ave., Suite
1450
Phoenix, Arizona 85073
(602) 261-3882

PITTSBURGH, AO
1000 Liberty Ave., Rm. 2038 A
Pittsburgh, Pennsylvania 15222
(412) 644-3444

RALEIGH, AO
414 Fayetteville St.
Raleigh, North Carolina 27608
(919) 755-4064

RICHMOND, AO
400 North Eighth St., Rm. 6213
Richmond, Virginia 23240
(804) 771-2692

SAN ANTONIO, AO
727 East Durango, Suite B-601
San Antonio, Texas 78206
(512) 229-6051

SAN DIEGO, AO
880 Front St.
San Diego, California 92188
(714) 293-6288

SAN FRANCISCO, DO
1390 Market St., Suite 325
San Francisco, California 94102
(415) 556-0260

SAN JOSE, AO
84 West Santa Clara Ave., Rm.
300
San Jose, California 95113
(408) 275-7352

SEATTLE, DO
710 Second Ave., 7th floor
Seattle, Washington 98104
(206) 442-0968

ST. LOUIS, DO
625 North Euclid St.
St. Louis, Missouri 63108
(314) 425-5571

TAMPA, AO
700 Twiggs St., Rm. 302
Tampa, Florida 33602
(813) 228-2310

WASHINGTON, AO
1717 H St., NW, Suite 402
Washington, District of Columbia 20006
(202) 653-6197

Health and Safety in the Workplace

Numerous changes benefiting workers have occurred in the area of health and safety. Federal and state laws have recently been passed which allow employees the right to refuse dangerous work or receive accurate reports concerning toxic substances in their working environment. The law also grants employees the right to work in a smoke-free environment. Other changes have allowed employees to circumvent Workers' Compensation and sue bosses directly for their injuries. In addition, increased activity by labor unions and the federal Occupational Safety and Health Administration (OSHA) has protected employees from unsafe working conditions.

This section will discuss the important health and safety rights that workers are currently receiving.

Your Rights under OSHA

The 1970 Occupational Safety and Health Act requires every American employer to provide a safe and healthful workplace. The Occupational Safety and Health Administration is the federal agency created to enforce this law. The agency issues regulations on worker safety that employers must follow. OSHA inspectors visit work sites to be sure that employers adhere to the rules. Penalties are sometimes imposed (e.g., fines up to $10,000 for each violation and/or imprisonment up to six months) for employers who willfully or repeatedly violate OSHA laws or fail to correct hazards within fixed time limits.

The Occupational Safety and Health Act allows workers the right:

- To refuse to perform work in a dangerous environment (e.g., in the presence of toxic substances, fumes, or radioactive materials)
- To strike to protest unsafe conditions
- To initiate an OSHA inspection of dangerous working conditions by filing a safety complaint
- To participate in OSHA inspections, pre-hearing conferences, and review inspection hearings
- To assist the OSHA compliance officer in determining that violations have been corrected

One of the most important aspects of the law is that employers cannot punish workers (through firings, demotions, or transfers) who assert their health and safety rights to a union, OSHA, or any other federal, state, or local agency empowered to investigate or regulate such conditions. In one recent case, for example, seven machine-shop workers walked off their jobs claiming it was too cold to work. The company fired them, stating they violated company rules by stopping work without notifying the foreman. The workers filed a complaint and alleged this was an unfair labor practice. The U.S. Supreme Court ruled that the employees had a constitutional right to strike over health and safety conditions, and that the firing violated the law. The workers were awarded back pay and job reinstatement as a result.

(NOTE: Generally, you should not refuse to engage in work that you consider dangerous or unhealthy unless it would place you in imminent danger of serious injury or death. Rather than walking off the job, it is best to first complain about potentially dangerous or unhealthy conditions to your union, employer, or OSHA.)

If you believe you have been punished for exercising your safety and health rights, contact the nearest OSHA area office immediately. This should be done *within thirty (30) days* of the time you discover you have been punished. A union representative or attorney-in-fact can file the complaint if you are unable to do so.

Once you decide to take this action, you must provide an OSHA officer with the facts (e.g., what happened, and who was involved); OSHA will then investigate. OSHA will ask your employer to restore your job, earnings, and benefits if you have been illegally punished. If necessary, an OSHA representative may go to federal court to protect your rights.

The following table lists addresses and phone numbers of OSHA regional offices:

Boston—Region I (Connecticut, Maine, Massachusetts, New Hampshire, Rhode Island, and Vermont)

BOSTON REGIONAL OFFICE

Regional Administrator
U.S. Department of Labor—
OSHA
16–18 North Street
1 Dock Square Building, 4th Floor
Boston, Massachusetts 02109
Comm. Phone: (617) 223-6710
FTS Phone: 223-6710

BOSTON AREA OFFICE

Area Director
U.S. Department of Labor—
OSHA
400-2 Totten Pond Road, 2nd Floor
Waltham, Massachusetts 02154
Comm. Phone: (617) 890-1238
FTS Phone: 839-7691

SPRINGFIELD AREA OFFICE

Area Director
U.S. Department of Labor—
OSHA
1200 Main Street, Suite 513
Springfield, Massachusetts 01103
Comm. Phone: (413) 781-2420, Ext. 522
FTS Phone: 836-9522

CONCORD AREA OFFICE

Area Director
U.S. Department of Labor—
OSHA
Federal Building, Room 334
55 Pleasant Street
Concord, New Hampshire 03301
Comm. Phone: (603) 224-1995
FTS Phone: 834-4725/
                       4785

AUGUSTA AREA OFFICE

Area Director
U.S. Department of Labor—
OSHA
40 Western Avenue, Room 121
Augusta, Maine 04330
Comm. Phone: (207) 622-6171 Ext. 417
FTS Phone: 833-6417

PROVIDENCE AREA OFFICE

Area Director
U.S. Department of Labor—
OSHA
169 Weybosset Street, 5th Floor
Providence, Rhode Island 02903
Comm. Phone: (401) 528-4669
FTS Phone: 838-4667

HARTFORD AREA OFFICE

Area Director
U.S. Department of Labor—
OSHA
MDC Building, 2nd Floor
555 Main Street
Hartford, Connecticut 06103
Comm. Phone: (203) 244-2294
FTS Phone: 244-2294

New York City—Region II (New Jersey, New York, and Puerto Rico)

NEW YORK REGIONAL OFFICE

Regional Administrator
U.S. Department of Labor—
OSHA
1515 Broadway (1 Astor Plaza),
Room 3445
New York, New York 10036
Comm. Phone: (212) 944-3426
FTS Phone: 265-3426

MANHATTAN AREA OFFICE

Area Director
U.S. Department of Labor—
OSHA
90 Church Street, Room 1405
New York, New York 10007
Comm. Phone: (212) 264-9840
FTS Phone: 264-9840

QUEENS AREA OFFICE

Area Director
U.S. Department of Labor—
OSHA
136–21 Roosevelt Avenue, 3rd
Floor
Flushing, New York 11354
Comm. Phone: (212) 445-5005
FTS Phone: 662-3580

BELLE MEAD AREA OFFICE

Area Director
U.S. Department of Labor—
OSHA
Belle Mead GSA Depot Building
T3
Belle Mead, New Jersey 08502
Comm. Phone: (201) 359-2777
FTS Phone: 342-5323

CAMDEN AREA OFFICE

Area Director
U.S. Department of Labor—
OSHA
2101 Ferry Avenue, Room 403
Camden, New Jersey 08104
Comm. Phone: (609) 757-5181
FTS Phone: 488-5181

LONG ISLAND AREA OFFICE

Area Director
U.S. Department of Labor—
OSHA
990 Westbury Road
Westbury, New York 11590
Comm. Phone: (516) 334-3344
FTS Phone: 265-2909

DOVER AREA OFFICE

Area Director
U.S. Department of Labor—
OSHA
2 East Blackwell Street
Dover, New Jersey 07801
Comm. Phone: (201) 361-4050
FTS Phone: NONE

HASBROUCK HEIGHTS AREA
OFFICE

Area Director
U.S. Department of Labor—
OSHA
Teterboro Airport Professional
Building
877 Route 17, Room 206
Hasbrouck Heights, New Jersey
07604
Comm. Phone: (201) 288-1700
FTS Phone: NONE

PUERTO RICO AREA OFFICE

Area Director
U.S. Department of Labor—
OSHA
U.S. Courthouse & FOB
Carlos Chardon Avenue, Room
555
Hato Rey, Puerto Rico 00918
Comm. Phone: (809) 753-4457/
                    4072
FTS Phone: 753-4457
(through DC FTS)

BUFFALO AREA OFFICE

Area Director
U.S. Department of Labor—
OSHA
220 Delaware Avenue, Suite 509
Buffalo, New York 14202
Comm. Phone: (716) 846-4881
FTS Phone: 437-4881

SYRACUSE AREA OFFICE

Area Director
U.S. Department of Labor—
OSHA
100 South Clinton Street, Room
1267
Syracuse, New York 13260
Comm. Phone: (315) 423-5188
FTS Phone: 950-5188

ALBANY AREA OFFICE

Area Director
U.S. Department of Labor—
OSHA
Leo W. O'Brien Federal Build-
ing
Clinton Avenue & North Pearl
Street, Room 132
Albany, New York 12207
Comm. Phone: (518) 472-6085
FTS Phone: 562-6085

Philadelphia—Region III (Delaware, District of Columbia, Maryland, Pennsylvania, Virginia, and West Virginia)

PHILADELPHIA REGIONAL OFFICE

Regional Administrator
U.S. Department of Labor—
OSHA
Gateway Building, Suite 2100
3535 Market Street
Philadelphia, Pennsylvania
19104
Comm. Phone: (215) 596-1201
FTS Phone: 596-1201

PHILADELPHIA AREA OFFICE

Area Director
U.S. Department of Labor—
OSHA
U.S. Customs House, Rm. 242
Second & Chestnut Street
Philadelphia, Pennsylvania
19106
Comm. Phone: (215) 597-4955
FTS Phone: 597-4955

WILMINGTON DISTRICT OFFICE

District Supervisor
U.S. Department of Labor—
OSHA
Federal Office Building, Room 3007
844 King Street
Wilmington, Delaware 19801
Comm. Phone: (302) 573-6115
FTS Phone: 487-6115

WILKES-BARRE AREA OFFICE

Area Director
U.S. Department of Labor—
OSHA
Penn Place, Room 2005
20 North Pennsylvania Avenue
Wilkes-Barre, Pennsylvania
18701
Comm. Phone: (717) 826-6538
FTS Phone: 592-6538

CHARLESTON AREA OFFICE

Area Director
U.S. Department of Labor—
OSHA
500 Eagan Street, Room 303
Charleston, West Virginia 25301
Comm. Phone: (304) 347-5937
FTS Phone: 930-5937

PITTSBURGH AREA OFFICE

Area Director
U.S. Department of Labor—
OSHA
400 Penn Center Boulevard
Suite 600
Pittsburgh, Pennsylvania 15235
Comm. Phone: (412) 644-2905
FTS Phone: 722-2905

ERIE DISTRICT OFFICE

Supervisor
U.S. Department of Labor—
OSHA
147 West 18th Street
Erie, Pennsylvania 16501
Comm. Phone: (814) 453-4351
FTS Phone: 721-2242

BALTIMORE AREA OFFICE

Area Director
U.S. Department of Labor—
OSHA
Federal Building, Room 1110
Charles Center, 31 Hopkins
Plaza
Baltimore, Maryland 21201
Comm. Phone: (301) 962-2840
FTS Phone: 922-2840

HARRISBURG AREA OFFICE

Area Director
U.S. Department of Labor—
OSHA
Progress Plaza
49 North Progress Avenue
Harrisburg, Pennsylvania 17109
Comm. Phone: (717) 782-3902
FTS Phone: 590-3902

RICHMOND DISTRICT OFFICE

Area Director
U.S. Department of Labor—
OSHA
Federal Building, Room 6226
400 North 8th Street
PO Box 10186
Richmond, Virginia 23240
Comm. Phone: (804) 771-2864
FTS Phone: 925-2864

Atlanta—Region IV (Alabama, Florida, Georgia, Kentucky, Mississippi, North Carolina, South Carolina, and Tennessee)

ATLANTA REGIONAL OFFICE

Regional Administrator
U.S. Department of Labor—
OSHA
1375 Peachtree Street, NE, Suite 587
Atlanta, Georgia 30367
Comm. Phone: (404) 881-3573
FTS Phone: 257-3573/
                       2281

ATLANTA AREA OFFICE

Area Director
U.S. Department of Labor—
OSHA
Building 10, Suite 33
LaVista Perimeter Office Park
Tucker, Georgia 30084
Comm. Phone: (404) 221-4767
FTS Phone: 242-4767

COLUMBIA AREA OFFICE

Area Director
U.S. Department of Labor—
OSHA
1835 Assembly Street, Room 1468
Columbia, South Carolina 29201
Comm. Phone: (803) 765-5904
FTS Phone: 677-5904

SAVANNAH DISTRICT OFFICE

Supervisor
U.S. Department of Labor—
OSHA
400 Mall Boulevard, Suite J
Savannah, Georgia 31406
Comm. Phone: (912) 354-0733
FTS Phone: 248-4393

JACKSON AREA OFFICE

Area Director
U.S. Department of Labor—
OSHA
Federal Building, Suite 1445
100 West Capitol Street
Jackson, Mississippi 39269
Comm. Phone: (601) 960-4606
FTS Phone: 490-4606

BIRMINGHAM AREA OFFICE

Area Director
U.S. Department of Labor—
OSHA
Todd Mall
2047 Canyon Road
Birmingham, Alabama 35216
Comm. Phone: (205) 822-7100
FTS Phone: 229-1541

MOBILE DISTRICT OFFICE

Supervisor
U.S. Department of Labor—
OSHA
951 Government Street, Suite
511
Mobile, Alabama 36604
Comm. Phone: (205) 690-2131
FTS Phone: 537-2131
                      537-7163

FORT LAUDERDALE AREA OFFICE

Area Director
U.S. Department of Labor—
OSHA
Federal Building, Room 302
299 East Broward Boulevard
Fort Lauderdale, Florida 33301
Comm. Phone: (305) 527-7292
FTS Phone: 820-7292

FRANKFORT AREA OFFICE

Area Director
U.S. Department of Labor—
OSHA
John C. Watts Federal Building,
Room 127
330 W. Broadway
Frankfort, Kentucky 40601
Comm. Phone: (502) 227-7024
FTS Phone: NONE

JACKSONVILLE AREA OFFICE

Area Director
U.S. Department of Labor—
OSHA
Art Museum Plaza, Suite 4
2809 Art Museum Drive
Jacksonville, Florida 32207
Comm. Phone: (904) 791-2895
FTS Phone: 946-2895

RALEIGH AREA OFFICE

Area Director
U.S. Department of Labor—
OSHA
Federal Office Building, Room
406
310 New Bern Avenue
Raleigh, North Carolina 27601
Comm. Phone: (919) 755-4770
FTS Phone: 672-4770

TAMPA AREA OFFICE

Area Director
U.S. Department of Labor—
OSHA
700 Twiggs Street, Room 624
Tampa, Florida 33602
Comm. Phone: (813) 228-2821
FTS Phone: 826-2821

NASHVILLE AREA OFFICE

Area Director
U.S. Department of Labor—
OSHA
1720 West End Avenue, Suite
302
Nashville, Tennessee 37203
Comm. Phone: (615) 251-5313
FTS Phone: 852-5313

Chicago—Region V (Indiana, Illinois, Michigan, Minnesota, Ohio, and Wisconsin)

CHICAGO REGIONAL OFFICE

Regional Administrator
U.S. Department of Labor—
OSHA
230 South Dearborn Street,
32nd Floor, Room 3244
Chicago, Illinois 60604
Comm. Phone: (312) 353-2220
FTS Phone: 353-2220

CALUMET CITY AREA OFFICE

Area Director
U.S. Department of Labor—
OSHA
1400 Torrence Avenue, 2nd
Floor
Calumet City, Illinois 60409
Comm. Phone: (312) 891-3800
FTS Phone: NONE

CLEVELAND AREA OFFICE

Area Director
U.S. Department of Labor—
OSHA
Federal Office Building, Room
899
1240 East 9th Street
Cleveland, Ohio 44199
Comm. Phone: (216) 522-3818
FTS Phone: 293-3818

NILES AREA OFFICE

Area Director
U.S. Department of Labor—
OSHA
6000 West Touhy Avenue
Niles, Illinois 60648
Comm. Phone: (312) 631-8200/
8535   8535
FTS Phone: NONE

COLUMBUS AREA OFFICE

Area Director
U.S. Department of Labor—
OSHA
Federal Office Building, Room
634
200 North High Street
Columbus, Ohio 43215
Comm. Phone: (614) 469-5582
FTS Phone: 943-5582

AURORA AREA OFFICE

Area Director
U.S. Department of Labor—
OSHA
344 Smoke Tree Business Park
North Aurora, Illinois 60542
Comm. Phone: (312) 896-8700
FTS Phone: NONE

INDIANAPOLIS AREA OFFICE

Area Director
U.S. Department of Labor—
OSHA
USPO & Courthouse, Room 422
46 East Ohio Street
Indianapolis, Indiana 46204
Comm. Phone: (317) 269-7290
FTS Phone: 331-7290

CINCINNATI AREA OFFICE

Area Director
U.S. Department of Labor—
OSHA
Federal Office Building, Room
4028
550 Main Street
Cincinnati, Ohio 45202
Comm. Phone: (513) 684-2354
FTS Phone: 684-3784

EAU CLAIRE DISTRICT OFFICE

Supervisor
U.S. Department of Labor—
OSHA
Federal Building, U.S. Court-
house
500 Barstow Street, Room B-9
Eau Claire, Wisconisin 54701
Comm. Phone: (715) 832-9019
FTS Phone: 784-9231

MILWAUKEE AREA OFFICE

Area Director
U.S. Department of Labor—
OSHA
Clark Building, Room 400
633 West Wisconsin Avenue
Milwaukee, Wisconsin 53203
Comm. Phone: (414) 291-3315
FTS Phone: 362-3315

MADISON DISTRICT OFFICE

Supervisor
U.S. Department of Labor—
OSHA
2934 Fish Hatchery Road, Suite
220
Madison, Wisconsin 53713
Comm. Phone: (608) 264-5388
FTS Phone: 364-5388

APPLETON AREA OFFICE

Area Director
U.S. Department of Labor—
OSHA
2618 North Ballard Road
Appleton, Wisconsin 54911
Comm. Phone: (414) 734-4521
FTS Phone: 362-6218

MINNEAPOLIS AREA OFFICE

Area Director
U.S. Department of Labor—
OSHA
801 Butler Square Building
100 North 6th Street
Minneapolis, Minnesota 55403
Comm. Phone: (612) 725-2571
FTS Phone: 725-2571

PEORIA AREA OFFICE

Area Director
U.S. Department of Labor—
OSHA
3024 West Lake St.
Peoria, Illinois 61615
Comm. Phone: (309) 671-7033
FTS Phone: 360-7033

BELLEVILLE DISTRICT OFFICE

Supervisor
U.S. Department of Labor—
OSHA
218A Main Street
Belleville, Illinois 62220
Comm. Phone: (618) 277-5300
FTS Phone: 955-4200
(Springfield Operator)

TOLEDO AREA OFFICE

Area Director
U.S. Department of Labor—
OSHA
Federal Office Building, Room
734
234 North Summit Street
Toledo, Ohio 43604
Comm. Phone: (419) 259-7542
FTS Phone: 979-7542

DETROIT AREA OFFICE

Area Director
U.S. Department of Labor—
OSHA
231 West Lafayette, Room 628
Detroit, Michigan 48226
Comm. Phone: (313) 226-6720
FTS Phone: 226-6720

Dallas—Region VI (Arkansas, Louisiana, New Mexico, Oklahoma, and Texas)

DALLAS REGIONAL OFFICE

Regional Administrator
U.S. Department of Labor—
OSHA
555 Griffin Square Building,
Room 602
Dallas, Texas 75202
Comm. Phone: (214) 767-4731
FTS Phone: 729-4731

DALLAS AREA OFFICE

Area Director
U.S. Department of Labor—
OSHA
1425 West Pioneer Drive
Irving, Texas 75061
Comm. Phone: (214) 767-5347
FTS Phone: 729-5347

AUSTIN AREA OFFICE

Area Director
U.S. Department of Labor—
OSHA
303 Grant Bldg.
611 East 6th Street
Austin, Texas 78701
Comm. Phone: (512) 397-5783
FTS Phone: 734-5783

ALBUQUERQUE AREA OFFICE

Area Director
U.S. Department of Labor—
OSHA
Western Bank Building, Room
1407
505 Marquette Avenue, NW
Albuquerque, New Mexico
87102
Comm. Phone: (505) 776-3411
FTS Phone: 474-3411

CORPUS CHRISTI AREA OFFICE

Area Director
U.S. Department of Labor—
OSHA
4455 S. Padre Drive, Suite 105
Corpus Christi, Texas 78411
Comm. Phone: (512) 888-3257
FTS Phone: 734-3257

HOUSTON AREA OFFICE

Area Director
U.S. Department of Labor—
OSHA
2320 LaBranch Street, Room
2118
Houston, Texas 77004
Comm. Phone: (713) 750-1727
FTS Phone: 526-6727

LITTLE ROCK AREA OFFICE

Area Director
U.S. Department of Labor—
OSHA
West Mark Building, Suite 212
4120 West Markham
Little Rock, Arkansas 72205
Comm. Phone: (501) 378-6291
FTS Phone: 740-6291

BATON ROUGE AREA OFFICE

Area Director
U.S. Department of Labor—
OSHA
Hoover Annex Suite 200
2156 Wooddale Boulevard
Baton Rouge, Louisiana 70806
Comm. Phone: (504) 389-0474
FTS Phone: 687-0474

LUBBOCK AREA OFFICE

Area Director
U.S. Department of Labor—
OSHA
Federal Building, Room 421
1205 Texas Avenue
Lubbock, Texas 79401
Comm. Phone: (806) 762-7681
FTS Phone: 738-7681

OKLAHOMA CITY AREA OFFICE

Area Director
U.S. Department of Labor—
OSHA
50 Penn Place, Suite 408
Oklahoma City, Oklahoma
73118
Comm. Phone: (405) 231-5351
FTS Phone: 736-5351

Kansas City—Region VII (Iowa, Kansas, Missouri, and Nebraska)

KANSAS CITY REGIONAL OFFICE

Regional Director
U.S. Department of Labor—
OSHA
911 Walnut Street, Room 406
Kansas City, Missouri 64106
Comm. Phone: (816) 374-5861
FTS Phone: 758-5861

KANSAS CITY AREA OFFICE

Area Director
U.S. Department of Labor—
OSHA
1150 Grand Avenue, 6th Floor,
Room 606
Kansas City, Missouri 64106
Comm. Phone: (816) 374-2756
FTS Phone: 758-2756

ST. LOUIS AREA OFFICE

Area Director
U.S. Department of Labor—
OSHA
4300 Goodfellow Boulevard,
Building 105E
St. Louis, Missouri 63120
Comm. Phone: (314) 263-2749
FTS Phone: 273-2749

DES MOINES AREA OFFICE

Area Director
U.S. Department of Labor—
OSHA
210 Walnut Street, Room 815
Des Moines, Iowa 50309
Comm. Phone: (515) 284-4794
FTS Phone: 862-4794

WICHITA AREA OFFICE

Area Director
U.S. Department of Labor—
OSHA
216 North Waco, Suite B
Wichita, Kansas 67202
Comm. Phone: (316) 269-6644
FTS Phone: 752-6644

OMAHA DISTRICT OFFICE

District Supervisor
U.S. Department of Labor—
OSHA
Overland-Wolf Building, Room
100
6910 Pacific Street
Omaha, Nebraska 68106
Comm. Phone: (402) 221-9341
FTS Phone: 864-9341

Denver—Region VIII (Colorado, Montana, North Dakota, South Dakota, Utah, and Wyoming)

DENVER REGIONAL OFFICE

Regional Administrator
U.S. Department of Labor—
OSHA
Federal Building, Room 1554
1961 Stout Street
Denver, Colorado 80294
Comm. Phone: (303) 837-3883
FTS Phone: 327-3883

BILLINGS AREA OFFICE

Area Director
U.S. Department of Labor—
OSHA
Petroleum Building, Suite 210
2812 1st Avenue North
Billings, Montana 59101
Comm. Phone: (406) 657-6649
FTS Phone: 585-6649

SALT LAKE CITY AREA OFFICE

Area Director
U.S. Department of Labor—
OSHA
U.S. Post Office Building, Room 505
350 South Main Street
Salt Lake City, Utah 84101
Comm. Phone: (801) 524-5080
FTS Phone: 588-5080

BISMARCK AREA OFFICE

Area Director
U.S. Department of Labor—
OSHA
Federal Building, Room 348
PO Box 2439
Bismarck, North Dakota 58501
Comm. Phone: (701) 255-4011,
Ext. 521
FTS Phone: 783-4521

DENVER AREA OFFICE

Area Director
U.S. Department of Labor—
OSHA
Tremont Center, 1st Floor
333 West Colfax
Denver, Colorado 80204
Comm. Phone: (303) 837-5285
FTS Phone: 327-5285

San Francisco—Region IX (American Samoa, Arizona, California, Guam, Hawaii, Nevada, Trust Territory of the Pacific Islands)

SAN FRANCISCO REGIONAL OFFICE

Regional Administrator
U.S. Department of Labor—
OSHA
11349 Federal Building
450 Golden Gate Avenue
P.O. Box 36017
San Francisco, California 94102
Comm. Phone: (415) 556-0586
FTS Phone: 556-0586

LONG BEACH AREA OFFICE

Area Director
U.S. Department of Labor—
OSHA
400 Oceangate, Suite 530
Long Beach, California 90802
Comm. Phone: (213) 432-3434
FTS Phone: 796-2431

HONOLULU AREA OFFICE

Area Director
U.S. Department of Labor—
OSHA
300 Ala Moana Boulevard, Suite 5122
P.O. Box 50072
Honolulu, Hawaii 96850
Comm. Phone: (808) 546-3157
FTS Phone: 556-0220
(FTS Operator)

SAN FRANCISCO DISTRICT OFFICE

Area Director
U.S. Department of Labor—
OSHA
11341 Federal Building
450 Golden Gate Avenue
San Francisco, California 94102
Comm. Phone: (415) 556-7260
FTS Phone: 556-7260

PHOENIX AREA OFFICE

Area Director
U.S. Department of Labor—
OSHA
Amerco Towers, Suite 300
2721 North Central Avenue
Phoenix, Arizona 85004
Comm. Phone: (602) 241-2007
FTS Phone: 261-2007

CARSON CITY AREA OFFICE

Area Director
U.S. Department of Labor—
OSHA
1050 East William Street, Suite
402
Carson City, Nevada 89701
Comm. Phone: (702) 883-1226
FTS Phone: NONE

Seattle—Region X (Alaska, Idaho, Oregon, and Washington)

SEATTLE REGIONAL OFFICE

Regional Administrator
U.S. Department of Labor—
OSHA
Federal Office Building, Room
6003
909 1st Avenue
Seattle, Washington 98174
Comm. Phone: (206) 442-5930
FTS Phone: 399-5930

ANCHORAGE AREA OFFICE

Area Director
U.S. Department of Labor—
OSHA
Federal Building
701 C Street, Box 29
Anchorage, Alaska 99513
Comm. Phone: (907) 271-5152
FTS Phone: NONE

OSHA TRAINING INSTITUTE

OSHA Training Institute
U.S. Department of Labor
1555 Times Drive
Des Plaines, Illinois 60018
Comm. Phone: (312) 297-4810
FTS Phone: 353-2500

BELLEVUE AREA OFFICE

Area Director
U.S. Department of Labor—
OSHA
121 107th Street, NE
Bellevue, Washington 98004
Comm. Phone: (206) 442-7520
FTS Phone: 399-7520

CINCINNATI LABORATORY

OSHA Cincinnati Laboratory
U.S.P.O. Building, Room 108
5th & Walnut Streets
Cincinnati, Ohio 45202
Comm. Phone: (513) 684-2531
FTS Phone: 684-2531

BOISE AREA OFFICE

Area Director
U.S. Department of Labor—
OSHA
1315 West Idaho Street
Boise, Idaho 83702
Comm. Phone: (208) 384-1867
FTS Phone: 554-1867

PORTLAND AREA OFFICE

Area Director
U.S. Department of Labor—
OSHA
1220 Southwest 3rd Street,
Room 640
Portland, Oregon 97204
Comm. Phone: (503) 221-2251
FTS Phone: 423-2251

SALT LAKE CITY LABORATORY

SLC Analytical Laboratory
390 Wakara Way, Research Park
Salt Lake City, Utah 84108
Comm. Phone: (801) 524-5287
FTS Phone: 588-5287

SALT LAKE CITY HEALTH
RESPONSE UNIT

Health Response Unit—OSHA
390 Wakara Way
Salt Lake City, Utah 84108
Comm. Phone: (801) 524-5896
FTS Phone: 588-5896

On-the-Job Injuries and Workers' Compensation

Recent developments in Workers' Compensation cases are allowing some employees to sue bosses directly in court for their injuries. Workers may benefit substantially if this trend continues. The reason is that under Workers' Compensation, employees are given a predetermined amount of compensation for their injuries and nothing more. Critics of the system claim that money paid to injured workers is less than average jury verdicts for similar injuries outside the workplace.

New legal theories are being asserted to circumvent Workers' Compensation. For example, in one recent case, an employee working for a scaffold manufacturer was injured by a defective scaffold. The worker sued the company directly for his injuries. His lawyer asserted that the company was accountable as a manufacturer, not an employer. The court agreed.

Other states are allowing employers to be sued for intentionally causing worker injuries. One employee proved that he contracted asbestosis on the job. The employee claimed the company was liable because it fraudulently concealed the origins of his disease; he was able to recover damages directly from the company for his injuries.

Thus, be aware that Workers' Compensation may *not* preclude you from recovering additional damages, no matter what anyone tells you. That is why it is best to contact a lawyer immediately if you are injured while working.

Working in a Smoke-Free Environment

Many workers are demanding the right to work in a smoke-free environment. This right is being upheld with increasing regularity through the passage of state laws, city ordinances, federal legislation, and case decisions. Several states, including Missouri and New Jersey, have adopted the view that employers are required to provide a smoke-free workplace for employees who are sensitive to smoke. Other states (i.e., Colorado, Minnesota, Montana, Nebraska, Oregon, and Utah) have laws specifically dealing with smoke in the workplace. Various federal agencies, including the Merit Board and the Equal Employment Opportunity Commission, have also ruled that employers must take reasonable steps to keep smoke away from workers who are sensitive to it.

The result of these laws and regulations varies. Some employees have been successful in banning smoking in the office where they work. Others are suing for and receiving unemployment compensation after resigning from their jobs. Still others are seeking disability pay. In one recent case, a woman was awarded $20,000 in disability pay because she developed asthmatic bronchitis after being transferred to an office with several smokers. The court also ruled that unless her employer (the government) transferred her to a job in a smoke-free office within sixty days, she would be eligible for disability retirement benefits of $500 per month.

The following strategies may help you if you desire to work in a smoke-free environment.

In order to protect your rights and increase the chances of a successful lawsuit, an aggrieved worker can do the following:

1. *Gather the facts.* Document the environment conditions of your work location to support your request. For example, it is important to determine the number of smokers, type of ventilation, physical arrangement of desks, how often people smoke, etc.

2. *Acquire medical proof.* Visit a doctor if you suffer an illness from working in a smoke-filled environment. Note the prescriptions and amount of time lost from work. It is also a good idea to visit your employer's medical department to document your condition.

3. *Speak to management.* Present management with a letter from your personal doctor stating your need to work in a smoke-free area. If possible, request the transfer collectively with other workers.

4. *Confirm your grievance in writing.* After the initial discussion, you may wish to document your request by presenting management with a letter similar to the following:

(Date)

(Name & Title)
(Department)
(Company Name & Address)

Dear (Name):

This will confirm the conversations we have had regarding the need to provide me (us) with a work environment free of tobacco smoke. Enclosed is information to support the request to eliminate smoking in work areas.

Also enclosed is a petition signed by employees in our work location. (If this is an individual request and there is no petition, then use the second paragraph of the same petition in this letter as the second paragraph.)

As my (our) ability to work is constantly undermined by the unhealthy, toxic pollutants to which I (we) am (are) chronically exposed, I (we) will appreciate your giving this request priority. May I (we) expect a reply by (date)?

Very truly yours,

(Send copies to whatever level management seems appropriate from verbal contacts, union representative at local level, and personal physician.)

Wait a few days after sending this letter. Then, if a satisfactory response is not made, you may wish to send an additional letter similar to the following:

(Date)

(Name & Title)
(Department)
(Company Name & Address)

Dear (Name):

As of this date, I (we) have received no reply to my (our) request of (date).

(If temporary or interim measures have been tried but are not successful, identify them here, i.e., the additional ventilation you have introduced has not been sufficient to clear the air and has caused employees to work in cold drafts. In view of the high cost of energy, it would seem in everyone's best interest to proceed without delay to re-stricted smoking in work areas.)

To protect my (our) health while in your employ it is vital that the company provide me (us) with a smoke-free work area to comply with the common law requirements of this state. I (we) have asked organizations who are expert in this area of occupational health to provide you with addi-tional information on my (our) behalf.

I (we) will be most appreciative of your immediate re-sponse to this urgent matter.

Sincerely,

(Send copies to middle management, president of company and medical director of company; also union representative and personal physician.)

5. *Speak to a lawyer.* If you receive a negative response, you may wish to consult a lawyer to determine your rights. The lawyer can assert several options on your behalf. For example, she can assist you in presenting demands directly to the employer or union representative, file an action in court, contact OSHA, or sue the employer under the Equal Employment Opportunity Act. Legal fees are sometimes paid to successful litigants under these acts.

(NOTE: Although such action is probably illegal, be aware that your employer may fire or penalize you for enforcing your rights. This possibility should be considered before you decide to retain a lawyer.)

6. *Contact an appropriate agency for further information.* Your regional Department of Labor, Department of Health, or OSHA office will provide you with more information. In addition, you may wish to contact the New Jersey Group Against Smoking Pollution. GASP maintains a list of perti-nent cases, regulations, and lawyers who are knowledgeable in this area.

7. *Speak to a doctor about Worker's Compensation.* If you incur medical expenses due to smoke-related on-the-job illness, discuss filing a Worker's Compensation claim with your doctor.

Protecting Valuable Ideas

Are you entitled to compensation if you develop a valuable idea which is used by your employer?

The answer depends on a number of factors. For example, Jonathan develops a manufacturing process which he thinks will save his company money. Jonathan tells his boss, and the idea is incorporated into the company's production process. Jonathan is not compensated for the idea. He resigns and sues to recover a percentage of the money saved by the idea's use.

Jonathan's case is not as strong as it appears. The reason is that ideas, plans, methods, and procedures for business operations cannot be copyrighted. This is also true with respect to certain ideas for intellectual property (story outlines, etc.).

The law generally states that ideas belong to no one and are there for the taking. In addition, an idea is presumed to be a work made for hire and property of the employer if an employee offers it voluntarily without contracting to receive additional compensation. Thus, for example, if Jonathan can prove that the idea was his own original, unique creation and was furnished with the understanding that he would be promoted or compensated once it was used, he may have a stronger case.

Many workers are unknowingly exploited because they give away their ideas without understanding their rights. Review the following strategies if you wish to avoid being exploited in this area.

1. *Crystallize your ideas, method, or process in writing.* This is essential because it is difficult to prove you are the creator of a valuable idea unless it is in writing.

2. *Be sure the writing is detailed and specific.* This can increase your chances of proving the idea is a protectable property interest. For example, if you write a proposal for a unique and original television show, be sure to fully describe the characters, budget, and script dialogue rather than briefly discussing the concept of the show.

3. *Avoid volunteering ideas.* In one famous case, a homemaker mailed an unsolicited cheesecake recipe to a baking company. The recipe was used and became a popular money-maker. Although the woman sued the company for damages, she lost. The court ruled that no recovery was obtainable because the homemaker voluntarily gave her idea to the company.

4. *Negotiate a predetermined method of compensation.* Always crystallize your compensation arrangement in writing. The following sample agreement contains many important points which should be clarified.

Acknowledgment of Receipt of Idea

On this day, received from (employee's name) an idea concerning _____, which was presented in the form of _____ .

The company acknowledges that it has not used the idea in the past. If used, (employee's name) will be compensated according to the following: _____ _____ .*

The employer agrees to maintain the confidentiality of the material submitted to us by (employee's name) and

---

* NOTE: If compensation is difficult to determine at the time the acknowledgment is prepared, it can state that the employee will be compensated in a manner mutually agreed upon by the parties and that the idea will remain the property of the employee until such formula is determined.

agrees not to disclose it, or the ideas upon which it is based, to any person, firm, or entity without the employee's consent.

_____   By: _____
(Date)   (Employer)

                    By: _____
                         (Employee)

5. *Get a receipt.* If you cannot obtain an acknowledgment, it is important to prove you gave your valuable idea to another. One way to accomplish this is by sending a certified letter which states:

- That you submitted an idea
- That the idea was offered in confidence
- That you would be paid if the idea was used
- That the idea could not be used without your consent

The following letter is an illustration:

(Date)

(Name)
Vice President
LMN Pictures Corp.
(Address)

Re: The Submission of My Original Screenplay Proposal "The Life of Mr. X"

Dear (Name):

I enjoyed speaking to your about my original screenplay proposal. Based on our conversation, enclosed please find:

1. My 250-page script entitled "The Life of Mr. X"

2. My 20-page plot outline
3. My 35-page character sketches

You have agreed to review my materials in confidence, and not disclose the contents to any other person, firm, or entity without my consent. Furthermore, in the event the screenplay is accepted, it is agreed that I shall have the first option of writing the movie screenplay.

I look forward to hearing from you.

Sincerely,

(Send certified mail, return receipt requested.)

6. *Avoid signing releases.* Some companies and individuals ask creators to sign releases stating they assume no obligation in reading the material. *Avoid signing such releases.* However, you still may be able to protect yourself even if you sign one. Wait a few days, then send a certified letter to the organization reminding them you are the original creator of the idea which you submitted. This may help protect you in the event the idea is used without your consent.

7. *Make copies.* Keep copies of all materials and letters that you send to others. Some people mail an unopened copy of the package back to themselves for this purpose. The postmark date on the front of the envelope may establish you were the original creator on the postmark date.

8. *Speak to a lawyer.* It is best to consult a lawyer whenever you wish to protect a valuable idea. This is especially true if you develop an idea that is capable of being patented.

Summary of Steps to Take while Working for Your Employer

1. Save all correspondence, copies of records, and other documents

2. Notify your employer immediately if you discover errors in your salary, bonus, or commissions

3. Avoid accepting reductions in your salary or other benefits, particularly if you have a written contract which prohibits oral modifications of important terms

4. Enforce your rights immediately in the event you are exploited.

5. Recognize your rights to privacy, unionize, health and safety in the workplace

Asserting Your Post-Termination Rights

The third phase of your employment relationship—the post-employment phase—is just as important as knowing how to be hired properly and enforcing your on-the-job rights. Many workers are fired unfairly, yet bow their heads and shuffle their feet out the door. In fact, millions of dollars in post-termination benefits are squandered each year by people who fail to recognize what they are legally entitled to. This section will help you recognize and assert your post-termination rights.

Unfair Discharge

There are many state and federal laws that protect workers from unfair discharge. For example, dismissals based on the following are illegal and you can receive money damages by proving you were fired primarily for any of these reasons. This is true even if you were hired at will without a written contract.

- Age
- Sex

- Race, national origin, or religion
- Union membership or participation in union or political activity
- Group activity to protest unsafe work conditions
- Refusal to commit an unlawful act on the employer's behalf (e.g., commit perjury or fix prices)
- Reporting alleged violations of the law ("whistle-blowing")
- Performing a public obligation (e.g., attending jury duty or supplying information about a fellow employee to the police)
- Being sued for nonpayment of a debt or wage garnishment
- Exercising statutory rights or privileges (e.g., filing a Workers' Compensation claim)

The following four common causes of unfair firings deserve special mention:

Whistleblowing

The law protects workers who tattle on abuses of authority. For example, the state of Michigan has a "Whistle-blower's Protection Act" which protects employees from retaliation after they report suspected violations of laws or regulations. This statute provides specific remedies, including reinstatement with back pay, restoration of seniority and lost fringe benefits, litigation costs, attorney fees, and a $500 fine. Other states have similar laws.

People who work for federal agencies are also protected from whistleblowing. In one recent case a nurse was dismissed after reporting abuses of patients at a Veterans' Administration Medical Center. She sought reinstatement and damages before a federal review panel. The panel ordered that she be reinstated and awarded her $7,500 in back pay.

Firing to Deny Accrued Benefits

The law obligates employers to deal in good faith with long-time employees. Workers with seniority sometimes receive money damages when they prove this covenant is violated. For example, one man with forty years of service claimed he was fired so his company would avoid paying commissions otherwise due on a $5 million sale. A court found this to be true, and awarded him substantial money even though he had been hired at will. Another employee was fired after working thirteen years without a written contract. The court ruled that the company did this to deprive him of the vesting of pension benefits in his fifteenth year of service. The employee was awarded $75,000 in damages.

Actual cases such as these demonstrate the right of employees to receive the fruits of their labors. If you are fired just before you are supposed to receive anticipated benefits (e.g., accrued pension, profit-sharing, or commissions due), and have reason to suspect you were fired to be denied these benefits, consult a lawyer immediately to protect your rights.

(NOTE: If an employer fires you for a lawful reason, i.e., for cause, the fact that you are about to become eligible for a substantial benefit may not make the firing illegal.)

Absence from Work

You can be fired for absence from work due to illness unless your union or written employment contract prohibits this. However, you cannot be fired for asserting a workers' compensation claim. If you are penalized after making such a claim, contact your local Workers' Compensation Board for the purpose of filing a formal complaint.

Maternity Leave

Childbirth leave and pregnancy-related disability are protected by numerous federal and state laws. These laws prohibit employers from firing or demoting workers on the basis of pregnancy. Many states provide disability and sick leave benefits to pregnant mothers, while in other states, an extended unpaid maternity leave or child care leave can only be granted at the discretion of the employer. If the employer permits extended child care leave, guidelines promulgated by the Equal Employment Opportunity Commission require male employees to receive the same benefits.

(REMINDER: If you work without a written contract of a fixed duration, are not a tenured public employee or civil servant, or do not belong to a union, your employer is generally free to fire you *for any reason at all,* provided the reason does not involve discrimination, or is based upon a form of protected conduct. That is why, if possible, it is important to obtain a written employment contract which specifies that you can only be fired *for cause.*)

What to Do when You Are Fired

Most employers fire workers without warning. This is done to deprive them of the opportunity to carefully consider their options. However, the fact that you are axed suddenly does not mean you should accept less benefits than you deserve. The following strategies can help increase severance benefits and/or damages in the event you are fired.

1. *Stall for time.* Do not panic or scream at your boss when informed of the bad news. Request time to think things over. Additional time may help you learn important facts and negotiate a better settlement. *Thus, avoid accepting the company's first offer, if possible.*

2. *Review your employment contract.* If you signed a written contract, re-read it. Review what it says about termination. For example, can you be fired at any time without cause, or must the employer send you written notice before

the effective termination date? It is essential to know what the contract says in order to map out an effective action plan.

(NOTE: If you belong to a union or work for the federal government, you are probably required to follow internal grievance procedures specified in the collective bargaining agreement unless you will be damaged by not taking immediate private action.)

3. *Discover why you are fired.* This can help in the event you decide to sue your former employer. For example, once you receive reasons why you are fired, the employer may be precluded from offering additional reasons at a trial or arbitration. Thus, it is a good idea to request a written explanation of why you were discharged. The following letter illustrates the kind of request that can be made.

(Date)

(Name)
President
ABC Company
(Address)

Re: My termination

Dear (Name):

On (date), ABC Corporation terminated my services as (title). I was told by (name of person) that my services were no longer required, effective (date).

(Name of person) never told me why I was terminated. Accordingly, I hereby request such information.

Thank you for your cooperation in this matter.

Sincerely,

(Send certified mail, return receipt requested)

You may have grounds to commence a lawsuit if an employer refuses to tell you why you were fired. Some

states, including Missouri, have *service letter statutes*. These
are laws which require companies to specify *in writing* the
true reasons for an employee's termination.

4. *Learn who made the decision to fire you.* You may discover you were fired for petty reasons (e.g., jealousy), and
be reinstated. Usually, however, there is little you can do
other than negotiate a better severance deal.

5. *Request to see your personnel file.*   Some states permit
terminated workers to review and copy the contents of their
personnel files. Sometimes these files do not support firing
decisions because they contain favorable recommendations
and comments. If you can only be fired for cause and the
company gives you specific reasons why you were fired,
your file may demonstrate that such reasons are factually
incorrect and/or legally insufficient. If this occurs, you may
have a strong case against the former employer for breach of
contract.

Thus, try to review your file. Even if you fail to discover
pertinent information, this will help you be better prepared
for future interviews. Make copies of all recommendations
and letters of praise. In addition, add your own explanations
and supporting documentation to the file if you discover
inaccurate comments.

6. *Reconstruct promises.* If promises were made by up-
per management, recall the time, place, and whether these
statements were made in the presence of witnesses. The
facts surrounding your employment history may justify a
finding that you were fired improperly.

For example, if the company president tells you at the
hiring interview, "Don't worry, we never fire anyone except
for cause," this statement may be sufficient to create rights in
the event you are fired. The following actual case demonstrates why:

> A company executive worked for thirty-two years without
> a written contract. The man was suddenly fired. He sued
> his company and argued that he had done nothing wrong
> to justify the firing. At the trial, the executive proved that:

1. The company president told him several times that he would continue to be employed if he did a good job

2. The company had a policy of not firing executives except for cause

3. He was never told, criticized, or warned that his job was in jeopardy

4. He had a commendable track record; his employment history was excellent, and he had received periodic merit bonuses, raises, and promotions

The executive won the case because the facts created an implied promise that the company could not arbitrarily terminate him.

Thus, try to reconstruct all promises that are made and write down everything you are told when you are hired. This should include what was said, who said it, where the words were spoken, and the names of any witnesses who were present. The reason is that some courts are ruling that oral promises of job security are binding even though employment is not for a definite term.

7. *Review employment manuals.* Language in company policy manuals is sometimes viewed as promises which employees may rely upon. Some courts have ruled that provisions in personnel manuals and handbooks distributed to employees *are* enforceable against employers. The following recent case is a good example:

A man working for a Fortune 500 company did not sign an employment contract when he was hired. However, during negotiations, he was assured that the job was secure because the company never terminated employees without just cause.

The man signed an application form which stated that employment was subject to the provisions of the company handbook on personnel policies and procedures. The manual stipulated "that employees would be fired for just and sufficient cause only" if internal steps toward rehabilitation were taken and failed.

For eight years, the employee received periodic raises and job promotions and turned down offers from other companies. However, the employee was suddenly fired without warning. He sued the company, claiming he had been wrongfully discharged. The company argued he was terminated properly, since he had been hired at will.

The court ruled in the employee's favor, and he won the right to sue the company for breach of contract. The court stated that the facts created a company obligation to terminate its employees in a manner stated in the manual.

If your employer publishes rules and work regulations, read them carefully. Look for answers to the following questions:

- Who is authorized to fire you?
- Must the firing decision be approved by a committee to be effective?
- Must you be given written reasons for the firing?
- Can you obtain a copy of your personnel file?
- Must formal procedures be followed (e.g., do you have the right to argue before a grievance committee)?
- Must you be given a final warning before the firing is effective?
- Must you first be asked if you would take a job demotion?
- Are there set rules regarding severance benefits?
- Must you be fired only for cause?

Thus, don't forget that handbooks and manuals can be used as bargaining tools to effectuate a better settlement. The reason is that if the employer fails to act in a manner specified in its manual, it may be violating an important contract obligation.

8. *Did you sign an employment application?* Employment applications sometimes contain important employment

terms. Be sure to read the employment application before you sign it, and save a copy for your files.

Always review this document after you are fired; you may discover that you were fired improperly.

9. *Avoid signing exit agreements.* Exit agreements, releases, and covenants not to sue are complicated documents and should never be signed until you speak to a lawyer. Some employers are afraid of using these agreements because they don't want the terminated employee to consult a lawyer. When a lawyer enters the picture, the employer may be forced to negotiate a less favorable settlement, particularly if the employee has a legitimate claim. Remember, you may be relinquishing valuable rights by signing exit agreements without proper guidance.

10. *Request a negotiating session.* Lower-level employees often have difficulty arranging an additional negotiating session after being notified they are fired. This is because many companies refuse to negotiate severance compensation. Some employers even request terminated workers to vacate the premises immediately. However, many executives are granted time to consider a company's first offer.

The following negotiation points will help you obtain a better severance arrangement whatever your situation.

Negotiating Points to Maximize Post-Termination Benefits

It is unlikely you will get your job back once the firing decision has been made. Your main concern is to receive clarification on the amount of accrued wages and available wage equivalents. It is essential to act in a professional manner; being vindictive or making threats won't solve anything. Many employers are fearful of the increasing amount of employee-related litigation and are flexible in easing the departure of terminated individuals. Thus, the trick is to discuss important details up front to receive the benefits you deserve.

The following points should be discussed with your ex-employer:

1. *Wages*. The amount of severance pay is an important item. According to personnel experts, the rule of thumb is one week of pay for each year on the job, but this varies by industry and company. However, consider these strategies:

   a. Try to stay on the payroll as long as possible
   b. Ask to receive severance pay in one lump sum, rather than installments
   c. Discuss relocation allowances, vacation pay, overtime and unused sick pay. Request additional payments as compensation for allowing the employer to fire you without notice

2. *Bonus*. How will your bonus be computed? If you were entitled to receive a bonus at the end of a full year, ask for it now. If the company refuses, argue that the termination deprived you of the right to receive the bonus. If that doesn't work, insist that your bonus be pro-rated accordingly to the amount of time you worked during the year.

3. *Pension and profit-sharing benefits.* The law requires employers to furnish employees with *precise* details regarding the nature and amount of their pension and profit-sharing benefits when they resign or are fired. Employers are obligated to pay "vested" pension and profit-sharing benefits even if an individual decides to sue his former employer. Thus, it is important to know the vesting rules of your plan. Consult your personnel office or union representative and be sure to read the summary of rules which your employer is required to give you by law.

4. *Medical Coverage.* Does medical coverage stop the day you are fired, or is there a grace period (typically thirty days)? Ask for a copy of the policy. Do you have the option of extending coverage beyond the grace period? If so, what is your contribution to the premium charge? Does it cover your wife and family? If no medical coverage extension is offered, speak to the company's group insurer representative. You may be able to obtain a reasonable medical *conversion policy.*

(NOTE: If you are married and your spouse is working, check to see if you are covered under your spouse's health policy. It may not be necessary to purchase additional coverage.)

5. *Life Insurance.* Inquire about life insurance coverage and ask for a copy of the policy. Some group life insurance plans permit terminated employees to convert the policy to other life insurance within a specific time period. Ask your ex-employer if there is such a plan. Be sure you know the manner and time period required to exercise the conversion privilege.

6. *Your cover story.* Clarify how the news of your departure will be announced. Discuss the story to be told to outsiders (e.g., that you resigned for "personal reasons"). Will your employer furnish you with favorable references when you look for a new job? This is important.

Some employees discover that an ex-employer is making inaccurate references which inhibit their chances of obtaining new employment. It is important to take affirmative action if this happens to you. For example, you should send a certified letter to the ex-employer to protect your rights. This may establish grounds for a defamation lawsuit if the employer continues to make inaccurate statements. The following is an example of a letter which will document your protest:

(Date)

(Name of Employer)
Anyplace, U.S.A.

Dear (Name):

On (date) I applied for a job with (name of potential employer). At the interview, I was told that your firm had submitted an inaccurate, unfavorable reference about me.

You supposedly said the reason I was fired was that I was an uncooperative and complaining worker.

This is untrue. In fact, after reviewing my personal file which I copied, there is not one derogatory comment about me in the entire file.

You are hereby requested to cease making such inaccurate statements about my job performance. If you do not comply, be assured that I will contact my lawyer and take appropriate legal action.

Thank you for your cooperation in this matter.

Sincerely,

(cc: To potential employer)
(Send certified mail, return receipt requested.)

7. *Don't be forced into retirement.* Under the federal Age Discrimination in Employment Act, you cannot be forced to retire before age seventy unless you are a top-level executive who receives at least $27,000 in benefits, or are required to retire because of the nature of the job (e.g., firefighter). Thus, think twice if you are offered the opportunity to resign rather than being fired. Although it sounds better, you may unknowingly be relinquishing valuable benefits, including unemployment compensation, contributory savings, and

other accrued benefits, by accepting the offer. For example, when you resign from a job, you may be entitled to receive money personally contributed to a pension plan. However, you generally *lose* any funds contributed by your employer except to the extent those contributions may have become "vested."

Thus, analyze your benefits package carefully before making such a decision.

8. *Other Perks.* Some employees receive office space, telephone, secretarial help, and the continued use of a company car while looking for employment. Discuss these points if you feel they are negotiable. Your employer might even agree to tide you over with a loan if you ask for it.

9. *Outplacement Guidance.* Many employers are providing résumé assistance, secretarial help, and job search expense money to dismissed workers. Others provide outplacement guidance and career counseling. Request such assistance if appropriate.

Additional Points to Remember when You Are Fired

1. *Confirm your agreement in writing.* After you have reached a severance agreement with your former employer, you should always send a certified letter to protect your rights. The letter may serve to clarify points that are still ambiguous as well as document the deal that has been made. In addition, if the former employer fails to abide by an important term, such a letter may increase your chances of success if you decide to sue for breach of contract.

The following letter is a good example:

(Date)

(Name of Corporate Officer)
Title
ABC Corp.
Anyplace, USA

Dear (Name):

This will confirm our agreement with respect to my severance:

1. I will be kept on the payroll through February 28, 1984, and will receive two (2) weeks vacation pay, which shall be included with my final check on that date.

2. ABC Corp. will pay my last year's bonus of $1,000 immediately.

3. ABC Corp. will purchase both my nonvested and vested company stock, totaling approximately 1200 shares (as of October, 1983) at the buy-in price of $17.75 per share, or at the market rate if it is higher at the time of re-purchase, no later than February 28, 1984.

4. ABC Corp. will continue to provide my major medical, disability, and life insurance policies up to February 28, 1984. If possible, it will assist in the conversion of said policies, to be borne at my own expense after that date.

5. I will be permitted full use of the company's premises at (location) from the hours of 9:00 A.M. to 5:00 P.M. This shall include use of a secretary, telephone, stationery, and other amenities to assist me in obtaining another position.

6. I will be permitted to continue using the automobile previously supplied to me through February 28, 1984, under the same terms and conditions presently in effect. On that date, I will return all sets of keys in my posses-

sion together with all other papers and documents belonging to the company.

7. ABC Corp. will reimburse me for all reasonable and necessary expenses related to the completion of company business after I submit appropriate vouchers and records.

8. ABC Corp. agrees to provide me with a favorable letter of recommendation and reference(s), and will announce to the trade that I am resigning for "personal reasons." I am enclosing a letter for that purpose.

9. Although unanticipated, ABC Corp. will not contest my filing for unemployment insurance after February 28, 1984, and will assist me in obtaining same if necessary.

10. If a position is found prior to February 28, 1984, a lump sum payment of my remaining severance will be paid. The stock program will be purchased as of the date of employment by another company if prior to February 28, 1984.

If any of the terms of this letter are incorrect, please advise me accordingly in writing. Otherwise, this letter shall set forth our understanding in this matter.

Bill, I want to personally thank you for your generous severance offer, and would like to take this opportunity to personally thank you for your assistance and cooperation.

I shall always look back at my years with ABC Corp. as positive ones.

Best wishes,

Enclosure

Sample of enclosure to be sent to the field sales force with severance agreement letter:

Memorandum

TO: Sales Force
FROM:
SUBJECT: Resignation of Steven Smith

I regret to inform you that Steven Smith has decided to pursue other interests and therefore has resigned from ABC Corp.

Steven has contributed greatly to the rapid growth of the Furniture Division over the past four and one half years.

Since there are some projects that Steven has intimate knowledge of, he has agreed to see these through to completion.

I wish Steven success in his new venture and at the same time thank him for his efforts in the past.

Then, send follow-up letters as your particular situation warrants. See the following sample:

(Date)

Name of Corporate Officer
Title
ABC Corp.
Anyplace, USA

Dear (Name):

As a follow-up to my letter of December 14, 1983, I am informing you of my employment by another company effective February 1, 1984.

Since I have been fortunate to find a position prior to February 28, 1984, I would like to put into effect item No. 10 of my

December 14 letter. Therefore, I will expect to receive a lump sum payout of salaries due to me through February 28 plus two weeks vacation pay. The Executive Stock Program should be finalized as soon as is practical, using February 1 as the reference day for quoted stock price and payout.

With this letter, I am including my American Express card. As of this day I have returned all keys to the office. I will be in touch to return the company car.

I have also included the last of my company-related expenses.

Thank you very much for your help.

Best wishes,

Enclosure

2. *Apply for unemployment benefits.* Unemployment benefits will help tide you over until you obtain another job. If you are denied benefits because it is determined that

- You voluntarily left your job
- You were fired for misconduct
- You refused a valid job offer

Ask for a hearing to appeal the denial of benefits.

3. *Look for work.* Whenever an employee is fired, the law requires him to make a good faith attempt to get another job. If an employee is fired illegally, but does not make a good faith effort to obtain employment, a court may reduce damages by the amount he could have earned in his new job. This is called mitigation of damages.

Many employees who are wrongfully terminated think they can sit back while suing their former employers. This is not true. The law requires you to accept a job with a comparable rate of salary and other duties if one is offered.

However, you are not required to move across the country or accept a job in a different line of work. In addition, if you do not secure employment, but make reasonable efforts to obtain a similar job, you will be entitled to all damages under the terms of your contract.

How to Resign Properly

Most employees do not know how to resign properly. The slightest mistake can expose you to a lawsuit and cause you to forfeit valuable benefits. Careful planning may provide a smooth transition without legal repercussion. Thus, review the following strategies whenever you consider resigning from a job.

1. *Plan ahead.*

2. *Sign a written contract with your new employer. This is essential.* Never resign from a job until you sign a written employment contract with your new employer. A written contract is needed to protect you if the new employer changes his mind and decides not to hire you, or fires you after a short period of time. *This often happens with devastating consequences.* Never leave your old job without first obtaining a signed written contract from you new employer.

3. *Review your prior contract or letter of agreement.* Learn what it says regarding termination. Be sure to comply with those terms. For example, if the contract states that you can resign provided written notice is sent certified mail sixty (60) days prior to the effective termination date, you must send timely notice before you resign. The failure to do so could cause the employer to sue you for breach of contract.

4. *Offer notice.* It is best to offer notice even if it isn't required. This courtesy will give the employer time to seek a

replacement. It will also give you additional time to negotiate a satisfactory settlement before you walk out the door.

5. *Should you resign by letter?* Contrary to popular belief, it is not necessary to resign by letter. In fact, it may be advantageous not to do so. However, if you want to clarify your resignation benefits, or put yourself on record that your resignation will not take effect for several weeks, confirm this is writing. Keep the letter brief. Avoid giving specific reasons for the resignation because this can preclude you from offering other reasons or tipping your hand in the event of a lawsuit.

The following resignation letter is an example of the kind of letter that should be sent:

(Date)

Name
Title
XYZ Company
(Address)

Re: My Resignation

Dear (Name):

You are hereby notified that I am resigning as (title) with your company, effective (date).

Please be advised that I will return (describe any company property in your possession) by (date).

I look forward to discussing my termination benefits and aiding you in a smooth transition.

Sincerely yours,

(Send certified mail, return receipt requested.)

6. *Review your benefits package.* Be sure you know what you are entitled to.

7. *Keep quiet.* Announce the move to friends and business associates *after* you've told the employer, never before.

8. *Avoid badmouthing.* Keep the details of the resignation to yourself, especially if the parting is less than amicable. Workers who badmouth former employers sometimes wind up being sued for business slander and product disparagement. Other companies withhold severance benefits as a way of getting even. Thus, keep your lips sealed.

9. *Return company property immediately.* Post-resignation disputes often arise when automobile keys, samples, promotional materials, confidential lists, etc., are not immediately returned. Be sure to return all items to avoid claims of misappropriation, fraud, and breach of contract. When returning items by mail, be sure to get a receipt to prove delivery. If the company owes you money, you may consider holding the company's property to force a settlement. However, speak to a lawyer before taking such action. Some states permit employees to retain company property as a lien; others do not.

10. *Should you sign a release?* Releases extinguish potential claims between employees. Many companies ask their employees to sign releases when they resign. You should consider asking for a written release if your contract contains a restrictive covenant or other unfavorable provisions. On the other hand, never sign a release if you believe the employer has mistreated you.

The example on the facing page is a standard release.

11. *Enforce your rights.* Speak to a lawyer immediately if you cannot receive what you are entitled to. If you are owed a small sum (e.g., $750), it may be desirable to commence an action in Small Claims Court in the county where the employer resides or does business. Consult chapter 7, entitled "How to Sue in Small Claims Court," to learn more about this. In any event, you should pursue your rights immediately to preserve your claim.

B 111—General Release by Corporation: 6-76 JULIUS BLUMBERG, INC., LAW BLANK PUBLISHERS

To all to whom these Presents shall come or may Concern,
Know That

A corporation organized under the laws of the State of , as RELEASOR,

in consideration of the sum of

($),

received from

as RELEASEE,

receipt whereof is hereby acknowledged, releases and discharges

the RELEASEE, RELEASEE'S heirs, executors, adminis-
trators, successors and assigns from all actions, causes of action, suits, debts, dues, sums of money, accounts, reckonings, bonds,
bills, specialties, covenants, contracts, controversies, agreements, promises, variances, trespasses, damages, judgments, extents,
executions, claims, and demands whatsoever, in law, admiralty or equity, which against the RELEASEE, the RELEASOR,
RELEASOR'S heirs, executors, administrators, successors and assigns ever had, now have or hereafter can, shall or may, have
for, upon, or by reason of any matter, cause or thing whatsoever from the beginning of the world to the day of the date of this
RELEASE.

Whenever the text hereof requires, the use of singular number shall include the appropriate plural number as the text of
the within instrument may require.

This RELEASE may not be changed orally.

In Witness Whereof, the RELEASOR has *caused this RELEASE to be executed by its duly authorized officers
and its corporate seal to be hereunto affixed* on 19 .

In presence of:

....

By...

STATE OF *, COUNTY OF* *ss.:*

On 19 before me personally came
to me known, who, by me duly sworn, did depose and say that deponent resides at

that deponent is the of
the corporation described in, and which executed the foregoing RELEASE, that deponent knows the seal of the corporation,
that the seal affixed to the RELEASE is the corporate seal, that it was affixed by order of the board of
of the corporation; and that deponent signed deponent's name by like order.

....

If the party making payment is not the same as the party released, delete words "as RELEASEE" and add names of parties released after the word "discharges."

Forms may be purchased from Julius Blumberg, Inc., NYC 10013, or any of its dealers. Reproduction prohibited.

Summary of Steps to Take after
You Resign or Are Fired

1. Enforce your rights immediately
2. Request a final negotiating session to increase your severance compensation
3. Try to resolve your differences amicably before resorting to litigation
4. Ask for a favorable recommendation and cover story
5. Insist on receiving a final statement of commissions, bonus, pension, and profit-sharing, and other benefits to determine if you are owed any money
6. Be sure you know exactly what you are owed before signing a release and settling with the employer
7. Contact a lawyer to determine your rights if you are fired
8. Collect all pertinent records to help the lawyer determine the merits of your case
9. If you are owed a small amount of money, you may institute proceedings in Small Claims Court
10. If you are owed more than $1,500, cannot calculate how much money you are owed, or believe you were fired unfairly, do *not* see the employer in Small Claims Court. Rather, consult a lawyer to protect your rights

These federal laws prohibiting retaliation contain provisions prohibiting reprisals against employees for reporting violations of, or asserting rights under, those laws:

Age Discrimination in Employment Act of 1967, 29 U.S.C. §623.
Asbestos School Hazard Detection & Control Act, 20 U.S.C. §3608.
Civil Rights Act of 1964, Title VII, 42 U.S.C. §2000e-3.

Civil Rights of Institutionalized Persons Act, 42 U.S.C. §1997(d).
Civil Service Reform Act of 1978, 5 U.S.C. §§2301, 2302, 7102, 7116.
Clean Air Act Amendments of 1977, 42 U.S.C. §§7401, 7622.
Comprehensive Environment Response, Comp. & Liability Act of 1980, 42 U.S.C. §9610.
Conspiracy to Obstruct Justice Act, 15 U.S.C. §1985(2).
Consumer Credit Protection Act of 1968, 15 USC §1674.
Employment Retirement Income Security Act of 1974 (Pension Reform Act), 29 U.S.C. §§1140, 1141.
Energy Reorganization Act Amendment of 1978, 42 U.S.C. §5851.
Fair Labor Standards Act, 29 U.S.C. §215.
Farm Labor Contractor Registration Act Amendments of 1974, 7 U.S.C. §2050(b).
Federal Mine Safety and Health Act Amendment of 1977, 30 U.S.C. §§815, 820(b).
Federal Railroad Safety Act Amendment, 45 U.S.C. §441.
Federal Water Pollution Control Act of 1972, 33 U.S.C. §1367.
International Safe Container Act of 1977, 46 U.S.C. §1506.
Jury Duty Act, 28 U.S.C. §1875.
Longshoremen's and Harbor Workers' Compensation Act of 1972, 33 U.S.C. §948(a).
National Labor Relations Act, 29 U.S.C. §158.
Occupational Safety and Health Act of 1970, 29 U.S.C. §660.
Railroad Employers Act of 1908, 45 U.S.C. §60.
Safe Drinking Water Act of 1974, 42 U.S.C. §300j-9.
Solid Waste Disposal Act of 1976, 42 U.S.C. §6972.
Surface Mining Control and Reclamation Act of 1977, 30 U.S.C. §§1201, 1293.
Toxic Substances Control Act of 1976, 15 U.S.C. §2622.
Also, to bring it up to date, it should include a new statute, Migrant and Seasonal Agricultural Worker Protection Act of 1983, 29 U.S.C. Sec. 1855.
Reprinted by permission of the Nassau County Chapter of the New York Civil Liberties Union.

II

Strategies
to Protect
Your Money

2

You and the IRS

- **Introduction** 122
- **How a Dispute Arises** 122
- **How Returns Are Selected for Audit** 124
- **What Are Your Chances of an IRS Audit?** 126
- **What to Do if You Are Notified of an Audit** 126
- **Your Rights to an Appeal** 130
- **What is the Best Appeals Route?** 132
- **Summary of Tax Rules to Save Money and Reduce Tax Audits** 133
    - Auto Use 134
    - Business Gifts 134
    - Parties 135
    - Travel Expenses 136
    - Convention Expenses and Business Seminars 136
    - Business Meals and Entertainment Expenses 137
- **How Long Should You Save Your Records?** 138

Introduction

Each year, the Internal Revenue Service audits more than 2 percent of all returns. However, if your income exceeds $50,000 per year, or if you claim large deductions, invest in tax shelters, own a small business, participate in barter clubs, or make an error on the return, you stand a greater chance of being audited.

Tax audits are time-consuming, costly, and nerve-wracking. However, knowledge of IRS procedures can significantly reduce (1) the odds of being audited, and (2) the amount of tax owed in the event of a dispute.

This chapter will tell you all about the IRS. You will learn how disputes arise and how the IRS selects returns for audits. A checklist of practical suggestions is provided to tell you what to do if you are notified of an audit. In addition, you will discover how to appeal an IRS audit decision and will learn how to maintain proper records to substantiate deductions.

How a Dispute Arises

Most disputes arise after a return is filed. Returns must be filed on time; the deadline for individuals is April 15. Penalties are imposed for late returns unless a taxpayer can demonstrate a valid reason for the delay. The following are valid reasons for filing a late return:

1. Death or serious illness of the taxpayer or an immediate family member
2. Unavoidable absence by the taxpayer
3. Destruction by fire or other casualty of the taxpayer's place of business or business records
4. Circumstances which make the taxpayer's accountant unable to complete the return
5. Circumstances where a taxpayer was unable to get essential assistance despite timely efforts

Most extensions for filing late returns are limited to sixty days. The IRS will not grant extensions greater than 180 days except for taxpayers who are abroad, or who can justify why additional time is needed to file.

A taxpayer can generally obtain an automatic two-month extension of time for filing his return by submitting an appropriate document at the IRS Service Center where the tax return will be filed, *together with the payment of any tax owed for the year*. However, be aware that the payment of tax is not extended beyond April 15, and additional interest and penalties are imposed on taxpayers who fail to pay the appropriate tax when the extension is filed. Just to be safe, familiarize yourself with the rules of your state when filing a federal tax return extension. Some states automatically extend the due date of the state return; others require a separate application. Thus, speak to your accountant if appropriate.

Tax returns are first reviewed at one of ten IRS Regional Service Centers. The return is checked for form, execution, and mathematical accuracy. Withholding statements are matched to the return and estimated tax returns are verified. Math errors are corrected and the taxpayer is sent a notice of the error. If the correction favors the IRS, additional tax is requested; if the correction favors the taxpayer, a refund is made.

Information on the return is then recorded on computer tape and transmitted to the IRS Center in Martinsburg, West Virginia. There the master computer codes all items on the return and assigns scores. If the final score exceeds a predetermined number, the return is sent back to a Regional Center for review. Revenue agents then select the most blatant returns for office and field examination audits.

How Returns Are Selected for Audit

According to the contents of a confidential IRS handbook, the following items are "red flags" which attract special attention by the master computer and internal auditors.

1. *Unreimbursed business deductions used for personal matters.* These include travel and entertainment, automobile and business gifts

2. *Tax shelter deductions.* The IRS is currently auditing the majority of returns claiming tax shelter deductions

3. *Unincorporated businesses.* According to the IRS, many small business owners fail to report income. The computer is instructed to carefully analyze returns of small business owner taxpayers who file income tax returns with large gross incomes, but who claim large expenses

4. *Married, filing separately.* Many husbands and wives file separate returns before the divorce is finalized. Often each parent claims all the children as dependents to take advantage of the deduction. The computer is instructed to pick this up

5. *Charitable contributions.* If you contribute property in excess of $500 (e.g., a stamp collection, painting, or

Bible) to charity, the IRS scrutinizes the transaction to be sure that the *fair market value* of the item is not overstated. Taxpayers frequently purchase items at a low cost, obtain written appraisals with excessive fair market values, and donate them to charity to get large deductions

6. *Adjusted gross income in excess of $50,000.* The IRS is currently assigning approximately 35 percent of their auditors to individual returns (joint and single) with adjusted gross incomes exceeding $50,000

7. *Large casualty loss deductions.* Here taxpayers often claim deductions for the fair market value of items lost, destroyed, or stolen, and not the actual cost of the item. Under the law, you can only claim the *lesser of the two*

8. *Home-office deductions.* Most home-office deductions are scrutinized carefully. Under the law, the business part of your home:

   a. Is that part used solely for business and not personal use

   b. Must be located in your home or garage

   c. Must be used on a continuing basis for business purposes

Taxpayers meeting this test must divide the area allocated for business purposes by the entire area of their home. When they arrive at a figure, say 10 percent, they can deduct 10 percent of the expenses directly related to the business portion of the home. This includes depreciation, rent, utilities, and insurance. They can also fully deduct direct expenses made to that area (e.g., painting and repairs).

The IRS is aware that taxpayers often inflate the amount of space allocated for business purposes. Others claim home-office deductions, but aren't qualified to take them; auditors review these claims carefully

9. *Mortgage interest deductions.* Returns claiming mortgage interest deductions are sometimes audited for large deductions

10. *Medical expenses.* Some taxpayers claim deductions for medical insurance which they do not have

11. *Occupation.* The IRS believes that certain jobs (e.g., waitresses, cabdrivers, bartenders, etc.), allow taxpayers to hide income because they receive cash tips which are not reported. Some experts believe the IRS scrutinizes these returns more closely

What Are Your Chances of an IRS Audit?

The following table compiles the odds of audits for taxpayers in various tax brackets:

INCOME	# OF TAX FILERS IN MILLIONS	# OF AUDITS EXPRESSED AS A %
Under $10,000 short form	27.5	.35
Under $10,000 long form	8.5	.98
$10,000–40,000 short form	21.2	.57
$10,000–20,000 long form	11.2	2.45
$25,000–50,000	17.7	2.90
$50,000 and up	3.3	5.68

Source: *Time,* March 28, 1983.

What to Do if You Are Notified of an Audit

There are two types of audits: *office examinations* and *field examinations.* Office examinations are conducted through correspondence with the taxpayer or through an in-person interview at an IRS District Office. Some audits are conducted by correspondence only. This is typically done for the convenience of the taxpayer in minor disputes. Here the taxpayer sends his explanation and supporting evidence to the IRS District Office by mail. If the taxpayer and IRS fail to agree on an adjustment, an in-person interview is then required.

Field examinations are conducted in person at the taxpayer's home or office and pertinent books and records are inspected on the taxpayer's premises.

Once you are chosen for an audit, there is no escape—you cannot be excused even if you were never audited before. However, you can protect yourself by acting properly. The following strategies will tell you what to do if you are notified of an office or field examination:

1. *Check to see if the notice is correct.* The IRS sometimes sends out incorrect form letters to taxpayers. Read the notice carefully to be sure it is accurate. Notify the IRS immediately if you believe you received the wrong notification letter.

2. *Be prepared.* It is a good idea to be familiar with the actual manuals used by Internal Revenue Service tax staffers when they conduct an audit. As a result of the Freedom of Information Act, the following handbooks are available to the public from the Freedom of Information Reading Room, Internal Revenue Service, 1111 Constitution Avenue, N.W., Room 1569, Washington, D.C. 20224:

- "Income Tax Examination Handbook" ($5.25)
- "Audit Guidelines Relating to Specialized Industries" (insurance, mining/timber, auto, textiles, brokers, railroads, real estate, banking, public utilities) ($1.00 each)
- "Tax Audit Guidelines—Individuals, Partnerships, Estates and Trusts, and Corporations" ($2.25)
- "Tax Audit Guidelines and Techniques for Tax Technicians" ($1.75)
- "Technique Handbook for In-Depth Audit Investigations" ($1.75)

- "Examinations Tax Shelter Handbook" ($1.00)
- "Audit Technique Handbook for Estate Tax Examiners ($3.00)
- "Handbook for Audit Reveiwers" ($.75)
- "Employment Tax Procedures" ($1.25)
- "Excise Tax Procedures" ($1.00)
- "Handbook for Audit Group Managers" ($.75)
- "Exempt Organizations Audit Procedures ($4.00)

3. *Put your records in order.* All deductions must be substantiated. This does not mean you are automatically liable for additional taxes if your records are not complete. Agents must report unsubstantiated deductions, but they have discretion in determining deficiencies. However, the more complete and accurate your records, the better.

4. *Bring all relevant records and substantiation to the audit.* Find out what records should be brought to the examination. You are not required to bring records from past returns unless requested to do so. Thus, *never bring more than is requested.*

Usually the auditor will require personal information (i.e., your age, marital status, and number of dependents). A birth certificate, draft card, or marriage license can prove these items. To support your claim, travel, entertainment, and transportation expenses should be substantiated in an account book or diary with corresponding documentation. For example, entries in a desk calendar require evidence for proper substantiation.

5. *Schedule the audit at your tax preparer's office.* An agent's judgment may be affected by the kind of house and furnishings you own. In addition, the agent will be unable to talk to family members or business associates. *Damaging information is sometimes obtained this way.* Thus, problems can be avoided by conducting the audit at your preparer's office, rather than your home.

6. *Never volunteer information.* Answer all questions, but do not talk excessively to the agent. Take your time when answering questions. Do not answer any question if you are unsure of its meaning. Instruct your accountant or tax preparer to answer or explain the question if you don't understand it. You have the right to do this. Your preparer can even stand in for you at the audit if you give him *power of attorney*. Remember this.

7. *Conduct yourself properly.* Dress in a businesslike manner, act professional, and stick to the issues. The revenue agent is not interested in excuses or sob stories. His job is to gather the facts and apply them according to IRS policies. Thus, never *argue* with the agent. The agent does not have the authority to settle issues contrary to IRS rulings and regulations, so save your arguments for the appeal. However, the agent can negotiate a better settlement on your behalf, so *avoid aggravating him.*

8. *Never be intimidated.* Taxpayers have the following rights which can be asserted during the audit examination:

- The initial meeting can be conducted in private
- You may change the agent assigned to your case if you have valid cause
- You can stop the examination to call your lawyer if you feel uncomfortable or believe that audit is being conducted to further a *criminal investigation*

An IRS Special Agent will contact you in the case of criminal investigation. If criminal fraud is indicated by the appearance of a Special Agent, remain silent and contact a lawyer immediately. Do not provide the Special Agent with your records without first getting approval from your lawyer.

If this is your second audit in several years and the first resulted in no additional tax paid, you may have the right to cancel the examination. Discuss this with a lawyer if appropriate.

9. *Try to settle your claim.* It is best to attempt a settlement with the revenue agent at the initial office or field examination. By settling the claim early on, you avoid the expense and anxiety of further proceedings and may reduce the possibility that IRS agents will discover *other areas of tax avoidance.*

Your Rights to an Appeal

Once the taxpayer agrees with the agent's findings, he signs a form and is granted time to pay the additional tax, interest, and penalties. If there is a disagreement, the taxpayer can appeal the findings or schedule a meeting with the examining agent's supervisor. Agreements are often reached at these supplementary meetings. If an agreement is not reached, the IRS will send you an examination report. The report states the position of the IRS. Taxpayers may agree with the findings and pay the assessed tax or file an appeal within thirty days.

The first step in the appeals process is an appeals conference. This is an informal hearing conducted by an appeals officer who has broad authority to settle most cases. You can represent yourself (which is unwise), or you can be represented by a certified public accountant, a tax lawyer, or a qualified former IRS agent at the hearing.

A settlement at the appeals conference is a final disposition of the case. If settlement is not reached or the conference is waived, the IRS then issues a statutory *Notice of Deficiency.* The Notice sets forth the IRS claim for additional tax and is commonly called the "ninety-day letter."

After receiving the "ninety-day letter," taxpayers have one of four options:

1. Settle the claim by paying the tax

2. Schedule an additional appeals conference to effectuate a settlement

3. Pay the tax and seek a refund by filing an action in District Court or the Court of Claims

4. File a petition to the Tax Court within ninety days from the date you received the deficiency note.

By paying the disputed tax, interest, and penalties, you have the option of bringing suit to obtain a refund in either a local U.S. District Court or Claims Court. This must be done no later than two years after the claim is disallowed. If you go this route, you cannot bring suit later in Tax Court.

The advantage of the District Court is that cases are resolved quickly and can be appealed. However, practically all taxpayers prefer to contest the claim in Tax Court. The reason is that taxpayers are *not* required to pay the disputed tax in order to sue.

(NOTE: Only 2 percent of all 1981 tax deficiency cases were filed in Claims Court; 5 percent were filed in U.S. District Court, and 93 percent in Tax Court. In fact, 31,000 pending Tax Court cases were filed in 1982—up from 23,000 in 1980.)

The following steps outline the procedure in Tax Court. A taxpayer:

• Petitions the Tax Court within ninety days after receiving the deficiency notice
• Receives the IRS response approximately sixty days thereafter
• Answers the IRS response within forty-five days
• Awaits scheduling of the hearing
• Appears at the hearing. The case is heard by a Tax Court judge and a written opinion is issued

If the dispute is under $5,000, a written opinion is not given and the decision is not appealable. Matters exceeding $5,000 in any given tax year are appealable to the U.S. Court of Appeals.

(A REMINDER: Although you are not required to pay the disputed tax up-front, interest and penalties continue to run. Tax Court cases often take up to four yours to be heard.

Thus, you may find yourself paying more in interest and other penalties than the original claim. Some taxpayers pay the tax after filing the petition to avoid this—you may wish to do the same.)

What Is the Best
Appeals Route?

The following strategies will help you in making the right decision about the appeals process:

1. *Attempt to settle the dispute after it reaches the litigation stage.* The IRS settles approximately 70 percent of all cases before reaching trial. If you settle the case, you avoid paying interest and other penalties. Under the Tax Equity and Fiscal Responsibility Act of 1982, for example, taxpayers are liable for penalties up to $5,000 for delaying or bringing frivolous claims in Tax Court. The interest on unpaid taxes is now pegged to the prime rate and the IRS can slap an additional 5 percent nondeductible penalty for underpayment due to "negligence or intentional disregard of IRS rules and regulations." Thus, filing a claim to gain time may not help. That is why it may be wise to settle.

2. *Know your odds.* The following table is a breakdown by court of taxpayers' 1980 win/loss record:

FISCAL 1980 CASES	TOTAL VICTORY	PARTIAL VICTORY	DEFEAT
Tax Court			
(a) Small tax cases	9.5%	37.1%	53.4%
(b) Regular tax cases	11.0%	38.0%	51.0%
District Court	22.4%	11.8%	65.8%
Court of Claims (now called Claims Court)	48.0%	6.0%	46.0%

(NOTE: A total victory means it was determined that no tax was owed. A defeat means that the taxpayer had to pay the full amount of tax claimed by the IRS. In partial victory cases, the taxpayer either paid less tax than was claimed or paid no or less tax on certain issues and full or less tax on others.)

As the chart demonstrates, the chances of success in Tax Court and District Court cases are not that great.

3. *Avoid representing yourself.* The old adage "He who represents himself has a fool for a client" makes sense. Avoid representing yourself (pro-se) in tax matters. The amount of money you save in professional fees may not be worth the amount of money you lose at the hearing.

4. *When in doubt, ask for a private IRS ruling.* Some taxpayers avoid litigating disputes by requesting private IRS letter rulings. The IRS sometimes offers its position on questions or actual problems raised by a taxpayer or his tax practitioner. It usually takes approximately four months to obtain a ruling and the IRS does not answer all requests. Critics remark that private IRS rulings have no precedental value. However, many tax lawyers rely on these opinions and use the information to restructure a questionable transaction before a dispute arises. Thus, ask your professional advisor if it is wise to obtain a private IRS ruling when in doubt.

Summary of Tax Rules to Save Money and Reduce Tax Audits

Many Americans suffer disallowances of legitimate expenses because they don't maintain accurate records and don't know the law.

The following information summarizes key areas where proper record substantiation is required. You will learn some of the tricks used by IRS agents when auditing returns in these areas. This will reduce the chances of an audit and maximize deductions to save your money.

Deductions

1. *Auto use.* Many professionals, independent contractors, small business owners and other self-employeds are entitled to deduct business-related transportation expenses. This includes the cost of operating and maintaining an automobile.

Deductible expenses include gasoline and oil bills, repairs, insurance, depreciation, interest required to purchase the car, taxes, licenses, garage rent, parking fees, and tolls when the car is used for business purposes.

(NOTE: Commuting expenses between your residence and principal place of business are *not* deductible.)

One way of computing the deduction is by the *standard method;* you take the number of business miles and multiply that by the current rate, e.g., $.22½ per mile for the first 15,000 business miles, and $.15 for each additional mile. The other way is by the *itemized method;* you total all business-related operating and fixed expenses, including depreciation.

IRS agents closely examine the following items to be sure *business* mileage claims are not exaggerated and that only business deductions are taken. Agents frequently ask to see the following items at an audit. Thus, be prepared:

- Repair bills—these sometimes record auto mileage
- Insurance policies are used to prove that family members also use the car
- Credit card receipts are often signed by family members, and may prove personal use
- Where you work—IRS agents exclude travel to and from work from business mileage; chances are you'll be questioned about this

2. *Business gifts.* Business gifts up to $25 per person per year are deductible provided the gift is ordinary, necessary, and incurred in connection with your trade or business. Ex-

amples of gifts include jewelry, packaged food, and beverages. You can deduct unlimited business gifts costing $4 or less which have your name or business engraved or printed on them. If you give a gift to the wife of a business associate, you cannot give an additional gift to the business associate and deduct $50 unless the wife does business with you separately.

In order to obtain the business gift deduction, the IRS agent will request proof of:

- The cost of the gift
- When the gift was made
- A description of the gift
- A valid reason why the gift was made
- Proof that the gift was made to a business associate and not a friend or relative

3. *Parties.* Parties are deductible provided they are business-related. IRS agents will carefully scrutinize your records to analyze the purpose of these parties. The following strategies will help prove legitimate deductions in this area:

- Save receipts of payments made to bartenders, maids, and domestic help
- Produce a guest list of business people who attended the party. Keep a record of the business, if any, that resulted from discussions at the party
- Purchase food, liquor, and beverages at a different store than where you usually go to purchase such items
- Ask for receipts. This will help prove that your purchases were not for personal consumption
- Match the amount of purchases with the amount of guests. By doing this, the agent cannot say you overbought to claim a larger deduction.

4. *Travel expenses.* Travel expenses are the ordinary and necessary expenditures incurred while traveling overnight in pursuit of your trade or business.

The IRS requires *strong* proof of travel expenses; approximations are not acceptable. Expenses cannot be lavish or extravagant, or incurred for personal or vacation purposes.

IRS agents always examine expenses which are charged via *credit cards.* To avoid problems, avoid mixing credit cards; use one card for business and one card for pleasure.

Save your ticket when you travel by airplane. Agents are instructed to examine airline tickets to look for the following:

- *Date of departure, return, and intermediate stops*—a long trip may prove that the trip was extended beyond business days
- *The cost*—did you claim too much?
- *Name of the passenger and company or individual who purchased the ticket*—were you reimbursed for the cost? If so, the IRS agent will ask you to prove that you treated the reimbursement as income. Be aware of this

IRS agents frequently scrutinize lodging receipts to be sure that expenses are not excessive. For example, did you reserve a room for double occupancy when a single room would have been sufficient? Did you run up a large tab that was not business-related? IRS agents are instructed to investigate third-party services, including hotel directories and reservation services, to identify and explain items on lodging receipts. So, be prepared.

5. *Convention expenses and business seminars.* Meals, lodging, and convention expenses are deductible, provided your attendance advances the interests of your trade or business.

IRS agents review convention and meeting agendas to determine if the seminar was business-related. The following items are examined closely in this area:

- The nature of the business conducted
- The amount of time spent attending the seminar
- The social events on the agenda
- The time and place of the meeting. This is done to determine if the convention was vacation-oriented

The best way to prove business seminar and convention expenses is to:

- *Save* all convention pamphlets and agenda receipts
- *Obtain* a certificate which states you attended the convention
- *Produce* sign-in sheets or other documents signed by a convention official to prove you had an excellent attendance record at the meetings

These strategies may help prove your claim.

6. *Business meals and entertainment expenses.* Business meals and entertainment expenses are deductible provided business was discussed with the person being entertained. You do not have to prove that business actually resulted from the expenditures; all that is necessary is that you had more than a general expectation of deriving benefits in the future. Thus, *save your meal checks* because IRS agents look at them. Meal checks should state the date, name, location, and amount. Be aware that IRS agents look at the number of persons served and try to ascertain if the dining was a reciprocal arrangement with social rather than business overtones.

(REMINDER: IRS agents may disallow the deduction if the meal occurred in a nightclub or other place where entertainment is a major attraction. Most business meals are deductible only if you can demonstrate that they occurred in an atmosphere conducive to business discussions.)

Final Points

Here are some additional points to remember about the IRS:

- *Audit notices*—examining officers can audit individual tax returns up to twenty months after the filing date.
- *Delinquent accounts*—the IRS levies assets of delinquent taxpayers. Social security benefits, pensions, etc., are not exempt from levy unless it would cause severe hardship to the individual.
- *Installment payments*—the IRS allows installment payments if payment in full imposes undue hardship or loss. However, the IRS will try to keep the payment period as short as possible (never more than six years).
- *Paid informants*—the IRS pays a "10 percent" bounty for information which leads to the recovery of tax from an individual or business. However, if an individual uncovers social security fraud, he is not entitled to a finder's fee on the money recovered as a result of the fraud. The Social Security Agency does not give financial rewards like the IRS.

How Long Should You Save Your Records?

Taxpayers can be asked to account for their income tax deductions up to three years after the April 15 deadline, up to six years if they accidentally fail to report 25 percent or more of gross income, and indefinitely, in cases involving tax fraud.

The following comprehensive list of record retention guidelines was prepared from U.S. government publications and other articles. For additional information about specialized industries, contact the Office of the Federal Register in Washington, D.C., to obtain the latest edition of the *Guide to Record Retention Requirements*.

I. Personal Documents to Hold Indefinitely

1. Wills; keep current wills only
2. Passports, military discharge certificates, birth certificates, marriage licenses, naturalization papers, etc.

II. Financial Records to Hold Indefinitely

1. Deeds, leases, mortgages
2. Stock certificates, bonds, and other securities
3. Pension and profit-sharing plans, IRA, KEOUGH, and other retirement plans
4. Insurance policies—accident and health, auto, homeowners, life, etc.; keep current policies only
5. Automobile, boat, and airplane titles; receipts and canceled checks for large purchases, home improvements, as long as you own items

III. Tax Records to Hold Indefinitely

1. Tax returns and canceled checks (federal, state, and local)

IV. Insurance Records

1. Accident reports	6 years
2. Claims—settled	3 years
3. Fire inspection reports	6 years
4. Safety records—reports	6 years

V. Corporate Records (for those who own their own business)

1. Articles of Incorporation	Permanent
2. By-laws	Permanent
3. Charter	Permanent
4. Contracts and agreements—employment, labor partnership, government, etc.	Permanent
5. Copyrights and trademarks—all registrations	Permanent
6. Deeds and easements	Permanent
7. Leases, expired	3 years
8. Legal correspondence of any kind	Permanent
9. Minutes and minute books	Permanent
10. Mortgages and notes	6 years
11. Patents	Permanent
12. Pension and other retirement plans: IRS letter of approval	Permanent
Plan and trust agreement(s)	Permanent
Ledgers, journals and all other accounting records	Permanent
Actuarial reports	Permanent
Financial statements	Permanent
Individual employee acct. records	Permanent
Anything else related to the plan	Permanent
13. Personnel records and files	4 years
14. Property records	Permanent
15. Proxies	Permanent
16. Stock and bond records—certificates, transfer lists—anything relating to stock issued and corporate indebtedness	Permanent
17. Stockholder lists	6 years

VI. Other Business Records (Particularly for Employers)

PERSONNEL

1. Contracts and agreements	Permanent
2. Daily time reports	4 years

3. Disability or sick benefits   4 years
4. Timecards   4 years
5. Withholding statements and *all other* payroll 4 years
   records

VII. Accounting Records

1. Bank statements   3 years
2. Budgets   2 years
3. Canceled checks
    Dividends paid   4 years
    General   3 years
    Payroll   3 years
    Taxes—payroll   4 years
    Taxes—income   Permanent
    Taxes—others   4 years

COMMENT: major expenditures of permanent Permanent
noteworthiness—use your own judg-
ment and keep the checks

4. Cash disbursements journal   Permanent
5. Cash receipts journal   Permanent
6. Commission statements to salesmen and Permanent
   representatives
7. Contracts—sales or purchases   3 years
8. Credit memos   3 years
9. Deposit slips   3 years
10. Depreciation records   3 years
11. Expense reports—salesmen and others   3 years
12. Financial statements—annual   Permanent
13. General ledger and general journal   Permanent
14. Inventories   3 years
15. Invoices   3 years
16. Payroll records, payroll journal, individual 4 years
    earnings records, W-2, W-4, etc.
17. Petty cash vouchers   3 years
18. Purchase journal   Permanent
19. Sales journal   Permanent

20. Subsidiary ledgers—accounts receivable, ac-   6 years
    counts payable
21. Timecards   4 years
22. Trial balances—monthly   3 years

These suggested retention guidelines begin with the filing of a particular income tax return. Since the law varies throughout the fifty states, and valid business or legal requirements may change, consult with your accountant or lawyer for further information.

3

Avoiding
Phony Business and
Investment Schemes

- **Introduction**   144
- **Abusive Tax Shelters**   144
- **Investment and Business Opportunity Frauds**   147
- **Avoiding Franchise Abuses**   149
- **Land Fraud and Other Real Estate Ripoffs**   154
- **Avoiding Problems with Real Estate Brokers**   159
- **Home Improvement and Building Contractor Abuses**   165
- **What You Should Know about Mail Fraud**   174
- **Used-Car Abuses**   178
- **Avoiding Car Repair Abuses**   183
- **Employment Agency, Search Firm, and Career Counseling Abuses**   186

Introduction

Thousands of phony business schemes circulate our country every day. A recent Senate Committee investigating consumer fraud reported that Americans are defrauded of billions of dollars each year. According to the study, unsophisticated investors and elderly individuals are most prone to being victimized by phony business opportunities, franchise ripoffs, mail and land fraud, abusive tax shelters, and investment schemes.

This chapter will examine many blatant schemes, scams, and swindles on the market today. The following strategies should be read *before* investing in any financial or business venture; by doing so, you can protect yourself from making a decision you may later regret.

Abusive Tax Shelters

People desire ways to keep more of the money they make. One effective technique of tax savings may be by investing in a legitimate tax shelter. In 1982, it was estimated that $47 billion dollars was raised through public and private tax shelter offerings.

The typical tax shelter works this way: An investor in a high tax bracket puts up cash and buys an interest in a business structured in the form of a limited partnership. The limited partnership generates large tax-deductible losses. These losses arise from such items as property taxes, interest on loans, rapid depreciation write-offs, and other business expenses.

The investor shares in a percentage of these tax deductible losses as a limited partner. The losses are then used to offset his income from other sources including salary, dividends, and interest that would otherwise be heavily taxed. However, the amount of losses used to shelter income is typically limited to the actual amount of money the individual has invested in the tax shelter (referred to as the amount "at risk").

Legitimate tax shelters enable investors to pay less income tax and own a share of a new business. When the business becomes profitable, the investor then receives a predetermined percentage of the profits. However, tax shelters are extremely complicated investments and must be analyzed carefully.

The recent proliferation of tax shelter schemes has resulted in the loss of billions of dollars of potential tax payments to the U.S. Treasury. As a result, the IRS is auditing many tax shelters and limited partner investors on the market today. In fact, approximately 300,000 tax shelter returns are currently being examined.

Investors are also being exploited by dishonest promoters. A growing number of unscrupulous operators are resorting to outrageous asset or service value overstatements, nonexistent or rigged "transactions," and other fraudulent schemes. Promises of write-offs greatly exceeding a person's initial investment and guarantees of immediate profits are frequently made but don't materialize.

Thus, read the following material carefully before you decide to invest in a tax shelter.

1. *Choose a tax shelter with low business risk.* The evaluation of a tax shelter requires a proper analysis of the business that underlies the shelter. Ask yourself if the shelter will eventually make money. Abusive tax shelters derive almost

all their benefits through tax write-offs and are not sound investments. Nonabusive tax shelters involve transactions where the economic benefits outweigh the tax benefits. Thus, select a shelter that stands a decent chance of making money.

2. *Choose a shelter with a low tax risk.* The IRS looks favorably on traditional tax shelters (e.g., real estate, oil and gas shelters, etc.). Other ventures (e.g., leasing of lithographs or master recordings) are being disallowed. Thus, be careful. The IRS is currently imposing severe penalties for investors who participate in abusive shelters. For example, interest is imposed at above-market rates and investors are required to return all the tax advantages gained by the shelter.

3. *Choose a shelter with reputable promoters and general partners.* Most public shelters are sold through national brokerage houses and financial advisory organizations. Investing in a shelter promoted by a reputable brokerage house may eliminate problems.

Always investigate the background of the sponsors and general partners. The general partner usually runs the business of the limited partnership (e.g., collects revenue, pays bills, etc.), and is paid a fee. In addition, the general partner may share in the profits of the venture after the investors are repaid their original investment. Limited partners have practically no say in how the business should be run. Thus, it is important to invest in a tax shelter run by honest general partners with successful track records. Avoid investing in shelters which disburse excessive compensation to general partners because this ultimately affects the business's profitability.

4. *Examine the offering prospectus carefully.* Tax shelter offering statements are complicated documents. They usually contain a variety of documents and an opinion which justifies the legality of the shelter. *Always* consult a lawyer to be sure the opinion is accurate. Be aware that documents are sometimes backdated, affidavits are forged, appraisals are

inflated, and nonexistent records are created in many fraudulent tax shelters.

5. *Choose a shelter that fits your personal finances.* Select a tax shelter that makes economic sense. If you think you will remain in a high tax bracket for several years, invest in a shelter that is certain to throw off large losses for at least three years. Conversely, avoid investing in a long-term shelter if your income fluctuates markedly from year to year.

6. *Be prepared to lose your investment.* Despite glowing assurances by salespeople, most tax shelters fail to make money. Thus, never invest in a tax shelter unless you can afford to lose your investment. Experts suggest people should only consider investing in a tax shelter who have a net worth exceeding $250,000, or have income of $60,000 per year and a net worth of at least $80,000, excluding personal assets.

7. *Consult your lawyer, accountant, or other financial advisor.* Always seek professional advice *before* investing in a tax shelter. You may find ways to reduce taxable income through devices other than tax shelters, so don't forget to discuss this with your advisors.

Investment and Business Opportunity Frauds

Promoter P. T. Barnum was once quoted as saying: "There's a sucker born every minute." This is particularly true with respect to phony business opportunity and investment frauds (the most common form of consumer exploitation).

The following guidelines can protect you no matter what form of investment you are contemplating. Review these rules *before* sinking your money into a business or investment offering and you may significantly reduce the chances of being swindled.

- *First Commandment:* Never rely on promises from people you don't know

- *Second Commandment:* Be wary of people who offer deals over the telephone

- *Third Commandment:* Be suspicious of deals which offer large returns to anonymous investors

- *Fourth Commandment:* Be skeptical of deals offered in newspaper and magazine ads—most legitimate business opportunities are not marketed this way

- *Fifth Commandment:* Never be pressured into making a quick decision. This is the way phonies typically operate. If you are told a "once-in-a-lifetime" deal will pass by unless you act quickly, chances are good that you are being swindled

- *Sixth Commandment:* Never invest in a deal until you receive written information. Read the literature thoroughly *before* making any decision

- *Seventh Commandment:* Investigate the identity of the promoters, organizers, general partners, and other individuals involved in the deal. Do they have a successful track record in other ventures? Ask for bank and credit references of these people; review them carefully

- *Eighth Commandment:* Analyze how your money will be used. Is it secured? What is it being invested in? Are the organizers receiving an unfair share?

- *Ninth Commandment:* Consult a lawyer, accountant, financial advisor, or other professional before sinking large sums in a venture

- *Tenth Commandment:* Contact the FTC or FBI if you have doubts. These agencies maintain a list of companies and individuals who have been indicted and convicted for investment fraud. One phone call can tell you if you are about to be swindled. Always take such precautions when necessary

Avoiding Franchise Abuses

It is estimated that nearly one third of all U.S. retail sales (amounting to approximately $439 billion in products and services) are conducted from 600,000 franchise locations. More than 4.6 million people are employed in franchise operations and 20,000 additional franchises commence business each year.

The popularity of franchising is due to its unique method of conducting business. For an agreed-upon price, a franchisor grants the right to market products and operate a franchise in a specific location. The franchisee may acquire use of the name, designs, equipment, start-up assistance, and selling methods. Ownership of the venture may or may not remain with the franchisor; more often it does not.

However, despite the success of franchises, abuses are prevalent. Unsophisticated investors are exploited because they are unable to evaluate franchise offers properly. People launch successful businesses but lose them through recapture tactics asserted by franchisors. Others mortgage their homes and invest their life savings in franchises that fail because they have been misled by exaggerated claims of potential profitability.

There are no federal laws governing the franchising industry at the present time. This adds to the risk of abuse. While some states have laws protecting potential investors from misrepresentation, false and misleading advertising, and fraudulent franchise schemes, others do not.

Thus, it is up to each investor to recognize the many forms of franchise abuse. The following information will give you a better idea of points to consider before investing in a franchise operation.

1. *Beware of misleading ads promising high returns.* Franchise operators often place deceptive advertisements to attract investors. The following is a typical example:

FABULOUS BUSINESS OPPORTUNITY THROUGH
OWNERSHIP OF YOUR OWN FRANCHISE

ABC Company, the innovator in mattress and bedding franchises, is offering area franchises to select investors. Fantastic return on investment. Guaranteed $1 million sales in the first year. Experience not required. Our employees will train and assist in the start-up. Call for an appointment.

This ad may be misleading in several respects:

a. Investors may be required to pay additional money for equipment, training, and start-up assistance—the ad doesn't say this.

b. Bogus franchises may be sold to anyone who puts up the cash—rigorous interviewing and credit references may not be necessary.

c. Exclusive territories may be promised but not allotted.

d. Guaranteed sales may be nonexistent, or based on inaccurate figures.

Thus, the first step in analyzing franchise ventures is to examine *all* sales promotion literature and advertisements. Be sure to scrutinize claims telling you what to expect in profits, sales, and earnings.

2. *Investigate the franchise.* There are many items to discuss with the franchisor's representative before beginning serious negotiations. For example, you should ask for:

a. Financial statements, bank references, credit references, and other written materials concerning the franchisor, officers, and key executives. Review these thoroughly.

b. Facts about the negative as well as the positive aspects of the venture.

   c. Books and records revealing the sales figures of other franchisees. One of the major reasons franchises fail is that investors receive misleading profit projections; reviewing the actual books and records may protect you in this area.

   d. A copy of the franchise circular.

   e. The names of other franchisees. Make an appointment to speak to them about their business. Better still, visit their operation if possible.

3. *Analyze the key points of the deal.* Unsophisticated investors sometimes lose large sums of money because they sign franchise agreements without understanding all the ramifications. You should know answers to the following questions to protect your investment:

   a. Is a down payment required before negotiations begin? Most legitimate franchisors do not ask for a deposit until the contract is signed. *Be aware of this.*

   b. Can the franchise be terminated without your consent? If so, under what conditions? Some franchisees lose their businesses as a result of unfair termination provisions in franchise agreements (e.g., failure to meet sales quotas or pass sanitary inspections, etc.). Avoid this if possible.

   c. How long can you operate your franchise? Some investors successfully build their franchise, but are required to give the business back after a definite number of years. Resist this.

   d. What is the *entire* fee for your investment?

   e. How much down payment is required?

   f. Are royalty, licensing, and advertising allowances included in the fee, or are they extra? These charges are often overlooked and can be substantial. If a royalty is not included (e.g., 10 percent of the annual gross sales), be sure you know whether the business will be able to sustain profitability while paying these fees. You must calculate the effect of these expenses on your business before you decide to invest.

g. Will the franchisor provide assistance? (e.g., architectural and location site assistance, job training for managers, etc.). If so, do you have to pay extra for this?

h. Can the franchisor exercise control over your business? If so, to what degree?

i. Must you buy equipment from the franchisor in order to commence business? If so, what is the *entire* fee? Is it fair? Are there exorbitant interest payments?

j. Are you prohibited from starting the franchise in the location of your choice?

k. Can the franchisor refuse to renew the franchise and/or purchase it back from you? If so, how much money, if any, will you receive? How will it be paid? Is the price fair?

l. Can you invest in the franchisor's business? If so, will you obtain a more favorable price for the franchisor's stock?

m. Are you required to purchase product exclusively from the franchisor? If so, do you anticipate delivery problems?

n. Are you obligated to do business or pay commissions to third parties?

o. Are you or members of your immediate family required to work at the franchise site?

p. Are you relying on specific promises or guarantees? If so, be sure to include these in the agreement. For example, if the franchisor makes claims about your potential earnings, insist that you receive:

- Appropriate figures to prove the accuracy of all claims
- Statistics about the number of franchises and the amount of failures
- The number of franchises that earn *below* the earning claims

q. Will the franchisor provide loan assistance?

All of these points should be clearly understood before investing in a franchise.

4. *Consult the services of a competent advisor.* It is important to speak to a lawyer, accountant, or financial advisor before you buy. Representing yourself in the purchase of a franchise enterprise may be a foolish mistake. A competent lawyer should negotiate and review your franchise contract because franchise agreements are complicated documents. They are usually prepared by franchisors and contain unfavorable clauses.

5. *Contact a lawyer or your state's Attorney General's Office immediately if you believe you have been exploited.* Franchisees have certain rights under state and federal laws. For example, fifteen states have franchise registration statutes which obligate franchisors to file offering statements before selling franchises. Some states have laws which require franchisors to provide franchise-offering documents to potential investors *before* a franchise contract can be signed. These laws disallow the sale in the event that the franchise-offering documents are not distributed. In addition, the Federal Trade Commission requires that a franchisor must provide a prospective franchisee with an offering circular no later than the first serious meeting or ten days prior to the execution of the contract.

Franchisees can also seek remedies under antitrust and common law actions in fraud, misrepresentation, and breach of warranty. Thus, it is important to take immediate action to preserve your rights.

Land Fraud and Other Real Estate Ripoffs

Vast acreage of unimproved land is being subdivided and offered for sale as homesites and retirement spots. You have probably seen slick advertisements proclaiming the advantages of accessible leisure communities, and urging people to purchase "a place in the sun." However, this kind of information is often misleading. The average out-of-state purchaser is unfamiliar with the topography and history of the plot, and frequently overpays for his parcel. In many cases, developers abandon projects before completing elaborate facilities. Promoters mislead purchasers by stating that water is available, or that the land is furnished with adequate sewage disposal, road maintenance, electricity, gas, and accessible transportation, when this is not true.

Out-of-state land sales will total more than $4 billion this year, much of this for undeveloped land. This section will offer strategies telling you how to avoid investing in fraudulent land schemes.

Avoiding Fraudulent Land Deals

The following information should be considered before investing in any land deal:

1. *Question the accuracy of all promotional claims and advertising literature.* Unethical promotions are the modus operandi of unscrupulous land developers. The following advertisement is typical of the kind that appears in magazines and newspapers throughout the country:

SUNFLOWER RANCHES IN BOOMING NEVADA
6 ACRES

$2895 Full Price—No Interest
Only $50 down and $20 a month

Near Reno—Fun City of the Southwest

Less than a day's drive from California—America's largest state

Your place in the sun—your stake in the future

But time is growing short. Look at the following facts:

1. Nevada's free land is being bought at alarming rates
2. Land values in Nevada are rising rapidly
3. During the last ten years, Nevada's population increased by 240%
4. The climate is spectacular—no smog or snow—only sun
5. Each ranch is located near major highways; electricity and water are also provided
6. The developer is about to complete a fabulous 18-hole golf course and clubhouse
7. Title guaranteed by warranty deed and title insurance

Perfect for investment. However, you must move fast because each 6-acre tract is going up to $3,495 on October 1.

Come out to our headquarters and personally view the property. We will pay for your lodging and meals while you are here.

Many states have no legislation protecting consumers from this type of advertising. Although some states require developers to submit advertisements for approval before they can be released to the public, dishonest promoters still manage to disseminate false and misleading advertising which often avoids detection. Sometimes the schemes are discovered only after investors have lost thousands of dol-

156   Don't Get Taken!

lars to promoters who have disappeared from the scene, or have circumvented legal liability.

Thus, scrutinize all claims *before* speaking to a developer or his sales staff. Unscrupulous developers use a variety of tactics to induce you to buy. One is the "rush game" (e.g., "Price will go up tremendously on October 1, so buy now"). Another is the "free inducement offer" ("If you travel to our development site, we will pay for your lodging expenses while you are here."). The problem with the free inducement offer is that customers are manipulated by fast-talking salespeople once they have traveled to the site. Also, some promoters renege on their promise to pay for lodging expenses; others house prospective buyers in inadequate lodging facilities. *Thus, be aware of these tactics.*

2. *Ask for written documentation to support advertising and promotional claims.* One of the best ways to determine if you are dealing with a legitimate land developer is to request copies of documents which are required to be filed by law. Review these documents *before* you travel to the development site or sign the contract.

The following is a list of documents that must be filed with appropriate agencies under many state and federal laws:

   a. A purchase agreement embodied in the sales program

   b. A county engineer's report which describes the physical characteristics of the land proposed for development

   c. A title insurance policy

   d. A certificate of registration

   e. The deed and opinion of title

   f. Reports submitted by licensed engineers regarding draining, accessibility to roads, and the availability of potable water

g. A schedule and timetable of all improvements to be performed by the developer

h. A report from the county stating that the streets and other public places in the subdivided plot will be maintained

i. A copy of the proposed offering statement

You are also entitled to receive a copy of the Property Report. According to the federal Interstate Land Sales Full Disclosure Act, developers must file a Statement of Record and Property Report with the Secretary of Housing and Urban Development (HUD) in Washington. This must be done before large subdivided plots can be sold to the public. In order to be approved by HUD, all statements contained in these documents must be substantiated by supporting affidavits and exhibits. Once approval is obtained, a copy of the Property Report must be given to each prospective purchaser. If a copy of the Property Report is *not* given to you before the signing of the contract, the law allows you to rescind the transaction or sue for damages. *Be aware of this.*

3. Investigate the developer before purchasing. Problems can be reduced if you inquire into the financial resources and reputation of the developer. Start out by asking what associations, if any, the developer belongs to. Contact these organizations to learn about the qualifications for membership, and how long the developer has been a member. You should also call the Attorney General's Office in the state where the land is located. A staff member may be able to tell you if the developer has ever been charged with land fraud or other illegal practices.

When you meet with the developer or his representative, don't forget to ask the following questions *before* beginning serious negotiations:

a. Has a performance bond or other security been posted to assure the completion of facilities or improvements? If so, with whom? Request a copy.

b. Who is the lawful owner of the land? If title is held by a corporation or limited partnership, who are the partners? Are there any judgments, liens, or encumbrances against the owner of record?

c. What is the track record of the developer? Has he completed other developments? If so, investigate them.

d. Who is the authorized sales agent? Where are they located? How long have they been in business? Have they worked with the developer on past projects?

4. *Investigate the land you will be purchasing.* Once you are satisfied with the developer's reputation, you should familiarize yourself with the physical characteristics and other features of the land. For example, you should know the amount of yearly property taxes and whether there are other hidden costs. The following is a detailed checklist of important points to consider:

a. What is the total purchase price?

b. How much money is required as a deposit? Is it refundable?

c. What is the down payment?

d. What kind of deed and other assurances are you receiving from the seller?

e. What are the monthly payments and financing charges?

f. Is Time of the Essence?

g. Has the land been zoned for special use?

h. If the property to be acquired is income producing, do existing leases comply with all federal and state regulations?

i. Have special assessments been imposed for local improvements?

j. Does the seller have legal authority to sign the contract if he is not the real owner (e.g., power of
attorney)?

k. Have you received a detailed description of the
premises? Have you reviewed it to be sure it is accurate?

l. What is the range of selling prices within the development?

m. Does the community offer potential for future
growth?

n. Are there provisions for water, drainage, electricity,
gas, telephone lines, and sewage disposal?

o. Is there access to main roads?

p. Are there recreational and common facilities?

q. Are there municipal services (e.g., fire and police
protection, medical and dental facilities, public
transportation, schools, and shopping)?

r. Will personal property be used in connection with
the operation of the premises? If so, have you been
given a complete and accurate description?

s. Are the premises sold subject to an existing mortgage, or can you obtain your own mortgage?

5. *Consult a lawyer to review all documents and represent you
at the closing.* If you are satisfied with the developer's reputation and the land you are about to purchase, discuss the deal
with an experienced lawyer. This is essential in any large
real estate transaction.

Avoiding Problems with Real Estate Brokers

Although most real estate brokers, agents, and salespeople conduct business in an ethical fashion, consumers

are sometimes exploited in their dealings with these professionals. There are several points you must remember whenever you are buying real estate and dealing with a broker:

1. Avoid signing binder agreements if at all possible
2. Be wary of broker misrepresentation and other illegal practices

The following information will discuss these points in greater detail.

Binders

Binders are written agreements prepared by realtors that set forth key terms of the proposed sale. These agreements have legal consequences; they obligate sellers to pay realtor commissions when the broker produces a willing, able, and ready purchaser. Many unsuspecting sellers of homes and other real estate have been held liable for the broker's commission after the transaction has fallen through *by no fault of their own!* For example, I recently served as an arbitrator in a case where a couple was sued for $8,000. This sum represented the broker's commission on a deal that was never consummated. The couple signed the broker's standard binder agreement which stated that the couple agreed to sell their home for $120,000. A day after the agreement was signed, the broker located a suitable purchaser. However, the couple notified the broker that day that they had second thoughts about selling their house and wished to take their house off the market. The couple was sued by the broker and lost the case.

Similar cases such as this illustrate that you should never sign a binder before consulting a lawyer. If an agent insists that you sign such a document, you may wish to insert language similar to the following for your protection:

The full brokerage commission to be earned shall be $XXX. However, said commission is not to be considered earned until the full purchase price is paid to the seller and the deed is delivered to the purchaser. If this is not accomplished for any reason whatsoever, the broker shall have no claim for commission or compensation in connection with this transaction and shall promptly refund all money held as a deposit.

This clause may protect you from paying a commission if the sale is never consumated.

Other Illegal Practices

An increasing amount of consumer complaints regarding illegal practices of brokers, agents, and salespeople are being reported. The forms of exploitation vary. Some consumers are reporting that realtors are engaging in "real-tease" misrepresentation. For example, prospective buyers visit houses and learn that advertised bedrooms are only walk-in closets, or that a den is really a small foyer. Others are victims of discrimination. The following strategies may reduce the chances of being exploited.

To avoid problems:

1. *Deal only with a reputable broker.* Only 600,000 of the 2.5 million individuals licensed to sell real estate are members of the National Association of Realtors (NAR). However, members of this group are required to abide by a strict ethics code. Local chapters of the NAR police their members and conduct formal hearings once complaints are received. Realtors who misappropriate money or engage in illegal practices are subject to strict disciplinary sanctions including removal from access to multiple listing services, fines, and suspension from the association. Thus, by dealing with a

realtor who is a good-standing member in this organization, you may eliminate problems before they occur.

2. *Interview the broker before hiring him/her.* Select an experienced broker with a good reputation. Be aware that you can negotiate the amount of commission and the length of representation. Many independent brokers are willing to bend their fees when they don't have to share commissions with other brokers, so don't be afraid to ask for a reduction of the broker's commission before agreeing to representation. Confirm the terms of your arrangement in writing to avoid misunderstandings. For example, it is a good idea to send the broker a letter certified mail, return receipt requested, after you have agreed on essential terms. The following is an example:

(Date)

(Name of Broker)
SMS Brokerage Agency
(Address)

Dear (Name):

This will confirm that I agree to appoint you as my exclusive real estate broker effective (date) through (date).

You agree to use your best efforts to locate a willing, able, and ready purchaser for my home, located at (address).

It is agreed that the minimum acceptable price for my house will be $XXX. However, I have the right to withdraw my house for sale at any time, or change the acceptable terms of sale.

For your services, you will be paid a commission of XX percent of the purchase price. However, you undertake your responsibilities with the understanding that your commission will not be earned until the full purchase price is paid to me. If this is not accomplished for any reason whatsoever, you will have no claim for commission or compensation in connection with this transaction, and shall promptly refund all money held as a deposit.

As notice of your acceptance of this agreement, please sign this letter below where indicated, and return a signed copy to me immediately.

I look forward to working with you.

Sincerely,

Accepted and agreed to:
SMS Brokerage Agency

By: _____

(Send certified mail, return receipt requested.)

3. *Deal with real estate brokers rather than salespeople in complicated transactions.* In order to qualify as a broker, an individual must pass a state exam and possess a minimum number of education credits and years of selling experience. Salespeople usually must pass a less rigorous exam and are restricted to working under a broker's supervision. Thus, real estate brokers have more professional training than salespeople, and are typically more knowledgeable about available financing options and plans.

4. *Inspect the real estate before you decide to purchase.*

5. *Take immediate action if you have been exploited.* If you have a problem with a real estate broker, agent, or salesperson that cannot be resolved, contact the Regional Board of Realtors in your state as well as the local chapter of the National Association of Realtors. These local boards may investigate your written complaint and conduct a formal hearing on your behalf.

The following illustrates the type of letter that should be sent:

(Date)

Chairman
(Name of County or State) Board of Realtors
Anyplace, USA

Re: Formal Complaint against
(Name of Broker or Salesperson)

Dear Mr. Chairman:

I believe I have been the victim of several unethical practices perpetrated by (name of broker or salesperson). Please
treat this as a formal complaint against the above-named.

On (date), I inspected a house at (address). (Name of
broker or agent) told me that the house was built on filled
ground. When I asked for an engineer's report (name of
broker or salesperson) furnished me with a copy of the report.

I purchased the home on (date). However, in the past
two months, my home has been flooded on three separate
occasions. Further investigation has revealed that the engineer's report given to me was false because there is no engineer by that name in this state.

Kindly investigate this matter on my behalf. I understand that under state law, the board has the authority to
convene a formal hearing and impose sanctions against
(name of broker or salesperson) notwithstanding any legal
action I may independently take.

To date, I have suffered $6,000 in damages as a direct
result of such misrepresentation. I am supplying you with
documentation to support my claim.

Feel free to contact me at (work address, home address, work telephone number, home telephone number) if you require additional information or assistance in this matter.

I look forward to hearing from you.

Sincerely,

cc: Local chapter of NAR and real estate broker, agent, or salesperson

(Send certified mail, return receipt requested.)

Wait a few days, then call the board to discuss the appropriate action to be taken. Of course, you can also sue the realtor in court if you desire. Thus, it is best to speak to a lawyer to explore your options.

ADDITIONAL POINT: If you are looking for an apartment in a city with a tight housing market and are dealing with a broker, be sure that:

1. The broker does not misrepresent important terms (e.g., the condition of the apartment, actual date of occupancy, etc.)

2. You only pay a broker's fee if you rent an apartment found by that broker. For example, many complaints have been made by people who paid money to brokers who did not locate apartments for tenants or who misrepresented the terms of the deal. *Be aware of this*

Home Improvement and Building Contractor Abuses

Americans spend more than $11 billion a year in building renovation and home improvements. Many people are exploited by unqualified, unlicensed, and dishonest contractors. According to a nationwide survey conducted by the Better Business Bureau, more contractor-related complaints are received than any other form of complaint.

Abuses are endless. For example, salespeople pressure consumers into signing inadequate contracts which fail to incorporate oral promises, contractors purchase inferior materials which do not satisfy building code requirements, or consumers are overcharged for jobs that are never completed to their satisfaction.

The following information will tell you how to hire a contractor properly. Whether you desire to employ a general contractor or a specialist (e.g., plumber, carpenter, etc.) to perform work on your house, apartment, or business, these strategies can protect you from being a victim and tell you how to enforce your rights.

Choosing a Contractor

Problems in this area can be reduced by:

1. *Dealing with a licensed contractor only.* Most Department of Consumer Affairs and/or Better Business Bureaus require that contractors be licensed. Some require that contractors post a bond and sign affidavits before issuing licenses. Thus, contact these agencies to discover whether a particular contractor is licensed. A license does not guarantee the reliability or competence of a contractor, but it is a step in the right direction. Don't forget to inquire whether any complaints or lawsuits have been lodged against the contractor in the recent past.

2. *Avoiding hiring contractors* who solicit door-to-door, use a post office box as an address, or travel in an unmarked van or truck.

3. *Avoiding hiring contractors* who offer unbelievable bargains or require *full* payment before starting work.

4. *Asking for a written estimate.* The written estimate should include a description of materials to be purchased (the color, size, weight, and grade). Try to obtain written estimates from several contractors in order to make a valid comparison. However, some contractors charge money for written estimates, so be sure you know how much the estimate will cost *before* asking for it.

5. *Asking for references from customers and suppliers.* Confirm all references after they are received.

6. *Recognizing common schemes.* Dishonest contractors employ a variety of schemes to take your money. You can avoid being exploited by recognizing common illegal practices. The following are examples:

a. Farming out work to unqualified subcontractors. This can be avoided if you inquire who will eventually do the work *before* you hire the contractor and include this in the contract for your protection

b. Resorting to low-price bait ads. Unscrupulous contractors sometimes agree to provide inexpensive work, but send an "engineer" to persuade you to accept a more expensive package. This is a common scheme, so be aware of it

c. Offering rebates, discounts, or free gifts. If you are relying on promises of free gifts when accepting a contractor's bid, include this in the contract for your protection. For example, the contract should say when you will receive such gift or rebate

d. Offering claims of "lifetime guarantees" on building materials. Promises of lifetime guarantees may not be enforceable by law. Be aware of this

e. Charging exorbitant financing expenses. Dishonest contractors sometimes charge outrageous finance and interest expenses. For example, in one case, a couple was advanced $500 to purchase aluminum siding and other improvements from a contractor.

After signing the contract, the couple discovered that they were obligated to pay 84 monthly installments which collectively totaled $4,000 for a $1,900 job. Thus, always check your arithmetic and be aware of all hidden financing and interest expenses before accepting a home improvement loan from a building contractor.

Signing the Contract

Once you have selected a contractor, be sure to include all important terms in a written agreement. The following information will provide you with the important things to consider in a contract.

Your written agreement should state:

1. *The contractor's name, address, license, and telephone number.*

2. *The starting date of the job and the expected time of completion.* Is time of the essence? If so, the agreement should state that all work must be completed by a definite date because time is of the essence. Include a penalty if the job is not completed on time (e.g., 20 percent reduction of the contract price).

3. *That the contractor has procured all permits required by law* (e.g., certificates of insurance for Workers' Compensation, Public Liability and Property Damage), and that you will be provided a copy of these permits within forty-eight hours before work commences. The contract should also state that your deposit will be returned *immediately* if copies of these documents are not produced.

4. *A detailed description of all materials to be used.* This should include quantities, brand names, and model numbers. The contract should specify that the materials to be used are *fully warranted,* that labor and materials are guaranteed against defects and poor workmanship, and that all defects will be corrected at no extra charge.

5. *That there are no hidden charges to increase the cost of the job* (e.g., that the contractor agrees to move equipment and furniture back to its original location, clean up debris, post a performance bond, and return all unused materials to you at no additional cost).

6. *The manner of payment.* The best way to protect yourself against any problems is to keep the initial deposit as small as possible when negotiating payment terms. For example, it is best to avoid making substantial payments until the job is actually completed and you are satisfied with the work (e.g., 25 percent of the contract price upon signing, 25 percent during the actual work, and the balance upon satisfactory completion of the job).

7. *The method of financing.* Federal law requires that consumers be informed of all financing charges, the annual rate of interest expressed as a percent, the amount of each installment, the number of payments, and the penalties for late payment or default. Be sure to scrutinize all financing terms and figures.

(ADDITIONAL STRATEGY: Think twice before signing the contract if the contractor or salesperson rushes you into making a decision. *In many states, the law allows you to cancel the contract within a specified period* [e.g., three days in New York] for any reason *without penalty.* Some states even require a cancellation notice to be attached to the contract for this purpose. Thus, you may be able to cancel the contract if you have second thoughts, provided you act quickly.)

(REMINDER: After the contract is dated and signed by both parties obtain a legible copy and keep it in a safe place.)

While the Job Is in Progress

There are several things you should do while the job is in progress. First, match payments to the progress of the job. This will help you avoid paying for more work than you actually receive at any given time.

It is also important to observe the contractor's work to be sure the job is being done properly. Voice your immediate displeasure if you receive defective materials or shoddy workmanship. Be aware that if you obtained financing through a lending institution, you may be able to withhold installments until the problems are corrected.

Make your claims known by sending a letter certified mail, return receipt requested, to the contractor. The letter should state your reasons for job dissatisfaction, as well as clarifying what you contracted to receive, and what you are now receiving.

The following illustrates the kind of letter that should be sent:

Protest Letter Demanding Satisfaction

> (Your Name)
> (Your Address)
> (Telephone Number)
> (Date)

(Name of Contractor)
(Address)

Dear (Name):

I hereby make a formal demand for you to cure the breach of our written agreement dated _____.

Our contract specifically states that "Time Is of the Essence" and that you will finish the job (state what was agreed to) by (date).

You are now ten days late under the contract. Therefore, I demand (indicate what you want the contractor to do to remedy the situation, e.g., complete work immediately, reduce the final contract price, etc.).

Unless I hear from you immediately, I shall contact my attorney and file a formal complaint with the Department of Consumer Affairs.

Thank you for your cooperation in this matter.

Sincerely,

P.S. I am sending a copy of this letter to the Complaint Division of the Department of Consumer Affairs to remain on file.

(Send certified mail, return receipt requested.)

Most contractors are anxious to receive the final payment and will attempt to accommodate you if your demands are not unreasonable. Sending a letter should help.

(ADDITIONAL STRATEGY: Never agree to changes in the original contract unless the changes are agreed to in writing and initialed by both parties. This is for your protection.)

After Job Completion

The following points should be considered after the job is completed:

1. Never sign a completion certificate until you are sure the job has been completed

2. Never make final payment unless you are satisfied with the job

3. Never make final payment until the contractor provides you with *releases* from suppliers and persons employed on the job. Dishonest contractors sometimes pocket the money and fail to pay third parties, and the purchaser is often liable. *Demand releases to protect yourself*

If you made final payment and are dissatisfied with the job, be aware that several options are available. You can:

1. Sue the contractor in Small Claims Court
2. Hire a lawyer and sue the contractor in a regular court
3. Send a formal written complaint to the local Department of Consumer Affairs, Better Business Bureau, regional office of the Federal Trade Commission, or Attorney General's Office

These agencies frequently commence formal investigations after receiving written complaints. The advantage of filing a written complaint with an appropriate agency is that you may not have to pay money to hire a lawyer to obtain satisfaction. In New York City, for example, the Complaint Division of the Department of Consumer Affairs has the authority to schedule a hearing and impose penalties. These include fines, restitution, and orders requiring the contractor to complete the job in a satisfactory manner (or lose his license).

If you decide to file a formal complaint with an appropriate agency, send a letter certified mail, and include a telephone number where you can be reached during business hours. Attach copies (never originals) of all pertinent documents to prove your claim. This may include, for example, the contract, any letters of protest, advertisements, guarantees, sales literature, and other correspondence. If possible, take pictures to demonstrate the current condition of the premises; send these along with the complaint.

The following is an example of a formal complaint lodged with the Department of Consumer Affairs:

Formal Complaint Letter

(Your Name)
(Your Address)
(Date)

Director
Regional Office, Complaint Division
Department of Consumer Affairs
(Address)

Re: Request for Commencement of Investigation
against (Name of Contractor)

Dear (Name):

I hereby request you to commence a formal investigation of (name of contractor), located at (address), License number (#).

On (date), I signed a written contract with (name of contractor) to receive (specify work to be performed, where, at what price, etc.).

After the job was supposedly completed (state what happened, what you observed, etc.). I immediately contacted the contractor several times by phone and letter, and requested that he complete the job in the manner specified in our contract. On (date), I spoke with (name) and (state what you told the contractor, who you spoke with, what was said, etc.). On (date), I wrote a letter to the contractor.

To date, my requests have been ignored.

I enclose a copy of the contract, color photographs showing the condition of the premises as they currently exist, and additional correspondence, including a formal demand letter which I sent by certified mail, and which went unanswered.

It is my understanding that you have the authority to schedule a hearing. I would appreciate that this be done as quickly as possible because (state the reason why).

I am available at (give your telephone number) during business hours to assist you at your convenience. Kindly notify me of all developments in this matter.

Thank you for your cooperation and courtesies.

Very truly yours,

P.S. I am demanding (state how you have been damaged and what you wish to recover).

cc: Copy sent certified mail to contractor

(Send certified mail, return receipt requested.)

Wait a few days after sending the letter, then follow it up by calling the agency. If you do not receive appropriate action, consult a lawyer to determine your private legal rights and options.

What You Should Know about Mail Fraud

Many unscrupulous individuals conduct business through the mail. They use the mail to avoid personal access with victims and reduce the possibility of being caught. People are routinely exposed to a variety of mail fraud. This includes:

- False mail-order advertising
- Unsatisfactory mail-order transactions
- Exaggerated cosmetic, diet, medical, energy-saving products, and insurance offers
- Chain letters and pyramid sales promotions
- Deceptive billing tactics

The information in this section will tell you how to avoid becoming a mail fraud victim.

Mail Order Transactions

The following strategies should be reviewed whenever you decide to make a mail-order purchase:

1. *Comparison shop.* Find out if the merchandise is available from another mail-order source.

2. *Check the advertising claims.* Are they too good to be true? Reliable firms do not overpromise. Check the description of the product carefully and, if you send for it, keep a copy of the ad or catalog from which you ordered.

3. *Find out if there is a warranty.* Read it carefully. Does it offer your money back if you're not satisfied?

4. *Check the time limit on delivery.* If none is stated, the maximum length of time permitted by the Federal Trade Commission is thirty days. Mail-order transactions must be shipped within the time stated in the company's printed or broadcasted offer. If no time is stated, shipment must be within thirty days after the company receives the order unless you are contacted and agree to a delay.

5. *Ask the company for a more detailed description of the product or its guarantee if you have doubts.*

6. *Make sure your name and address are clearly marked on the order form.* If you are ordering a gift, be sure that the name and address of the person to whom you are sending it is legible.

7. *Keep a copy of your order form and any letters you send to the company.* Make sure you have the company's correct address for future reference.

8. *Never send cash.* Pay by check or money order to prove payment. Be sure to include extra charges, shipping, handling, and sales tax.

9. *Check the order immediately when you receive it.* Make sure it is what you wanted and ordered. If not, notify the company (it is best to do so in writing and keep a copy of your letter) and return the merchandise by certified mail for a refund or exchange.

10. *Contact your local Postmaster or Chief Postal Inspector if you have been victimized.* The Inspection Service of the U.S. Postal Office, headed by the Chief Postal Inspector, is the law enforcement and audit arm of the Postal Service. This office performs security, law enforcement, and audit functions. It is responsible for investigating potential violations. Direct any grievance to their attention.

The following is the kind of letter that should be sent:

> (Your Name)
> (Your Address)
> (Date)

Local Postmaster
Anyplace, USA

Dear Local Postmaster:

I believe I have been the victim of an illegal mail fraud.

On (date), I responded to an advertisement in _____ . The ad stated that I would obtain (name or product), provided I sent $29.95 to (address of company).

Over two months have passed and I have not received my purchase. In addition, I sent the company a letter dated _____ to document my protest, and I have not received a reply.

Please investigate this matter on my behalf. I can be reached at (telephone number) during business hours if you require additional assistance.

Thank you for your cooperation in this matter.

Sincerely,

Enclosures: Copy of ad, canceled check, letter of protest (Send certified mail, return receipt requested.)

(NOTE: If you wish to obtain more information on mail orders, write to the Federal Trade Commission, Washington, D.C., 20580, to receive a free copy of their publication, *Shopping by Mail.*)

Your local Department of Consumer Affairs and Better Business Bureau may be able to assist you in the event that you are exploited by a local business or individual. However, the assistance of the postal authorities is required if you are victimized by an out-of-state company.

Unordered Merchandise

It is a violation of the FTC Act to send unordered merchandise through the mail unless it is (1) a free sample marked as such, or (2) merchandise sent by a charitable organization asking for a contribution. Most states allow consumers to treat unordered merchandise as a gift. Persons sending unordered merchandise through the mail are prohibited from demanding payment. Moreover, billing for unordered merchandise may constitute mail fraud and/or misrepresentation, and the Postal Service can declare the receipt of unordered merchandise a gift.

If you are the victim of unordered merchandise, contact either your local postmaster, Chief Postal Inspector in Washington, D.C., or the Federal Trade Commission in Washington, D.C.

Unsolicited Mail

Individuals interested in stopping advertising mail, catalogs, and brochures from coming to their homes should contact the Direct Mail Marketing Association at 6 East 43rd Street, New York, N.Y. 10017. This organization can remove your name from the mailing lists of its members and stop most sweepstakes, contest offers, samples, coupons, and catalogs from coming to you.

Used-Car Abuses

Buying a used car can be a risky proposition. Many people buy used cars and enjoy years of trouble-free driving. Others, however, purchase vehicles which do not perform as promised. The following strategies will help protect your investment when buying a used car from a professional dealer or private individual.

Professional Dealers and Used-Car Salespeople

1. *Negotiate with licensed dealers only.*

2. *Inspect the vehicle thoroughly.* Never be pressured into buying a used car until you have carefully examined its internal and external features. Inspections should be made during the day when there is adequate light. Test drive the car, preferably alone, and be attentive for odd noises and other irregularities.

3. *Have the car inspected by your regular mechanic or diagnostic center.* This is important. Never buy a car from a seller who won't allow an independent inspection.

4. *Discuss key points to avoid misunderstandings.* The following items should be clarified *before* making your purchase:

a. What is the price of the car? Is tax, dealer preparation, and transportation included?

b. What are the terms of payment?

c. What are the financing charges for installment payments?

d. Will you be receiving a warranty? If so, for how long? Does the warranty cover parts and service? Who is giving the warranty (e.g., the manufacturer and/or the dealer)?

e. Who pays for transporting the car back to the dealer if it breaks down?

f. Will the dealer repair or replace defective parts *quickly* at no extra cost?

5. *Put all promises in writing.* A common form of exploitation arises when salespeople and dealers make promises which are not incorporated into the sales contract. *Be sure that all statements made about the condition of the car, service to be provided, and financial terms are put in writing.* The reason is that oral promises are hard to prove. Putting them in writing will increase the success of a lawsuit and discourage salespeople from making promises that management is unwilling to back.

6. *Read the fine print of the sales contract.* Salespeople and dealers often make generous promises which are never included in the agreement. For example, the fine print of many sales contracts states that the seller assumes no responsibility for the condition of the vehicle (e.g., "as is"), and that the written contract is the entire agreement between the two parties. Many agreements also state that no oral statements or representations made by the dealer or any salesperson are part of the contract. This protects the seller. Thus, if oral promises have been made, delete the "as is" clause, insert the promises that *have* been made and initial the changes in front of the salesperson or dealer.

7. *Receive the Certificate of Title, copy of the Bill of Sale, and other appropriate documents.*

8. *Keep records of mechanical problems which arise after purchase.* It is essential to keep accurate records to prove that your used car is defective. This includes:

- Your own notes
- Receipts from repair shops or the dealer's mechanic
- Records which show the date and mileage on the car in addition to the problem experienced
- Schedule of trips you made to the dealer's repair shop
- Copies of signed work orders, canceled checks, etc. These records will help your case if litigation becomes necessary

9. *Take immediate action to protect your rights.* Contact the dealer if you are unsatisfied with your purchase. This should be done immediately to protect your rights. Follow up telephone calls with a certified letter to document your protest. The letter should be written similar to the following:

(Date)
(Your Name)
(Address)

Mr. (Name), President
ABC Used Car Sales
Anyplace, USA

Re: My Defective Automobile

Dear (Name):

On (date), I bought a used (describe make, model, year, service number, color) for the sum of $XXX. At the time of the sale, you stated that the car was a "cream puff" in perfect mechanical condition.

It was agreed that your shop would perform any and all repairs if the car malfunctioned for any reason for a period of sixty days after the date of purchase. This was specifically inserted into the sales contract and initialed by both of us.

Last week, while I was driving the car to meet my wife in (location), the car broke down. An AAA representative towed the car back to my home. Despite several telephone calls to you, the car is sitting in my driveway while you keep telling me "to be patient" and that you will get around to repair it.

Please be advised that I require the use of an automobile for my business and that I am renting a replacement at the sum of $35 a day while your car is inoperative. Unless the car is repaired to my satisfaction immediately per our understanding, I will bring the matter to the attention of the Department of Consumer Affairs, the Consumer Fraud Division of the Attorney General's Office, and the Better Business Bureau as well as consider instituting legal action against you.

Thank you for your cooperation in this matter.

Sincerely,

(Send certified mail, return receipt requested.)

There are several options to explore if the dealer refuses to cooperate. In addition to instituting suit in Small Claims Court (see chapter 7 for information on how to do this), or a higher court, you should contact the Department of Consumer Affairs in your state, the Consumer Fraud Division of your state's Attorney General's Office and/or the Better Business Bureau. Settlements are often effectuated by these agencies.

Send the following type of letter to commence an investigation on your behalf:

(Date)
(Your Name)
(Address)

Dept. of Consumer Affairs
Anyplace, USA

Re: Formal Complaint against
ABC Used Car Sales,
License Number ____

To Whom it May Concern:

Please treat this letter as a formal complaint against the above-named.

On (date), I purchased a used car (describe make, model, year, serial number, color) from ABC Used Car Sales. A sales contract was signed which stated that ABC would perform satisfactory repairs at no extra charge for a period of sixty days from the date of the purchase.

On (date), the car broke down which ABC refuses to repair. This action has caused me significant damages including (specify).

Kindly investigate the matter on my behalf. I am enclosing a copy of the sales contract, letter of protest sent to ABC, costs of renting a replacement car, and other documentation for your review.

Feel free to contact me at (work address, work telephone number, home address, home telephone number) if you require any additional information or assistance.

Thank you for your prompt cooperation in this matter.

Sincerely,

cc: ABC Used Car Sales, Better Business Bureau, Consumer Fraud Division, Attorney General's Office.

(Send certified mail, return receipt requested.)

Private Individuals

The preceding strategies should also be followed when buying a car from a private individual. If you pay additional money for unexpected repairs, you may be able to recover the cost of these repairs in Small Claims Court. To do this you will have to prove:

1. That the individual made representations about the condition of the car to be sold (e.g., you were told "This car is in great shape; it was recently tuned up and inspected by a mechanic.")

2. That you bought the car on the basis of these representations

3. That these representations were false and that the individual knew they were false at the time they were made

4. That you were damaged as a result

(NOTE: Consult the appropriate section contained in the Small Claims Court chapter for further information.)

Avoiding Car Repair Abuses

Many people are exploited by unscrupulous mechanics and auto dealers. The following strategies will help reduce the chances of car repair abuses.

Before taking your car to a new dealer or repair shop:

1. *Talk to people who have patronized the firm.* Ask about the service they received. You can call the Better Business Bureau to discover if they have any complaints against the shop.

2. *Describe what is wrong with your car as completely and exactly as possible,* but don't tell the service manager or mechanic how to correct the problem. For example, if you brought your car in because the engine was running rough,

don't announce that you need a tune-up. You may only need to have the timing adjusted, a much less expensive job.

3. *Give the service manager or mechanic a* written list *of your car's problems* and keep a copy for yourself. This will reduce the chance of misunderstandings.

4. *Do not automatically agree to everything the service manager or mechanic recommends.* Do not sign a blank work order form when you leave your car at the garage. If the manager recommends work, ask for a detailed explanation of the work to be performed, and why it is needed.

5. *Obtain a written estimate of all repairs and service* before *leaving the car at the shop.* Get a second opinion before having expensive work done. Never authorize additional work over the telephone unless you trust the people you are dealing with.

6. *Shop around at specialty service shops before taking your car to a dealership for work.* Firms that specialize in certain kinds of work (e.g., muffler repair or brake jobs) may do the job at a lower cost.

7. *Ask for the parts that were replaced when picking up the car from the garage.* This can prove if work was actually done.

8. *Examine your receipt closely.* Question anything you don't understand before leaving the shop. Save a copy of the receipt in case problems develop.

9. *Complain to the service manager or shop owner immediately if the work was not done properly.* If you can't get satisfaction, send a letter certified mail to document your claim and consider filing a suit in Small Claims Court. The information contained in the Small Claims Court chapter will tell you how to effectuate this.

ADDITIONAL NOTE:
What to Do When You Buy a Lemon

Many states have recently passed "Lemon Law" statutes to protect buyers of defective new automobiles. This legislation has been enacted in California, Connecticut, New Jersey, and New York as a result of the hundreds of thousands of complaints from purchasers who bought new cars that malfunctioned and cannot be fixed. Other states are about to pass similar legislation.

The typical lemon law works this way: a new-car buyer who experiences a defect is required to notify the dealer or manufacturer and allow him to attempt to repair it. If after several attempts the condition is not alleviated, the car owner can resort to the company's arbitration program or bring an action to sue for the refund price of the car or a replacement.

The following steps can protect your claim in the event you purchase a "lemon."

1. *Write a letter to the manufacturer or dealer when you experience a problem.* State the model and vehicle identification number, the make of the car, and the date, purchase price, and place of purchase.

In most states, the buyer must notify the dealer and manufacturer of the defect within the warranty period, or one year of the date of delivery, *so don't delay.*

2. *In the letter, document the problem or defect that affects the car's use.* If possible, include a written statement from a mechanic or diagnostic center which confirms your claim.

3. *Schedule an appointment with the dealer to return the car.* After the car is repaired, ask for a copy of the bill which shows what repairs were performed.

4. *Save a copy of this document, together with your initial letter and all other pertinent records.* Prepare a diary of events which show the steps that were taken to maintain the car in proper working condition (e.g., that the car was inspected on a regular basis). This is because it is necessary to show that the defect in the car was not caused by your negligence or abuse.

5. *Bring the car back to the dealer if the problem is not corrected.* Check the law in your state to determine the appropriate course of action to take if the defect persists.

Employment Agency, Search Firm, and Career Counseling Abuses

In their anxious desire to obtain employment, many individuals are exploited by dishonest employment agencies, search firms, and career counselors. Reported cases indicate that some applicants are charged exorbitant placement fees. Others pay large, nonrefundable fees for job interviews that do not result in jobs. Still others are asked discriminatory questions at the initial interview, or are told to register in proscribed courses (for which the agency gets a fee) before they are permitted to interview.

The following recent case illustrates this problem:

A search firm placed an ad in *The New York Times.* The ad stated:

We Use Our Contacts, Methods, Experience, Research Facilities, and Equipment to Obtain Interviews for You in the Unpublished, Unadvertised Job Marketplace; Positions Are Available for qualified executives, managers, and professionals in the $20,000 to $60,000 range in corporations, associations, and foundations.

The ad attracted several hundred individuals who reportedly paid advance fees from $500 to $8,000. Most of these people never received any placement assistance or contacts.

Unfortunate incidents such as this can be avoided if you take proper steps. The following strategies can protect you from unethical and illegal employment practices:

1. *Know the difference between employment agencies, search firms, and career counselors.* Employment agencies offer different services to job applicants than search firms and career counselors. The primary function of employment agencies is to obtain a job for a client; career counselors and search firms perform a variety of services, including résumé and letter

preparation, successful interviewing techniques, and leads for job openings. Career counselors do *not* obtain jobs for applicants. It is important to understand this distinction before you discuss your needs with an agency or firm.

2. *Understand the ramifications of your arrangement.* Ask the following questions before you agree to be represented by an employment agency, search firm, or career counselor:

a. Is the firm licensed? In New York State, for example, all private employment agencies must be licensed and regulated by the Department of Consumer Affairs. To obtain a license, the agency must fill out a detailed application, post a performance bond, maintain accurate records, and avoid engaging in illegal acts. Career counselors do not have to be licensed to conduct business.

b. What are the precise services the firm or individual will render?

c. What is required of the job applicant (e.g., prepare a résumé, buy an interviewing suit, etc.)?

d. When will the firm or individual earn its fee (e.g., when you are offered a job by an acceptable firm, when you accept the job, when you work a minimum amount of time, etc.)?

e. What is the maximum fee to be charged?

f. Who will pay for the fee (e.g., you or the employer)? When is it payable?

g. What happens if you decide not to accept a job that is offered?

h. Is a deposit required once a job is accepted? If so, by whom?

i. Who pays for the cost of transportation to the interview?

j. Will you receive a detailed composite of each potential employer before you go on an interview (e.g., the name, address, kind of work to be performed, title, amount of wages or compensation, hours, whether the work is temporary or permanent, etc.)?

k. Will the agency investigate whether the potential employer has defaulted in the payment of salaries to others during the past five years (particularly in the entertainment industry)?

l. What happens to the fee if you resign or are fired within a short period of time?

m. Will the agency help you obtain another job if you are terminated?

n. Does the agency have the right to represent you on an exclusive basis?

o. What happens to the fee if you become disabled and cannot work?

2. *Confirm your arrangement in writing.* Most reputable firms will confirm your arrangement in writing. Insist on nothing less. If you receive an agreement, read it carefully. Question all ambiguous terms. Never sign the agreement until it is understood to your satisfaction.

3. *Avoid paying money in advance.* It is illegal for employment agencies to charge a fee *before* employment is procured. However, career counseling and search firms are permitted by law to charge a fee up front. Resist this if possible. The reason is that many people pay money to firms but never receive services which are promised. One popular variation of this scheme is perpetrated by modeling agencies. The agency places an impressive ad in a local newspaper. The ad says that the agency is looking for attractive children. Mothers from hundreds of miles away bring their children in hopes of establishing them in a show business career. The agency agrees to represent the children, provided the parent spends several hundred dollars for pictures and promotional material.

The unsuspecting parent pays the money. Weeks later, a few black-and white photographs of the children are received, but that is the last time the parent hears from the modeling agency.

There are many illegal schemes similar to this one. The best way to avoid them is not pay money up front (or until you are satisfied that the firm is working hard on your behalf).

4. *Recognize abuses before they occur.* Another way to protect yourself is to be aware of some of the common illegal practices that have surfaced in the past.

The following is a list of employment agency acts which are prohibited under New York law. Many states have similar laws. This list will help you know when you are being victimized.

Under New York law, it is illegal for an employment agency to:

a. Induce an employee to terminate his job so the agency can obtain new employment for him

b. Publish false or misleading ads

c. Advertise in newspapers without providing the name and address of the agency

d. Send an applicant to an employer without obtaining a job order from the employer

e. Make false representations or promises

f. Require applicants to subscribe to publications, pay for advertising costs, enroll in special courses, or pay for additional services

g. Charge a placement fee when the agency represents that it was a fee-paid job

h. Discriminate on the basis of sex, race, religion, or age

i. Require the applicant to complete applications forms that are designed to obtain different information than applicants of the opposite sex

Many of these abuses are also applicable to search firms and career counseling services. *Thus, be aware of them.*

5. *Seek immediate assistance if you have been exploited.* If you believe you have been exploited, you should take immediate action to protect your rights. One way is to send a certified letter to the firm to document your protest. The letter should state the reasons for your dissatisfaction and the manner you would like the problem resolved.

The following is an example of the kind of protest letter that should be sent:

(Your Name)
(Address)
(Date)

(Name of Firm)
(Address)

Dear (Name):

On (date) I responded to an advertisement that your firm ran in (name of magazine). The ad specifically promised that your firm could find a job for me as a salesperson in the cosmetics industry. The ad stated that a $250 advance was fully refundable in the event I could not obtain a job paying more than $20,000 per year.

Per your request, and after several telephone conversations, I sent you a check for $250. That was four months ago. Since that time, I received one letter from you, dated ____, which states you are reviewing my employment history.

In view of the fact that I have not obtained full-time employment, I hereby make formal demand for the return of my $250, per our agreement.

If I do not receive the money within fourteen days from the date of this letter, I shall contact the Department of Consumer Affairs, Better Business Bureau, frauds division of the Attorney General's Office, and my private lawyer to commence a formal investigation of this matter. For your edification, these agencies can suspend and cancel your license in addition to imposing other fines and penalties.

All of this will be avoided by making a timely return of my payment.

Thank you for your cooperation in this matter.

Sincerely,

(Send certified mail, return receipt requested.)

If the problem is not resolved to your satisfaction, your next step should be to contact your local Department of Consumer Affairs and Better Business Bureau. You may wish to send a letter similar to the following:

(Your Name)
(Address)
(Date)

Commissioner
Department of Consumer Affairs
Anywhere, USA

Re: Formal Complaint against
ABC Employment Agency,
License #____

Dear Commissioner:

I hereby make a formal complaint against (name of employment agency). I believe that the firm has committed the following illegal acts (state what they are).

The facts on which I base my allegations are as follows: (state the facts).

On (date), I sent the agency a formal demand letter requesting the return of my deposit. This letter was sent by certified mail, and I received no response. I enclose a copy of said letter for your review.

I request that you convene a formal hearing regarding this matter.

Feel free to contact me at (business and home address, business and home telephone numbers) for any further assistance or information.

Thank you for your cooperation.

Sincerely,

P.S. I am enclosing the following documentation for your review (include).

(Copy sent certified mail, return receipt requested to agency accused of committing illegal acts.)

(Send certified mail)

Wait a few days, and then contact the Department of Consumer Affairs to discover how your matter is progressing. You may also wish to discuss the matter with an attorney or consider commencing an action in Small Claims Court to recover damages.

4

Protecting Yourself when Purchasing a Computer for Your Business or Home

- **Introduction**   194
- **Avoiding Exploitation before Making Your Purchase**   195
- **Specific Negotiating Points to Consider**   197
    Software   197
    Hardware   199
    Service Bureau Contracts   201
- **How to Avoid Problems before They Occur**   204

Introduction

Recent advances in computer technology are affecting many aspects of our lives. The most simple computers perform complex accounting, bookkeeping, and payroll computations, turn data into useful charts and graphs, keep track of personal expenses and phone calls, and do countless other computer functions.

Most of these remarkable advances have occurred within the past twenty years. However, the rapid development of computer technology has caused problems for consumers. People who bought computers several years ago now find that their hardware (the computer itself) has become outdated, is difficult and costly to maintain, and is not compatible with new software programs (the instructions telling the computer what to do). Others, not familiar with computer technology, are misled by high-pressure computer salespeople who offer systems promising to do specific chores, but which fail to deliver.

The number of computer-related lawsuits has increased dramatically. Hundreds of lawsuits, for example, are currently pending against a well-known manufacturer of small business computers. Thousands of other cases have been settled out of court, often for substantial sums. This is caused in part because sellers are not supplying the same quality of assistance and instructions as in the past, computer salespeople are making false promises to first-time users, and some computer companies are marketing defective products.

A substantial number of small businessmen, lured by the prospect of automating their operations electronically, are buying computer systems which fail to work as promised. In one recent case, for example, the president of a brewery sued a computer services supplier. The president alleged that his computer was erroneously reporting beer distributors and liquor stores as being delinquent in their payments. Under laws in some states, those distributors lost the rights to buy liquor on credit. The case was settled for $2.3 million.

It is important that such abuses do not happen to you. This chapter will tell you what points to negotiate and include in your sales contract, particularly when buying or renting a computer system for your business. In addition, you will learn the proper steps to recover damages in the event that the hardware, software, or service bureau fails to perform properly.

Avoiding Exploitation before Making Your Purchase

Before buying a computer, ask yourself if you really need one. Know what the system is supposed to accomplish. Familiarize yourself with simple computer phraseology. Talk to friends and business associates to learn what they use. Prepare a list of points to consider before speaking with a salesperson. This should include:

1. The software you wish to buy
2. The cost of the hardware and hidden service and installation charges
3. The system's power, reliability, speed, memory capacity, and potential for future expandability

4. The system's ease of operation, programming, and memory
5. The company's guarantees, warranty, and maintenance policies
6. The tax ramifications of your purchase

It is wise to comparison shop to get a better idea about the kinds of systems and deals available. Avoid taking your checkbook, cash, or credit cards on your first visit. This will reduce the chances of your being pressured into a decision you may later regret.

If you are unsophisticated and are going to make a sizeable investment, consider hiring a consultant—especially if you plan to purchase or rent a system for your business. Computer consultants act like real estate brokers. They shop around and help you select equipment to fill your needs. Thus, it is important to know what you need and give accurate information to the consultant; this will enable him to do the job properly.

Ask for references before hiring a consultant; check them out. Speak to past and present customers to learn more about the way he operates. Be sure you know exactly what his services will cost.

In general, approach computer salespeople carefully. Many are eager to close a sale and fail to provide first-time users with honest appraisals. Never feel intimidated when speaking to one. If he is arrogant, makes you feel ignorant, or answers your questions in technical language, talk to someone else. Avoid doing business with salespeople who also act as consultants, because they sometimes encourage customers to purchase systems regardless of their true needs.

Be flexible. Don't be turned off by young salespeople because they often know more than old-timers. *Write down all specific promises made by a salesperson* regarding how the system will perform, its capabilities, and what it will do. This move may help your lawyer in the event of a future dispute.

Be sure you understand the operating manual before you select a system; you may lose several months' *downtime* if you can't figure out how to use it. In addition, it is wise to get feedback from people who will operate your system. Tell employees that the equipment is not meant to replace them, but to assist them in their duties, and ask what they think about the system.

Specific Negotiating Points to Consider

Software

Software can be acquired several ways. Some computer users hire computer programmers to write programs specifically suited to their needs (i.e., custom software). Others hire outside consultants to perform the programming. The majority of purchasers use programs which have already been developed and tested (i.e., packaged software).

Regardless of the type of software used, legal problems frequently develop when:

1. The software cannot be implemented into the system properly
2. It fails to accomplish promised results
3. It is misused by the purchaser

Most lawsuits arise over the failure of the software to perform a specific job, rather than the reliability of the hardware. The parties often fail to clearly describe what specific functions the software will perform. Problems then develop after the user has not received promised benefits.

Consider the following legal points before selecting computer software and try to incorporate these points in the agreement for your protection:

1. *Functions.* Define what the program will accomplish. Include this in a schedule and attach it to the contract.

2. *Ownership.* Will the software be rented for one-time, multiple, or unlimited use? Can it be purchased, or is it being made available on some other basis?

3. *Revisions.* If the seller updates the software on a regular basis, ask if you will receive revised versions. If so, will you have to pay for this? How long will you receive program revisions? If additional training is required, who pays for this?

4. *Implementation.* Can the software be used in another computer system, or are you restricted to using it in one system only? If no restrictions are imposed, be sure that additional fees will *not* be charged.

Be aware that some companies charge storage fees for programs used more than once, but stored between uses.

5. *Assistance.* Will the seller provide assistance in the event the program isn't working properly?

Try to receive guarantees that the program will not become outdated or cause the hardware to break down.

6. *Assurances.* Is the program you are buying "error-free," or are you purchasing the program "as is"? If you are acquiring the program "as is," demand the right to a demonstration with your equipment and data *before paying* to be sure that the program works to your satisfaction.

7. *Payment.* Clarify the manner of payment. For example, will it be made upon signing of the contract, when the software program is delivered, after it is installed, or after you receive a satisfactory demonstration? You may find a *progress payment schedule* advantageous (i.e., one third of the amount on signing, one third upon installation, and the balance on satisfactory completion. *Consider this.*

8. *Time restraints.* Do you need the software by a specified date? If so, the agreement should state that *"Time Is of the Essence."* It should also say, if possible, that if you don't receive the functional software by a certain date, you can

cancel the agreement, recover your deposit, and sue for damages.

If you are to receive the software *in stages,* ask to receive periodic written reports to keep you posted. You will then be able to make alternative plans if it becomes apparent that the seller cannot make timely delivery.

9. *Liability.* The contract should state that:

a. The seller is not violating copyright and other laws by selling the program to you

b. The seller will indemnify and hold you harmless

c. The seller will pay for all costs of legal representation should you be sued by a third party through no fault of your own

10. *Assignment.* Can you transfer the software license to affiliates or business successors? Probably not, but inquire about this.

11. *Restrictions.* The seller will probably impose restrictions on your use. Most companies impose restrictions because they spend substantial sums of money to develop computer programs and do not permit purchasers to copy or disclose the contents or results to unauthorized third parties. Try to limit these restrictions. In any event, be sure they are not violated.

(ADDITIONAL POINT: Most experts believe it is wise to know what computer software you intend to use before purchasing the hardware. This is because the software tells the computer what to do; without it, the computer cannot do the job properly. Thus, try to acquire top quality programs that are *adaptable* into your hardware.)

Hardware

Select a hardware system that is compatible with your software. Many computer manufacturers sell adaptable software programs, but you are not limited to selecting programs from the same manufacturer. Try to buy a computer with:

- A large memory capacity
- Sufficient power
- Ability to be upgraded to handle more sophisticated software programs (like floppy disks). This is important

There are many pitfalls contained in standard computer hardware contracts. These pertain to installation, payment, shipment, warranties, and other important terms. The following material will tell you what to look for:

1. *Preparation costs.* Some computer contracts contain *installation clauses.* These specify that computer equipment is to be installed only in air-conditioned or dust-free areas. To avoid problems, insist that the seller inspect the premises where the equipment will be installed before the contract is signed.

2. *Geographic restrictions.* Some sellers prohibit installed equipment from being moved to other locations. This may cause a problem if your business wishes to relocate.

3. *Payment.* Study your payment options carefully. Speak with an advisor before committing yourself, especially if a large purchase is contemplated. There are a number of ways to structure the deal. These include an outright purchase for cash, a purchase with financing from the seller, bank, or lending institution, a close-end lease, or a lease with an option to purchase.

4. *Shipping instructions.* Who is paying for preparation, shipping costs, and transit insurance? Insist that the seller pay for these items. Try to take title only after the hardware has been delivered, assembled, and has become functional—never before.

Inspect the system immediately when you receive it to be sure that it wasn't damaged in transit. Request that it be assembled as soon as possible after delivery. This will increase your rights.

5. *Delivery date.* Include the date you expect the system to be delivered and installed. If *Time Is of the Essence,* specify this in the contract. Time the delivery and installation of the hardware to the approximate date you expect to receive your software program. By doing this, you may avoid paying for hardware that cannot be operated because essential software has not arrived.

6. *Disclaimer clauses.* Computer manufacturers often seek to limit their legal exposure in the event that the computer fails to function properly. This is called a *disclaimer* or *limitation of liability clause.* The following is an example:

> The manufacturer's entire liability and the customer's exclusive remedy shall be the adjustment, repair or replacement of defective equipment. The manufacturer's liability for damages to the customer for any cause whatsoever, and regardless of the form of action shall be limited to the greater of $5,000 of the purchase price stated within.

These clauses are unfair and are often included in computer contracts. But some judges, depending on the particular clause and factual circumstances, refuse to enforce them against unsophisticated consumers because they are *unconscionable.*

7. *Special training.* Some computers require trained personnel to install and run them properly. Does your computer require special training? If so, how will such training be provided? Who will pay for it?

Service Bureau Contracts

Service bureaus are companies which provide time-sharing and computerized data processing services. This eliminates the need to purchase or rent computer hardware and software because the service bureau does everything (e.g., takes your data, processes, and analyzes it). Service bureaus provide inventory control, billing chores, word processing, payroll, and weekly sales information.

Employing a service bureau has several advantages:

a. Large sums of money are not expended to acquire sophisticated equipment for short-term projects

b. No computer expertise is required

c. Organizational assistance is part of the set-up

d. There are no hidden costs

e. You start receiving processed data immediately and don't waste time getting involved in an area you may not know much about

There are also disadvantages:

a. *Turnaround time* may be involved (i.e., time delays in receiving the information from the bureau once it has been processed)

b. You can't change the program once it has been set

c. You may have no control over vital information being disclosed to unauthorized third parties

d. Mistakes can be made which are difficult to detect

Despite the disadvantages, the rapid growth of service bureaus demonstrates the successes that individuals and businesses have with them. Consider the following points before hiring a service bureau:

- *Reputation*—Ask the service bureau for references. Investigate them

- *Reliability*—How long has the service bureau been in business? What are the qualifications of the people running it?

- *Resources*—Is the service bureau in good financial shape? Ask to see a recent financial statement
- *Service*—What programs are offered? Will you receive reasonable turnaround service? Conversely, will you be paying for faster service than you need?
- *Rates*—Are the rates competitive? Can you extend payment for initial programming charges over several months?

(NOTE: Long-term contracts should be avoided because your data processing requirements may change.)

Most service contracts are negotiable. The following points should be discussed and included in your service bureau contract:

1. *Duties*. Determine what you need. For example, will you receive on-line sharing access to data maintained in the service bureau's computer, or will you receive a new software program? If a new program is required, specify the duties of the service bureau (e.g., software development, acceptance testing, system availability, and payment schedules).

2. *Record retention*. The contract should state that the service bureau will protect the confidentiality of your data. It should also discuss damages in the event that delays occur (e.g., failing to receive promised payroll checks which disrupt your business).

3. *Record recovery*. It is important to recover possession of your data if a dispute arises. This will enable you to receive processed information from another company while resolving the dispute. Many service bureaus seek to impose a lien on such information and refuse to return it to you. *Avoid this in the contract*.

4. *Software rights*. The program usually remains the property of the service bureau, but it is a good idea to state

that upon the happening of specified events, such as the service bureau's change in ownership or filing of bankruptcy, you will be able to acquire the software.

5. *Other duties. Backup tapes* should be maintained to protect you if the original becomes misplaced or destroyed. Also, define the steps to be taken to prevent the disclosure of your data to unauthorized third parties.

6. *Errors.* The contract should specify a procedure for handling errors (e.g., further processing should stop until the error is corrected).

7. *Ownership.* All programs developed specifically for your use should be owned by you. Don't allow the company to make the program available to other customers without your consent.

8. *Fees.* Service bureaus generally charge two types of fees, one for designing the program, and one for processing. The charge for designing a custom program is usually a one-time charge unless you later make changes in the program. The processing charge is usually calculated on an hourly basis. Typical charges for small businesses range from $300 to $1,000 per month, depending upon the number and length of reports. Extra services, such as storing data in the company's memory for future use, may add to the cost. *Inquire about this.*

How to Avoid Problems before They Occur

Most small businesses and first-time users do not have the time or resources to fight the giant computer corporations. Difficult legal obstacles often reduce their chances of success. For example, some computer sales contracts limit damages to the purchase price; consumers cut off their rights by signing such contracts. Additionally, many purchasers fail to keep adequate records and are unable to prove their claims.

The following strategies will help you avoid problems before they occur.

1. *Beware of sales misrepresentation*
   a. The sales talk is a good time to get answers to hard questions. Know what you want to ask. *Be prepared* when you shop
   b. Don't allow the salesperson to tell you what you need—tell him what you need
   c. Don't allow fancy color brochures or free drinks to persuade you. Demand to see a working prototype or program application before making an investment
   d. Never make a purchase on a salesperson's presentation alone. *Comparison shop*
   e. *Beware of promises.* Make it clear you are relying on the salesperson's expertise in selecting a system to fit your needs. Write down all specific promises made by the salesperson regarding the capabilities of your equipment and what it will do for you

Under the law, express warranties are created when a manufacturer (through its salespeople) makes statements of fact about the capabilities of a product or service. If a customer relies on these factual representations, purchases the product or service, and the statement proves to be false, the customer is entitled to recover damages because the product or service failed to live up to its warranty. Thus, writing down such statements (e.g., how the computer would perform under a certain situation, what it would do) may help you prove your claims.

2. *Sign a written contract to protect yourself*
   a. Be sure you consider the major points raised in this chapter
   b. Avoid signing standard contracts, particularly for purchases exceeding $10,000.00. Standard contracts are prepared by legal staffs of computer vendors and contain clauses which benefit the seller and do not necessarily benefit you
   c. Ask a lawyer or other professional to review any complicated agreement you are about to sign

    d. Negotiate expensive purchases. Most computer hardware and software manufacturers and dealers refuse to negotiate standard sales and service agreements in the $1,000–$5,000 range. These contracts seldom vary from one dealer to the next. As a result, consumers often have trouble shopping for better terms and warranties. However, you or your lawyer will probably be able to negotiate more favorable terms when an expensive purchase is involved. Remember this

    e. Never assume you are precluded from recovering damages in the event that problems develop and you signed a standard contract with a disclaimer limiting your remedies. Although the law varies considerably from state to state, many judges find such clauses *unconscionable*, and therefore *unenforceable*. In addition, some lawyers are able to circumvent the effect of these clauses. Thus, always try to negotiate, but recognize you have rights even if you sign a standard computer contract

3. *Avoid paying for the job up front*

    a. If possible, structure periodic payments to completed work

    b. The final payment should be made several months after installation (say ninety days), to be sure you are satisfied with the system. Avoid paying the final installment until all flaws are corrected

4. *Minimize internal espionage by employees.* For example, avoid retaining confidential information in your business computer for a long period of time. Modify your passwords and coding on a regular basis to minimize abuses. You may wish to speak to a consultant for further details

5. *Keep accurate records after you acquire the equipment*

    a. Accurate records (e.g., your contract, correspondence, letters of protest, lost business, etc.), will help prove your claim in the event of a dispute. This is essential

6. *Document all complaints in writing, and send such letters by certified mail, return receipt requested*

7. *Speak to a lawyer immediately when problems arise*

III

Strategies
to Protect
Your Family
and Home

5

All about Accidents

- **Introduction**   210
- **How to Prove Injuries**   211
- **Checklist of Recoverable Damages**   214
- **Proving Liability**   216
- **Shopping-Related Accidents**   216
- **Injuries from Faulty Products**   219
- **What to Do in an Auto Accident**   221
- **Accidents at Home**   224
- **On-the-Job Accidents**   227
- **Common Carrier Accidents**   229
- **Final Words on the Subject of Accidents**   230

Introduction

Although accidents are a part of life, many are caused by the negligence of others. The law cannot prevent accidents from happening, but it does provide remedies once they occur. Money is recoverable from the person or business who was the primary cause of the accident to pay for an injured's medical bills, lost earnings, and pain and suffering.

Millions of dollars are squandered each year by people who have legitimate personal injury claims but who fail to take proper steps to recover damages. Some decide not to contact a lawyer because they think the accident was their fault. Others fail to seek immediate medical treatment, and are unable to prove that the accident caused the injury. Still other people do not know the true value of their case. They foolishly accept a small settlement, sign a release, and are precluded from recovering additional money.

Mistakes such as these can be avoided. This chapter will tell you how to get the most for personal injury claims. Whether you are injured while shopping, stepping off a train, or vacationing in a hotel, you will learn how to protect yourself, prove your case, and increase the odds (and size) of a settlement offer.

Most of the strategies you are about to read are applicable in any situation. For example, whether you slip and fall in a restaurant, supermarket, or on a neighbor's property, it is wise to take color photographs and visit a doctor immediately to prove the extent of your injuries. Thus, re-read the information whenever you, a relative, or friend is injured in an accident. If you decide not to pursue a claim, the decision will be based on knowledge rather than a hunch. If you decide to proceed, you will have taken proper steps to increase your claim *before* contacting a lawyer.

(WARNING: No one should fake an injury in the hope of obtaining money. Lawyers, judges, juries, and insurance companies are capable of flushing out phonies. Remember, the vast majority of people who document phony claims and proceed with unworthy lawsuits seldom recover money for their efforts.)

How to Prove Injuries

Other than no-fault, which is discussed later in the chapter, an injured person must prove that the accident was caused by the negligence of another. This is decided by a judge or jury in a civil court trial. Once this is proved, the person is entitled to receive money as compensation for her loss. Part of the loss is for out-of-pocket expenses, including court costs, past and estimated future medical fees, hospital bills, and lost wages. Money is also awarded for pain and suffering, inconvenience, and disfigurement.

Most automobile owners, business establishments, innkeepers, and homeowners maintain insurance policies to protect them in the event of accidents. This obligates insurance companies to negotiate settlements, pay money to the specified maximum in the policy, and defend any claims brought against the negligent policyowner. In fact, the typical personal injury lawsuit is settled before the trial stage; approximately 95 percent of all cases are settled in private negotiations between the injured's lawyers and insurance company adjusters during a pre-trial conference, or before a jury renders its verdict.

Insurance adjusters occupy a powerful role in the settlement process. They are conservative in philosophy. Their job is to secure releases and settle claims at the minimal cost. They prefer to settle claims rather than go to trial. This is where doing your homework pays off. By taking the proper steps, you can obtain larger payments for your injuries. The following information tells you how to substantiate and justify a claim:

1. *See a doctor immediately.* Always seek immediate medical treatment when you are injured in an accident. Ask the doctor to document your injuries in a written report. A doctor's visit can help prove that the accident caused or worsened an earlier injury. This is because the further from the date of the accident the doctor sees you, the more difficult it is to prove that the accident caused the injury. For example, one woman broke her toe in a department store, but walked on the toe for several years before experiencing severe pain. She consulted a lawyer and discovered she was unable to sue the store because the appropriate time to commence a lawsuit (i.e., The Statute of Limitations) had expired. If the woman had visited her doctor immediately, she would have learned the true extent of her injuries, obtained proper medical care, and significantly increased her chances of recovering damages for her claim.

Ask the doctor if additional visits are necessary, and whether you should be referred to a specialist. Always obey the doctor's instructions regarding physical activities, particularly activities that can be observed by others. Insurance companies sometimes hire detectives to spy on claimants. Their job is to collect evidence to undermine serious injury claims. Thus, avoid participating in strenuous physical activities if you are not supposed to—you don't want to aggravate your injuries and give the insurance company any ammunition.

2. *Ask for help.* Avoid getting up if you are seriously injured. If necessary, request an ambulance to take you to the hospital. Never be ashamed to do this. The following true case demonstrates why:

Ten years ago, my grandmother slipped on a stringbean in a supermarket and broke her hip. She refused help, hobbled out of the store, and crossed the street to her apartment. At the trial, the storekeeper argued that her hip could have been broken or aggravated any time she was not in the store. My grandmother had little choice but to accept a settlement possibly ten times less than the amount she might have obtained had she remained on the supermarket floor and been taken by an ambulance to the nearest hospital emergency room.

3. *Avoid discussing your injuries.* Never minimize your injuries. Statements such as "It's all right, I'm okay," or "Nothing to worry about" may come back to haunt you. Days or weeks later your injuries can get worse, but the insurance adjuster in charge of settling the case may learn about these remarks from witnesses and offer less money in settlement.

4. *Take color photographs.* Always take color photographs immediately after any accident to prove the extent of your injuries. Untouched pictures are admissable evidence in court, and are often used by juries to award large verdicts. Months and years later, when your bruise, scar, or stitches have healed, the pictures will demonstrate your injuries at their worst. Never overlook this.

5. *Speak to a lawyer immediately.* Studies have shown that larger settlement offers are made to claimants represented by lawyers. Claims handled by lawyers are valued higher for purposes of negotiation and settlement. The unrepresented claimant sometimes makes incriminating statements and is ignorant about the kinds of damages he is entitled to. When people are represented by lawyers, adjusters know that settlements for valid claims must be paid. The adjuster also knows that threats to proceed to trial if a fair settlement offer is not made are more credible coming from a lawyer.

6. *Document your medical expenses and actual damages.* Proper substantiation of your damages will greatly increase

the amount of money offered in settlement. The following chart lists compensable items besides showing how to prove them:

ITEM	PROOF
Loss of regular wages, tips, overtime	Income tax returns, employment and payroll records, letters and affidavits from employer, fellow employees
Loss of job as a result of the accident	Affidavit or testimony from ex-employer, fellow employees
Loss of fringe benefits, commissions, promotion	Affidavit or testimony from employer, fellow employees, sales figures
Loss of profits or income from your own business	Profit-loss statements, books, payroll records of business
Loss of future earning capacity; special skills	Professional degrees, medical records, affidavits, testimony from expert witnesses
Expenses of a job search	Transportation receipts, interview record affidavits, testimony of interviewers
Medical and drug expenses	Canceled checks, receipts, unpaid bills
Inpatient or outpatient hospital care	Canceled checks, receipts, unpaid bills
Nursing care	Canceled checks, receipts, unpaid bills
Prosthetic devices	Canceled checks, receipts, unpaid bills
Special diet	Canceled checks, receipts, unpaid bills
Treatment for injury-induced pain	Authorized drug prescriptions, medical reports, detailed diary prepared by claimant, affidavits from nurses and attendants,

ITEM	PROOF
	color photographs, testimony from expert witnesses
Pain and suffering	Same
Shock, mental anguish, anxiety, embarrassment, humiliation	Same
Depression, neurosis, psychosis	Same
Loss of sexual pleasure	Same
Court costs, filing fees, witness fees, stenographic fees	Canceled checks, receipts, unpaid bills
Transportation costs for medical treatment	Canceled checks, receipts unpaid bills

You are entitled to reimbursement for all of the above expenses, provided they can be proved. Careful documentation of appropriate expenses builds a strong case.

7. *Avoid settling claims early.* Never accept settlements within a month of the accident as a general rule. The reason is that you need time to properly diagnose the extent of your injuries, determine whether prolonged medical treatment is necessary, and calculate the effects of the accident (e.g., lost business, profits, etc.). For example, many back injuries do not materialize until several months after an accident. Despite the temptation, avoid signing a release and accepting a quick settlement—you may regret this later.

8. *Take precautions.* Insurers often hire detectives to investigate the condition of injured claimants. Detectives speak to friends, employers, and witnesses to learn more about the actual condition of the claimant. They take pictures (which are admissable evidence) to undermine claims. Thus, alert people who may be questioned. Tell them not to discuss your injuries with anyone.

9. *Prepare a daily diary.* It is a good idea to prepare a daily diary. Include dates and times of all medical treatment,

hospital visits, prescription purchases, who you saw, what was said, how you felt, etc. The diary will help document your claim and refresh your recollection if you are required to testify at a trial.

10. *Don't consent freely to a medical examination.* Insurance companies have the right to examine you when a claim is filed. Doctors hired by insurance companies are paid to ask questions and find medical reasons minimizing your claim. One favorite tactic is to diagnose the injury as being caused by a prior condition rather than the accident. Thus, never agree to a physical examination unless you have consulted a lawyer; insist that your lawyer be present at the examination.

Proving Liability

In addition to proving injuries, it is necessary to show that the other party acted improperly (i.e., negligently) in order to recover. The following strategies demonstrate ways to prove negligence and reduce your exposure from lawsuits in a variety of common situations.

Shopping-Related Accidents

Think how easy it is to be injured while shopping. In pleasant or inclement weather, people walk through revolving and electrical doors, fight crowds, maneuver around aisles, carry purchases out of a store, and drive in designated parking lots. Storekeepers post signs asking customers not to touch displays, furnishings, and appliances. They keep their floors clean of debris, obstacles, and other foreign matter. Some maintain a constant vigil over the sidewalks in front of their store, particularly when there is snow or ice.

People are injured despite these precautions. Most storekeepers and their insurance carriers (particularly the large retail department stores) encourage out-of-court settlements. Although the vast majority of these injuries are minor, every injury requiring medical attention is compensable, provided storekeeper negligence can be proved.

Storekeepers owe a legal duty to their customers. The law requires them to keep their stores in a reasonably safe condition and warn customers of dangers on the premises which are not obvious. Liability only extends to persons to whom this legal duty is owed. For example, children and friends who accompany customers are included. So, too, are people who pass through a store with permission (e.g., as a short-cut to the street). If a person enters a store merely to use a public facility such as a toilet or telephone, the question of whether the proprietor owes a legal duty to this individual is not clear cut.

The fact that you are injured does not automatically mean you can receive compensation. As in all negligence cases, you must prove the following elements to be successful:

1. That you suffered an injury on property under the store's supervision and control (e.g., in the store or outside on store-owned, or managed property)

2. That you were owed a legal duty of care and the owner and/or his employees failed to act properly

3. That the failure to act properly was a direct cause of your injury

4. That your own conduct did not cause the accident

Proving these elements is not unduly complicated. This can be illustrated by examining one common shopping accident—the slip and fall accident. The following information is generally applicable to all business establishments (e.g., bowling alleys, supermarkets, restaurants, etc.) where a slip and fall accident can occur.

People slip and fall over large objects (e.g., boxes), small items (e.g., food, chewing gum, etc.), and slippery floor surfaces. Unless the person is distracted by a promotional display, he has a better chance of recovering damages after slipping on a small item because people are usually responsible for noticing larger objects and walking around them.

The fact that you slip and fall does not guarantee the recovery of damages for your injuries. Take the following case, for example:

> Victor and his wife, Trudy, went food shopping. Victor was observing several brands of chili while walking down the aisle of his local supermarket. He slipped on a banana peel which had been lying on the floor for twenty minutes. Victor's back was injured by the fall. Several people witnessed the accident and Trudy saved the banana peel Victor slipped on.

If you think Victor has an excellent chance of winning his case, you are probably mistaken. The law does *not* require storekeepers to constantly check and sweep their floors or place employees at entranceways with mops during snowy and rainy days.

To win a slip and fall case in court, you must prove that you were injured in an area under the store's control (i.e., that you slipped on a banana in the store) *and* that the object was lying on the floor for a sufficient period of time. A sufficient period of time must pass in order to make the storekeeper and his employees negligent for (1) failing to remove the object from the floor and/or (2) failing to discover its presence and warn customers about it. This is determined by a judge or jury if the case is tried in court. Thus, the longer it is proved the object remained on the floor, the better your chance of success. In Victor's case, twenty minutes would probably not be a sufficient length of time to impute negligence. However, if a witness testified that he saw a store employee drop the banana on the floor and consciously fail to remove it, Victor might receive a favorable verdict.

The following strategies help prove negligence in slip and fall cases:

1. *Document the cause of the accident.* Many people fail to recover damages because they cannot prove what they

slipped on. Whether it be olive oil, water, food items, etc., you must know what substance caused you to fall.

2. *Inspect the area where you fell.* Imperfections in the floor or rug surface should be examined and shown to witnesses and employees of the store immediately after the accident.

3. *Examine the object closely.* Look for signs of *age.* For example, if you slipped on a *brown* stringbean or lettuce leaf, the color might demonstrate that it had remained on the floor for some time. You may wish to take a color photograph of the object if possible for this purpose.

4. *Report the accident to the storekeeper to document your claim.* Listen to anything that is said. Volunteered statements may be used as admissions of liability. For example, if the sales manager told you "This is the second accident like this within the past month," this could increase your chances of winning the case.

5. *Gather names and addresses of witnesses who saw you fall.* Ask them if they remember where and what you slipped on.

Injuries from Faulty Products

People can recover damages when they are injured by a defective or faulty product. This is called products liability. An injured party can sue and recover from any seller in the distributive chain. Thus, the manufacturer, distributor, and even the retailer are potentially liable for product-causing injuries. It is not necessary to actually have purchased the product in order to sue; nonpurchasers are protected when they are foreseeable users (e.g., a roommate injured by her girlfriend's faulty hairdryer).

Thousands of consumers recover damages each year for faulty products. A recent study reported that the success rate for people bringing products liability lawsuits exceeded sixty-five percent, and the average trial verdict was $80,000. Verdicts were recovered for injuries from a variety of consumer products (e.g., drugs, food, machinery, sports equipment, beauty products, ladders and scaffolds, etc.). For example, one boy received $875,000 from a retailer and a shirt manufacturer when he suffered serious burns after his T-shirt caught fire. Another woman was awarded $2,000 when a soda container exploded in her hand while she was in a grocery store. The judge awarded the money after the woman testified she had recurring nightmares that giant soda bottles were chasing her!

The following chart describes what generally must be proved in a products liability case in order to be successful:

WHAT MUST BE PROVED	HOW TO PROVE IT
The existence and severity of an injury	Written medical reports, hospital records, testimony of witnesses
That the product caused the accident and injuries	Testimony, expert witnesses
That the product was defective by manufacture or design —or—	Examination of the product, testimony of expert witnesses, similar accidents to other users
That the product was unreasonably dangerous with inadequate safety features or improper warnings given; and	Examination of the product, testimony of expert witnesses, similar accidents to other users
That the user maintained the product properly, followed instructions, and used the product in the manner intended	Testimony of witnesses

Damages are recoverable under several legal theories in products liability cases. For example, if factual statements are made that induce you to buy a product and you are injured (e.g., a salesperson tells you "This is a safe, dependable product" or sales literature states "This drug is safe and nonaddicting"), you can sue on the grounds of misrepresentation. You may also be able to sue on the basis of negligence, strict liability, and breach of warranty. There is a fine distinction between these categories. A lawyer specializing in products liability law will properly advise you. Thus, if you are injured by a defective product, follow the steps outlined in the preceding pages to prove your injuries. Don't forget to contact a lawyer immediately.

What to Do in an Auto Accident

It is likely that every driver is involved in at least one serious automobile accident during his/her lifetime. Even if you suffer no personal injury or property damage, an auto accident can expose you to civil and criminal liability, suspension or revocation of your license, and serious financial loss.

By knowing what to do and say after an accident, you can reduce your exposure and increase the amount of money paid for your personal injuries and property damage claims. The following information will tell you how to protect yourself properly in the event of an automobile accident:

1. *Stay calm.* This is important because you must think clearly.

2. *Stop your car.* In most states, it is against the law to leave the scene of an accident. Whenever you are involved in an accident, pull over and get out of your car (if you can) as quickly as possible. If you drive away, go back to the scene immediately.

3. *Don't obstruct traffic.* Use reflectors and flares so that drivers will not hit you or other cars. People in minor accidents often cause additional accidents, and are sued for huge sums of money. You must take all precautions to avoid additional accidents.

4. *Help injured passengers.* The law requires you to assist the injured. This means calling for help to obtain the police, a doctor, or ambulance. It does *not* mean actively helping people (such as removing the injured from cars or applying tourniquets) unless you are a trained professional (e.g., a doctor, dentist, nurse), and the injured party is in a dangerous location (e.g., the car she's in is about to explode).

This is important. If you render medical or other assistance and your actions cause or worsen a person's injuries, *you are liable,* despite your good intentions. So it's best to call for help immediately—but don't leave the scene—and hope that it arrives quickly.

5. *Call the police.* Whenever you are in an accident and think you are not at fault, call the police. Police departments usually respond to even minor property accidents. After the police arrive, ask that an accident report be prepared. Accident reports help prove claims because they document the position of vehicles and other details, including weather and road conditions.

6. *Never make incriminating statements.* Never apologize or admit the accident was your fault. Doing this may unnecessarily expose you to a lawsuit. Later, many people unfortunately learn that the other driver was legally responsible for the accident, but that their incriminating remarks weakened the case and reduced the size of a settlement offer.

Thus, never admit fault. If the other driver screams that you caused the accident, *ignore such statements.* Merely give your name, address, and telephone number. Show your driver's license, registration, and insurance company card. Ask for the same information in return. Record the make, model, year, plate number, and vehicle identification number. Check the other driver's insurance card, and write the name of the insurer, policy number, and the expiration date. If insurance coverage has expired, copy the information on the card anyway, and ask if the driver is currently insured.

(NOTE: You may have problems collecting if there is no present insurance carrier. The processing of your claim could be delayed and the motorist may not have sufficient assets to satisfy the judgment if you sue.)

Avoid revealing prior traffic infractions when showing your license to the other motorist. This information is privileged, but these records are on the backs of licenses in some states. Be careful the other motorist does not see it.

If the other driver is uncooperative, record his license plate and call the police. The police will help you obtain the necessary information.

Always be careful when talking to police officers. Never volunteer unnecessary information. Answer all questions honestly. If you are asked a question you do not wish to answer, simply say, "I don't know." A police officer cannot force you to say anything. You have the right to remain silent until your lawyer is present.

7. *Speak to passengers and other witnesses.* By talking to witnesses, bystanders, and passengers, you may learn information that will be valuable to your case. Write down the names, addresses, phone numbers, and statements made by witnesses so you can contact them if necessary.

If you are involved in an accident with a commercial driver or company employee, speak to him and his passengers. Employees frequently pin liability on their company. A comment such as "I told the boss twice this month there was something wrong with the steering wheel," can be used to your advantage. Always write down such statements.

8. *Inspect the accident site.* Make a careful inspection of the accident site to help prove or defend your claim. Be sure to note the following:

- Traffic controls and stop signs
- The position and length of skid marks
- Damage to trees, dividers, and other items
- The point of impact and damage to autos. This may be important in determining fault
- The exact spot where the cars stopped

You have different options if you are injured in an auto accident. Most states have adopted no-fault insurance. No-fault is designed to ensure prompt payment for injuries arising from the accident. This includes compensation for medical bills, lost wages, and the cost of hiring replacement labor to run your business or home. Payment is made by the injured party's insurance company or the insurer of the car in which the injured passenger was riding, regardless of fault.

Pedestrians are paid by the insurance company of the owner of the car that hit them. Motorcycle riders are generally not covered under no-fault. However, you generally are *not* entitled to benefits if you are injured while intoxicated, committing a felony, racing, or operating a stolen vehicle.

No-fault laws vary on a state by state basis, and are not always beneficial. One problem is that the amount of recoverable damages is limited (for example, up to $50,000 in New York). Another problem is that no-fault does not pay damages for death, pain and suffering, property damage, and other noncash expenses.

(STRATEGY: Some no-fault states allow you to commence a private lawsuit to collect damages. Thus, always consult a lawyer in the event of serious injuries to determine the best course of action.)

(ADDITIONAL POINTS: Some states reduce damage awards if the injured driver or passenger did not wear seat belts. Thus, wear seat belts to reduce injuries and maximize claims. Be sure to equip your car with essential items. Keep a writing pad and pen handy to record important information. Store flares, flashlights, and reflectors in your trunk to warn other drivers of your whereabouts.)

Accidents at Home

Many accidents happen at home. Homeowners are liable to invited guests, employees, and independent contractors for injuries which occur on their premises. Studies show that more than 50 percent of all personal injury lawsuits brought against homeowners are successful. For example:

- If a friend slips on an icy step you have not cleared for three days and suffers head injuries
- If the babysitter trips over a stereo wire and breaks a leg
- If a neighbor's child is injured while swimming in your pool
- If the house painter's ladder slips and he breaks an arm

chances are you may be liable.

The following simple steps will help you reduce exposure to personal injury lawsuits arising from accidents on your premises.

1. *Examine your homeowners' insurance policy.* Do you have general liability coverage? Most states require that you do. If your minimum coverage is less than $50,000, talk to an insurance agent and review your policy. Additional coverage is inexpensive and *essential* because personal injury verdicts have risen drastically in the past few years. If you own a house and other assets, you are a prime target for a lawsuit.

2. *Hire workers who carry Workers' Compensation.* This is important. When hiring someone to work in your home, ask to see his certificate of insurance. Many states require independent contractors to carry Workers' Compensation and public liability insurance. This will protect you in the event the worker injures himself or someone else on your premises. Only hire workers who document this coverage.

3. *Are you liable to pay Workers' Compensation.* If you hire someone to work in your home on a regular basis, you may be required to carry Workers' Compensation coverage. Insurance companies frequently claim they are not required to defend and pay damages on behalf of homeowners who employ individuals on a steady basis. Thus, review your policy. Speak to your insurance agent to clarify this point if applicable.

4. *Warn workers, guests, and employees of hidden defects on your premises.* Homeowners have a legal duty to keep their home in reasonably safe condition and warn invitees of potential hazards. Failure to do so could make you liable in a lawsuit for negligence. The same is true for tenants. However, the duty to maintain safe premises extends only to the apartment and not to the common areas (e.g., hallways).

Homeowners are not liable for injuries caused by dangerous conditions which are difficult to detect. For example, if it snows during the night and a friend slips on your steps at 9:00 A.M. the next morning while you are asleep, you are probably not responsible. However, if snow remained on your steps for three days and you invited a friend to your home without warning him about it, you would probably be liable if an injury occurred.

5. *Don't admit liability.* Never incriminate yourself if a person is injured on your property. This includes acknowledging that the accident was your fault, or that you were aware of a dangerous condition that caused the accident. Remember, these statements can be used as admissable evidence against you.

6. *Protect guests from dangerous pets.* Homeowners are required to exercise control over dangerous pets. If you know your dog has bitten someone in the past, or has a reputation for being vicious, you will be liable if the dog bites a guest; warning a social guest or business invitee of the presence of your pet is not sufficient.

7. *Protect children from attractive nuisances.* Attractive nuisances are swimming pools, windmills, exotic trees, etc.—any object that attracts children and is potentially dangerous. If the object is on your property and a child gets hurt, you will probably be liable even if the child is a trespasser. The law requires homeowners to take extra precautions in protecting children from their own curiosity. Be aware of this.

On-the-Job Accidents

Employers have a legal duty to warn employees of dangers and provide a safe place to work. However, in most situations, you cannot sue an employer for negligence if you are injured on the job. The reason is you are entitled to Workers' Compensation for your injuries. Payment is made by the employer's insurance company. The only questions to be settled are whether the injury was caused by a job-related accident and the amount of compensation to be paid. What you receive depends upon the law in your state; the law spells out the amount of compensation allowable for each type of injury. Injured employees are generally reimbursed for costs of medical treatment, partial lost wages (e.g., 60 percent of the weekly gross salary), temporary disability to meet living expenses, and permanent disability if recovery is not complete. Partial disability may also be awarded if you return to work, but cannot work full-time.

It is essential to document the accident if you are injured on the job. Gather witnesses immediately. Report the accident to your supervisor, shop steward, or boss. Seek prompt medical attention. Ask your boss for a detailed explanation of your workers' compensation rights, and file a timely claim. The law requires your employer to notify the insurance carrier and direct you to the appropriate insurance company representative or claims officer once the accident is reported.

Call the nearest Workers' Compensation Bureau Office if you have any questions. An assistant will tell you how to file a claim or make an appeal. You are not obligated to accept the amount offered by your employer's insurance company. For example, if the insurer refuses to pay, or cuts off payments before you are able to go back to work, you can file an appeal and schedule a hearing before the Workers' Compensation Board. Although you can represent yourself at the hearing, it's best to have a lawyer present.

(NOTE: The lawyer's fee is set by most Workers' Compensation Statutes; typically, 20 percent of the money you receive and nothing if you lose. An assistant at your local Workers' Compensation Board will advise you of applicable fee regulations. *Never pay the lawyer more than he is legally entitled by law.*)

Injuries covered by Workers' Compensation need not only occur at the work site. If you are injured while going to or from work, or suffer an injury caused by stressful conditions on the job, you may be entitled to Workers' Compensation and other benefits. These include nonoccupational disability insurance from the employer, food stamps, and social security benefits. Contact your local Workers' Compensation Board for further details.

Despite the existence of Workers' Compensation, you are not precluded from filing a lawsuit in the following:

1. *If you are an independent contractor.* Independent contractors are considered agents, not employees, and employers are not required to maintain Workers' Compensation on their behalf. Examples of independent contractors include sales agents, domestic servants, owners of small businesses, and other self-employeds. There is no precise legal definition that explains what constitutes independent contractor status. When courts or Workers' Compensation Boards attempt to determine if a person is an employee or independent contractor, they analyze the facts of each case. The most significant factors include whether the individual controls his own work schedule, operates his own place of business, is not required to report to his employer on a daily basis, pays his own withholding and social security taxes, and whether the parties have an employment contract which states that the worker is an independent contractor.

2. *When your injury wasn't job-related.*

3. *When you are injured on the job by a product or machine.* If this occurs, you can file for Workers' Compensation and sue the manufacturer for your injuries. Be aware that if your

lawsuit is successful, you may be required to reimburse your employer for the amount of Workers' Compensation you received. This is called *subrogation.*

4. *If you are injured by a nonemployee.* You can collect Workers' Compensation and privately sue the individual for damages. However, if you are injured by a fellow employee in nonwork-related conduct (e.g., an assault), you cannot recover Workers' Compensation. You must sue the employee in a private lawsuit to recover.

5. *If you are a farm laborer, seaman, or railroad worker.* You may be permitted to sue an employer for negligence in a private lawsuit.

(COMMENT: It is illegal for an employer to fire, threaten, or discriminate against an employee who files a Workers' Compensation claim or testifies before the Workers' Compensation Board. Consult a lawyer immediately if you believe this happened to you.)

Common Carrier Accidents

Common carriers (e.g., cruiseships, airplanes, trains, taxis, etc.) owe paying passengers a high degree of care. The law requires them to use extraordinary vigilance and skill in transporting passengers safely.

It is easier to prove that a carrier and its employees acted negligently than other kinds of businesses. The following recent case illustrates why. An intoxicated passenger on a cruise jumped overboard and was injured. The cruiseship company was held liable. The judge ruled that even though the passenger's conduct caused his injuries, the cruiseship's employees were negligent because they failed to supervise the passenger after observing him act peculiarly.

Speak to a lawyer if you are injured while on or by a common carrier. Never be intimidated if language on the back of your ticket seems to exculpate the carrier from responsibility. People mistakenly believe they are precluded from recovering damages after buying a ticket which says, for example:

> The carrier assumes no liability for property loss, death, or physical injuries arising from the acts of its employees

Common carriers insert this language to deter people from investigating their rights. However, such clauses often have no legal effect. The obligation to transport passengers safely is so important that carriers cannot disclaim liability. For example, if the ticket says you must commence a lawsuit within one year, or notify the carrier of your claim within six months of the accident, the clause may be unenforceable.

Just to be safe, consult a lawyer to be sure this is the law in your case when applicable.

Final Words on the Subject of Accidents

Additional Strategies

1. Be sure the individual, government agency, corporation, etc., has sufficient assets or insurance to satisfy the judgment before deciding to sue for your injuries. The reasons are obvious. If you wish to sue an uninsured business entity or individual, contact a credit reporting agency or banking institution. They may be able to tell you more about the location and identity of real property and other assets.

2. Always speak to a lawyer before accepting a settlement and signing a release. Your lawyer will tell you what the case is worth. Select a lawyer with a good reputation who spends a significant amount of his time handling personal injury matters.

3. Calculate the total cost of the lawsuit before deciding to institute suit. Sign a retainer agreement with your lawyer. Discuss the effect, if any, subrogation will play in the ultimate award. You may discover it is not worthwhile to commence a lawsuit if you have to reimburse your insurance company or employer for money you have already received. Some lawyers forget to tell their clients about subrogation because their fee is earned *when money is recovered, regardless of whether the client is ultimately responsible* for reimbursement. Be sure to discuss this with your lawyer.

6

How to Get
the Most from
Your Lawyer

- Introduction 233
- Determining when You Need a Lawyer 234
- Finding a Lawyer 235
- The Initial Interview 236
- Should You Hire the Lawyer You Have Met? 241
- Confirming Your Arrangement 243
- Additional Points about Fees 248
- Documenting Legal Fees 249
- Other Items to Clarify at the Interview 250
- Problems Encountered after You Hire the Lawyer 252
- Should You Change Your Lawyer? 253
- Should You Appeal a Case? 255
- Summary of Steps to Use Your Lawyer Effectively 257

Introduction

Most people expect their lawyers to work miracles. This conception has been inspired by popular television shows and movies. In reality, however, miracles rarely happen. Few legal problems disappear at a lawyer's touch, and lawyers cannot significantly reduce the time a person must wait before receiving his day in court.

What lawyers can and should do is to zealously protect the interests of their clients. They should represent them in a competent fashion, keep them informed, and bill them reasonably for their services. The good lawyer fights for his client, protects him, and enriches him monetarily in the process.

Unfortunately, lawyer-client disputes sometimes arise because:

- Fee arrangements are not spelled out
- Clients are misled about the probability of success with their cases
- Client funds are used improperly by lawyers
- Clients are not consulted regarding settlement negotiations
- Phone calls are not promptly returned
- Work on legal matters is put off
- Potential conflicts of interest are not fully disclosed

These are just some of the common causes of client complaints.

This chapter will explain how to get the most out of your lawyer. You will learn how to pick a lawyer and avoid problems, regardless of the type of matter. You will become aware of what to bring and say at the initial interview, how to negotiate a fair fee arrangement, how to stay informed and keep your lawyer working on your case, and even how to change lawyers or commence disciplinary proceedings. Other chapters of this book offer strategies to protect yourself as an employee, businessperson, consumer, and citizen. This chapter will discuss your rights as a client.

Determining when
You Need a Lawyer

The impact of the law on our lives is mind-boggling. Laws in this country are unduly complicated and people need lawyers to guide them properly. Americans are exposed to hundreds of different kinds of commercial transactions (e.g., buying and selling real estate, signing contracts with important financial provisions, forming businesses, etc.), which require legal services. Additionally, lawyers have the responsibility of advising us about income tax and labor regulations, social security, administrative, and other legislative enactments. Some people experience marital difficulties, or run afoul of the law. Most require careful estate planning, including the preparation of wills. Thus, inevitably, the services of a lawyer are required.

The time to determine whether you need a lawyer is *before action is contemplated* (e.g., before being hired, before pleading guilty to a traffic ticket, before buying a computer for your business).

The best way to decide if you need a lawyer is to speak to one. Chances are you won't be charged for advice given over the telephone. The information in the following pages will tell you what to say, and how to protect yourself when an appointment is scheduled.

Finding a Lawyer

The best way to determine if you have a problem requiring legal attention is to speak to a lawyer and schedule an interview. This is not easy. Lawyers should be selected with care. The right choice can mean thousands of dollars in your pocket. The wrong choice can cost you money and aggravation.

1. *First step—call a lawyer you know.* The place to start is to call a lawyer you have already dealt with. Ask what he thinks about your problem, and whether an interview should be scheduled. However, you should recognize that many lawyers who competently represent clients in one area (e.g., preparing a will) are not qualified to represent the same client in an unrelated matter (e.g., a personal injury lawsuit). This is because most lawyers become familiar with certain types of cases which they handle promptly, efficiently, and profitably. For example, many competent lawyers refer injury, medical malpractice, and products liability lawsuits to the specialist because it is difficult to keep abreast of the latest developments in these fields.

When lawyers accept matters outside the realm of their daily practice, *the chances of making mistakes or postponing work increases.* Thus, ask the lawyer *what proportion of his working time* is spent dealing in the field of law related to your problem. Measure his response. Speak to another lawyer if you do not like his answer. If the lawyer tells you that he does not commonly handle your type of matter, ask for the names of other lawyers he is willing to recommend. Clients sometimes receive excellent assistance through lawyer referrals.

2. *Ask around for recommendations.* If you have never dealt with a lawyer before, ask friends or relatives if they can recommend someone. Lawyers often receive clients by word of mouth. However, *be careful* if a lawyer is recommended; you may have a problem in a different field, and the lawyer might not be qualified to represent you. In addition, be wary of recommendations from people such as bail bondsmen and

hospital attendants. These people sometimes receive illegal referral fees for recommending clients and their recommendations may be self-motivated.

3. *Call your local bar association.* Another way of finding a lawyer is to contact your local bar association, and ask for the names of lawyers who specialize in handling your particular problem. These associations are in the phone book and some maintain lists of lawyers who agree not to charge more than $15 to $25 for the first half-hour of consultation.

Personnel who handle incoming calls for these associations generally are unbiased when referring names of lawyers. However, both prominent and neophyte lawyers list their names and telephone numbers with such associations. If experience is important, be sure to tell the person handling your inquiry that you want to contact an experienced practitioner.

4. *Be wary of lawyer advertising.* A few lawyers have misled the public with their advertising. One common method is to run an ad which states that a particular matter only costs $XX. When a potential client meets the lawyer, he learns that court costs and filing fees are $XX, but lawyers' fees are extra. In addition, beware of ads that proclaim the lawyer is a "specialist." Most state bar associations have not adopted specialist certification programs. The proclamation of "specialist" is only the lawyer's personal opinion, nothing more.

(NOTE: Although some good lawyers advertise, many top lawyers don't—they get their cases from former clients and other lawyers. Be aware of this.)

The Initial Interview

The initial interview serves several important purposes. It helps you obtain a sound evaluation about your legal problem, and helps you decide if you should hire the lawyer you met. The initial interview is also the time to discuss important working details, such as the fee arrangement.

Bring all pertinent written information with you at the initial interview (e.g., copies of employment contracts, checks, letters, bills of sale, photographs, etc.). Tell the lawyer everything related to the matter. Try to communicate relevant information without inhibition because your discussion is privileged and confidential. All of this will facilitate the lawyer's work and time.

Once the lawyer receives all of the pertinent facts and a lawsuit is considered, he will then:

1. Decide whether your case has a fair probability of success after considering the law in the state where the suit will be brought

2. Give you some estimate as to how long the lawsuit will last

3. Make a determination of the approximate legal fees and disbursements

4. Tell you what legal papers will be filed, when, and what their purposes are

5. Discuss the defenses your opponent will probably raise, and how you will deal with them

If the lawyer sees weaknesses in your case and believes that litigation will be unduly expensive, he may advise you to compromise and settle the claim without resorting to litigation. In any event, the chosen course of action should be instituted without delay so that you may be able to receive remuneration quickly. This will also insure that the requisite time period to start the action, that is, the Statute of Limitations, will not have expired.

If a lawsuit is not involved, the lawyer should advise you what legal work needs to be done, how long it will take, and how much it will cost.

The lawyer should give you an unbiased evaluation as quickly as possible. Some lawyers neglect to give honest appraisals. Clients are then misled and spend large sums of money on losing causes. Be wary if your lawyer says "You have nothing to worry about." Optimistic statements such as this generally cause more harm than good. That is because prudent lawyers tell clients that "airtight" cases do not exist, and that the possibility of unforeseen circumstances and developments is always present.

One of the best ways to protect yourself is to request an *opinion letter*. Opinion letters spell out the pros and cons of a matter. They help prospective clients evaluate whether or not they should proceed and spend money to accomplish their objectives. Even if you are charged for the time it takes to draft the letter, an opinion letter can minimize future misunderstandings between you and your lawyer; it is usually worth the fee.

The following is an example of an opinion letter requested by an employer who wants to know his legal rights against a former employee. The employee resigned and began selling equipment to customers of the former company in violation of their written employment agreement.

June 15, 1983

(Name of Client)
President
ABC Manufacturing, Inc.
Atlanta, Georgia 95568

Re: Opinion Letter Regarding (name of employee
e.g., ficticious Cynthia Lynn)

Dear (Name):

After our initial meeting, I reviewed the papers you sent regarding the Cynthia Lynn matter. As I understand the situation, Ms. Lynn signed a written employment agreement with your company. The agreement stated that in the event of termination or resignation from her job as your sales associate, Ms. Lynn would not call upon or sell goods to any of your customers for a period of one year.

You have asked me to advise you about your rights, the chance of success, the amount of damages that may be recoverable, the costs involved, and my ability to represent you in this matter.

Rights of ABC against Ms. Lynn

When Ms. Lynn signed a written contract with your company, she agreed not to call upon any of your customers for a period of one year. This is called a *restrictive covenant*. To enforce your covenant against Ms. Lynn, you must bring an action against her and prove your case. You have a choice of forums in which to bring the action; federal district court or a state court. Since it is easier to obtain an *injunction* (an action to immediately stop her from selling to your customers) in a state court rather than a federal court, I would suggest the state court.

I must advise you that injunctions are largely discretionary with the court, and there are several factors here that might lead it not to grant one on your behalf. Since you waited eight months before threatening to sue Ms. Lynn, my guess is that you have about a twenty percent (20%) chance of obtaining an injunction.

Rights to and Amount of Damages

Your chances of obtaining money damages against Ms. Lynn are much greater than your chances for an injunction. From our discussion and the facts and evidence suggested in your papers, it appears that the amount of recoverable damages would be measured by the profits since the time Ms. Lynn began selling competitive products to your customers.

It should be understood that if we win our case, however, Ms. Lynn may not voluntarily pay the judgment. Thus, it may be necessary to enforce the judgment by having a sheriff or marshall seize and sell assets not exempt from execution. However, if Ms. Lynn does not own assets, such as real estate, money in bank accounts, stocks, etc., but only owns personal items exempt from execution under the laws of our state, then any judgment you obtain may not be worth much.

Negatives to Lawsuit

Besides the fact that you may lose a lawsuit against Ms. Lynn or that any judgment obtained would be uncollectable, there are other negative factors you should consider before bringing a lawsuit. These include court costs and attorney fees. Court costs are recoverable, but other costs, such as travel, the time lost when you are called to testify (or required to help us develop the case), and attorney fees, are *not* recoverable.

My Services

I am familiar with the nature of your manufacturing business and am qualified to represent you in this matter if you choose to proceed. My fee would be based on my normal hourly charge of $100 for myself and $75 for associates. Trial time is billed at $500 per day. The initial services of preparing a complaint and serving same would cost approximately $300. Preparing a request for an injunction and attending a hearing on the injunction would cost approximately $1,000.

It is entirely possible that Ms. Lynn would not retain her own counsel and not answer the complaint. This means that a default judgment could be taken without the necessity of a trial. Here, attorney fees would probably amount to no more than $750.

I require a $500 retainer to open a file and commence an action.

If you wish to proceed with this matter, I will need to know the full names and addresses of your customers to whom Ms. Lynn is presently selling and the estimated sales volume which you have lost.

If you have any questions, please call me.

Very truly yours,

A properly drafted opinion letter should provide you with all the essential facts necessary to evaluate a problem. Don't forget to ask for one when appropriate.

Should You Hire the Lawyer You Have Met?

It is important to leave the interview feeling that your lawyer is open and responsive to your needs, that he is genuinely interested in helping you, that your inquiries will be promptly returned, and that your case will be prepared and handled properly. Although it is difficult to predict how well the lawyer will perform, there are certain clues to look for during the interview. The following points are worth considering:

- Does the lawyer present an outward appearance of neatness and good grooming?
- Are you received on time at the appointed interview hour, or are you kept waiting? Some lawyers believe that if a client is kept waiting he will think that the lawyer is busy and, therefore, good. Keeping you waiting is merely a sign that the lawyer is inconsiderate
- Does the lawyer leave the room frequently during the interview, or permit telephone calls to intrude? You deserve his complete attention

- Does he demonstrate boredom or lack of interest by yawning or finger-tapping?
- Is he a clock-watcher?
- Does the lawyer try to impress you by narrating in detail other cases he has handled? Good lawyers do not have to boast to obtain clients
- Does he fail to discuss the fee arrangement with you up front? Some lawyers have a tendency to wait until all work is done before submitting large bills. The failure to discuss fee arrangements at the initial interview may be a sign that the lawyer operates this way

A lawyer's reputation is another factor to consider. Successful lawyers win cases and make money for their clients. However, don't be fooled by appearances. Plush offices, fancy cars, and expensive clothes might be a means to charge you exorbitant fees for routine legal services. In addition, don't be impressed by the school where the lawyer graduated. Most law schools do not give their graduates *practical training*. In fact, many less prestigious "local" law schools offer superior nuts and bolts training, and that is what you are paying for.

Be sure that the lawyer of your choice will be working on your matter. People often go to prestigious firms, expecting their matter to be handled by a partner. They pay large fees and sometimes wind up being represented in court by a junior associate. This is a common practice among some firms, so be aware of it. To avoid this, state in the retainer agreement that your matter will be handled by lawyer X (the lawyer of your choice).

The major factor in determining whether you should hire a particular lawyer should be the amount of experience and expertise he has in handling legal problems similar to yours. Use a lawyer who devotes at least 30 percent of his practice to problems in your area. *Avoid inexperienced lawyers if possible*. Novices charge less, but they often require more time to handle a problem. If you are being charged on an hourly basis, you may pay the same amount of money and not obtain the expertise of a pro.

(FINAL WORDS ON THE SUBJECT: When you choose a lawyer, you are hiring someone to guide you and protect your interests. Make your choice carefully. Select someone whom you think is honest. Hire a lawyer to whom you can relate. Ask the lawyer about his outside activities and professional associations. Inquire if you can speak to any of his previous clients; references will help you learn more about the lawyer. If you do not feel comfortable with the first lawyer you meet, shop around and schedule appointments with others. As always, it is better to be safe than sorry.)

Confirming Your Arrangement

After you have decided to retain a lawyer, you must discuss a variety of points to eliminate potential misunderstandings.

1. *The fee arrangement.* Most lawyers generally charge a nominal fee, if any, for a first visit to the office. Fees should be charged only when actual time is spent working on a matter. Charges are based on the amount of time and work involved, the difficulty of the problem, the dollar amount of the case, the result, the urgency of the problem (for example, a real estate closing which the lawyer must handle the day after he is contacted should command a higher fee than the same closing that takes place in a month), and the lawyer's expertise and reputation in handling your type of problem. Operating expenses and office overhead are elements which might also affect the fee arrangement.

Frequently, a lawyer cannot tell you exactly how much he will charge because he is unable to determine the amount of work that is involved. In such a case, ask the lawyer to estimate what the minimum and maximum limits of the fee will be. If a figure seems high, do not hesitate to question him about it. If necessary, tell him you intend to speak to other lawyers about fees.

The fee arrangement is comprised of several elements which must be clearly understood. For example, *costs* are expenses that the lawyer incurs while preparing your case or working on your matter. These include photocopying, telephone, mailing expenses, fees paid to the court for filing documents, and numerous other expenses. Be certain that the fee arrangement specifically mentions *in writing* which of these costs you must pay.

Different forms of fee arrangements are used by lawyers. These are the flat fee, flat fee plus time, hourly rate, and the contingency fee.

a. *The flat fee.* In a flat fee arrangement, you pay the lawyer a specified sum to get the job done. Most attorneys offer a number of services which are performed on a flat fee basis (e.g., preparation of a simple will, uncontested divorce, formation of a small corporation, adoption, preparation of certain commercial contracts, and other standard services)

b. *The flat fee plus time.* Here, a sum for a specified number of hours is charged. Once the lawyer works more hours than are specified, you are charged on an hourly basis. The following retainer agreement illustrates this:

(Date)

Name of Client
Anyplace, U.S.A.

Re: Retainer Agreement Regarding
Jones vs. Jones

Dear (Name):

This letter confirms that you have retained me as your attorney to negotiate a settlement agreement with your husband, if that is reasonably possible; or, if not, to represent you in a divorce action. You agree to pay to me promptly an initial retainer of $1,500, which is my minimum fee in this matter. If I devote more than 20 hours to this case based upon my time records commencing from the initial conference, you shall pay an additional fee counted at the rate of $100/hour.

If you should decide to discontinue my services in this matter at any time, you shall be liable for my time computed at the rate of $100/hour, except that the minimum fee shall in any event be $1,500.

These fees do not include any work in appellate courts, any other actions or proceedings or out-of-pocket disbursements. Out-of-pocket disbursements include but are not limited to costs of filing papers, court fees, process servers, witness fees, court reporters, long distance telephone calls, travel, parking, and photocopies normally made by me or requested by you, which disbursements shall be paid for or reimbursed to me upon my request.

You are aware of the hazards of litigation and that, despite my efforts on your behalf, there is no assurance or guarantee of the outcome of this matter.

Kindly indicate your understanding and acceptance of the above by signing this letter below where indicated. I look forward to serving you.

Sincerely yours,

I have read and understand the above letter, have received a copy, and accept all of its terms:

_____

   Barbara Jones

    c. *Hourly rate.* Many lawyers set their fees on an hourly basis. This hourly fee can range from $75 to $200 or more. Under this arrangement, you will be charged on a fixed hourly rate for all work done.

If you are billed by the hour, ask if *phone calls* between you and the lawyer are included. If they are, tell him you should only be charged for calls exceeding a certain number of hours per month. You can justify this by arguing that you shouldn't be charged when the lawyer calls to clarify a point, obtain additional information, or discuss news regarding the progress of your case. You will save money in legal bills by insisting on this.

d. *Contingency fee.*   Here your lawyer recovers a specified percentage of any money recovered via a lawsuit or settlement. Contingency fee arrangements are common in personal injury lawsuits. Many people favor contingency fee arrangements because they are not required to pay legal fees if their case is unsuccessful.

Some types of contingency fees are not permitted. For example, a lawyer cannot agree to structure the size of his fee on the type of verdict obtained for a client in a criminal proceeding. Contingency fees are also looked upon unfavorably by courts and disciplinary boards in matrimonial actions (because they are viewed as encouraging divorces). So, too, are contingency fees in personal injury suits that exceed maximum allowable percentages (typically 50 percent). If your lawyer proposed contingency fees in these areas, think twice before accepting the arrangement and hiring him.

To avoid problems, always spell out contingency arrangements in writing. The agreement should state who is responsible for *costs* in the event that you are unsuccessful. The following letter is an example of this:

(Date)

Name of Client
Anyplace, U.S.A.

Re: Retainer Agreement
Regarding James vs. Gilbert

Dear (Name):

This letter confirms that we will represent you in the prosecution of your claim for personal injuries sustained by you on February 16, 1984, as a result of an auto accident with Mr. (Name) in Cleveland, Ohio.

We will devote our efforts to this matter for a fee, the amount of which will depend upon the outcome of your claim:

1. If nothing is recovered, you will not be indebted to us for our services.

2. If we are successful, we will receive 25 percent of the amount obtained for you if no suit is filed, and 33 1/3 percent of any amount recovered after suit is filed.

3. Actual costs expending in reaching a settlement, if any, are to be paid by you.

4. Proceeds, if any, recovered by way of settlement judgment, or otherwise shall be disbursed as follows: All our costs which have not been reimbursed by you will be deducted; our fees, as set out in the percentage above, will be deducted and the balance will be paid to you.

5. Should you decide to discharge us and retain another law firm, we shall receive a reasonable percentage of the proceeds recovered by said firm as fees for our services.

If this letter correctly states our understanding, will you please so indicate by signing this agreement in the space provided below and returning it to us.

Sincerely yours,

_____

Robin James

Additional Points about Fees

There are distinct advantages and disadvantages in using different fee arrangements. For example, when you pay a flat fee you know how much will be charged, but you do not know how much care and attention will be spent on your matter. The hourly rate might be cheaper than a flat fee for routine work, but some dishonest lawyers "pad" timesheets to increase their fees. In addition, although contingency fee arrangements are beneficial to clients with weak cases, the contingency arrangements sometimes encourage lawyers to settle "winner" cases for less money rather than go to court. This is why, no matter what type of fee is agreed upon, it is essential to hire a lawyer who is honest and has your best interests in mind at all times.

Always insist that your fee arrangement be spelled out in writing. All provisions should be explained to you so that they are clearly understood and be sure to save a copy for your records. The lawyer may also ask you to pay a retainer at the interview. The retainer guarantees the availability of the lawyer to represent you and is an advance paid to demonstrate your desire to resolve your problem via legal recourse.

Ask for a receipt if you pay the retainer in cash. Inquire whether the retainer is to become part of the entire fee and whether it is refundable. In addition, ask if you can pay the retainer and other fees by credit card. Some states allow this. And, be sure that interest will not be imputed if you are late in paying fees. Some lawyers are beginning to charge interest on late payments, so be aware of this.

Request that all fees be billed periodically. Insist that billing statements be supported by detailed and complete time records which include the number of hours (or partial hours) worked, a report of the people contacted, and the services rendered. Some lawyers may be reluctant to do this, but by receiving these documents and statements on a regular basis, you will be able to question inconsistencies and errors before they get out of hand. You will also be aware of the amount of the bill as it accrues, and can pay for it over time if you choose.

Request your lawyer to send copies of all incoming and outgoing correspondence so that you will be able to follow the progress of your case. If your lawyer is reluctant to do this, tell him that you will come in once every month to Xerox your file. You will be amazed to see how fast he changes his mind!

Documenting Legal Fees

Legal fees are deductible provided they are ordinary and necessary business expenses. This means that you can deduct the cost of legal fees paid or incurred for the "production, collection, maintenance, or conservation of income" or property used in producing income. Deductions are also allowed for legal fees paid to collect, determine, or refund any tax which is owed.

Ask your lawyer whether fees paid to him are deductible. Request him to structure the fee arrangement to maximize your tax deduction and ask for a written statement which justifies the bill on the basis of time spent or some other allocation. This will help support your claim. Keep the statement in a safe place until tax time, and show it to your tax preparer. Accountants and other professionals often clip copies of the statement directly to the return so that the IRS won't question the deduction.

The following is a checklist of deductible legal fees:

1. Attorney fees paid to obtain estate planning, *including the preparation* of a will
2. Attorney fees paid to obtain a tax ruling
3. Attorney fees paid to perfect a patent application, copyright, or other intangible assets
4. Attorney fees paid to obtain support, property settlements, or tax advice incident to a divorce are deductible; fees paid to obtain the divorce itself are not
5. Attorney fees paid to address problems involving bankruptcy, antitrust (except if it relates to the imposition of a fine or penalty), or labor relations
6. Attorney fees paid to oppose a suspension or disbarment of a professional license
7. Attorney fees for services tending to increase or protect taxable business income (e.g., defending inherited stock)

Other Items to Clarify at the Interview

The following points should also be discussed with your lawyer before hiring him:

1. *Will he be available?* Complaints often arise because of poor communication. At the initial interview, ask the lawyer what his normal office hours are. Tell him it is important that he be available since you are paying for this service. Request that he return phone calls within 24 hours. Insist that his secretary or associate return your phone calls if he will be unavailable for extended periods of time.

(NOTE: Make it clear that you will not call him unnecessarily.)

2. *Will he work on your matter immediately?* Some lawyers fail to work promptly on legal matters, despite good inten-

tions. The legal system is often a slow process. Don't stall it further by hiring a procrastinating lawyer.

Insist that the lawyer begin working on your matter as quickly as possible. Ask him to specify when he estimates the matter will be resolved. *Include this is in the retainer agreement for your protection.*

3. *Are there hidden conflicts of interest?* One of the rules of professional ethics (which lawyers are bound to follow) states: "A lawyer should avoid even the appearance of impropriety." This means that a lawyer owes duties of loyalty and confidentiality to a client. For example, when a lawyer represents both a husband and a wife in a divorce, there is an inherent conflict which limits his ability to zealously promote the best interests of each of them.

Always ask the lawyer up front if he perceives any potential conflict of interest (e.g., is he related to, or was he ever employed by the person you are suing?).

(NOTE: A lawyer must decline representing a client when his professional judgment is likely to be affected by other business, financial, or personal interests. If a lawyer is disqualified, his associates and partners are also forbidden from serving you.)

4. *How will your funds be handled?* Lawyers are obligated to keep client funds in separate accounts. This includes unearned retainer fees.

The rules of professional conduct state that a lawyer cannot "commingle" client funds with his own. For example, bank accounts for client funds must be clearly marked as "Client Trust Accounts" or "Escrow Accounts."

A lawyer must notify you immediately when funds are received on your behalf. You must also receive *an accurate accounting* of these funds. This consists of a complete explanation of the amount of money held by the lawyer, its origin, and the reason for any deductions. *Insist on nothing less.*

(ADDITIONAL POINT: Tell the lawyer to place your funds in an *interest-bearing escrow account.* Later on, when your funds are remitted, be sure that the interest is included in the amount returned to you. Some lawyers neglect to return the interest portion to clients. *You may be entitled to the interest, so don't forget this.*)

Problems Encountered after You Hire the Lawyer

After a lawyer has been hired and begins to work, the following questions may arise:

1. *When should you settle a case?* Most people are unsure about settling cases. Some are intimidated by their lawyers and accept small settlements. Although every case is different and some people seek the personal satisfaction of going to court, the following points should be re-read if you are involved in a lawsuit and are considering settling the matter before it goes to trial.

Most civil actions take up to five years to be tried (usually two to three years). By accepting a fair settlement early on, you have use of the money and the proceeds can be invested to earn more money. You will eliminate large legal fees, court costs, and the possibility of eventually losing the case after a trial.

However, if you have a good case, it usually pays to wait before discussing and accepting a settlement. This is especially true in personal injury lawsuits. Most trial lawyers believe that larger settlements are obtained for their clients by waiting until a case reaches the courthouse steps. The reason seems to be that insurance companies do not negotiate in earnest until the moment before a case is tried. Time is on the side of the insurance company. It benefits them to wait and see if the case is *valid* (i.e., that it is properly prepared, that strong witnesses are ready to testify, that the evidence will prove the claim, etc.). Also, insurance companies make money by holding settlement funds and investing them up until the very last minute.

The decision whether to accept a settlement should always be made jointly with your lawyer. He knows the merits, pitfalls, and true value of the case better than you. However, do not allow him to pressure you into accepting a smaller settlement than you think you deserve. Some lawyers seek smaller settlements now, because they are lazy and the settlement represents money in the bank to them. Avoid this.

Instruct your lawyer to provide you with a detailed explanation about the pros and cons of settling your case. Inform him that you prefer to control your affairs—including the decision of settling your claim. Do not let your lawyer push you around. If you disagree, tell him so. Your lawyer cannot settle or compromise the case without your approval. If he does, he can be sued for malpractice. Remember, lawyers are paid to act on your behalf, never vice-versa.

Should You Change Your Lawyer?

You have the right to change lawyers any time if there is a valid reason. Valid reasons include improper or unethical conduct, conflicts of interest, malpractice by the lawyer, etc. However, you cannot change lawyers merely to stall time.

If you are dissatisfied with your lawyer's conduct or the way the matter is progressing, consult another lawyer for his opinion. Do this *before* taking action, because you need a professional opinion to tell you whether your lawyer acted correctly or improperly.

Never fire your lawyer until you have hired a replacement. By doing so, you may be unrepresented, and your case could accidentally be dismissed. If you fire your lawyer, you may be required to pay him for the value of work rendered. You may also have to go to court to settle the issue of legal fees. However, this should never impede you from taking action if warranted.

If you have evidence that your lawyer misused your funds for personal gain or committed fraud, you should file a complaint with the grievance committee of your state or local bar association. Don't be afraid to do this. All complaints are confidential. You cannot be sued for filing a complaint if it is later determined that the lawyer did nothing wrong.

Another alternative is to commence a malpractice lawsuit against your lawyer. Legal malpractice arises when a lawyer fails to use "Such skill or prudence as lawyers of ordinary skill commonly possess and experience in the performance of the tasks they undertake." This doesn't mean that you can sue if your lawyer gets beaten by a better lawyer. You can only sue if he fails to render work or assistance of *minimal competence* and you are damaged as a result. You can also sue for *malpractice* when there is a breach of ethics (like the failure to remit funds belonging to a client) in addition to suing for breach of contract and/or civil fraud.

The following are actual examples of lawyer malpractice:

- Settling a case without your consent
- Procrastinating work on a matter (for example, neglecting to prepare a will and the client dies)
- Charging improper fees
- Failing to file a claim within the requisite time period (The Statute of Limitations)
- Failing to include a wife's claim for a husband's military pension in a divorce matter in a community property state
- Failing to competently represent a defendant in a criminal matter

Speak to another lawyer before embarking on any of these courses of action. His advice is essential in advising you if you have a valid claim. He will also tell you what steps should be taken to protect your rights.

Should You Appeal a Case?

The vast majority of lawsuits never go to trial; they are either discontinued or settled. However, every case that is tried has a loser and the losing party must decide whether or not to appeal the unfavorable decision.

The appeals process works this way: Appeals judges read the transcript of the trial, together with legal documents (called briefs) to determine if the trial judge or jury erred in their decision. *This rarely happens.* Less than 20 percent of all criminal cases and 30 percent of all civil cases are reversed on appeal. However, some decisions do get reversed. If a person or business has spent several years and thousands of dollars pursuing or defending a valid claim, the additional money spent for an appeal may be worth it (particularly if the delay caused by the appeal process works to your advantage).

Talk to your lawyer immediately if you receive an unfavorable verdict. There is a limited period of time to file a notice that you intend to appeal and you must do this without delay to preserve your rights.

To evaluate the chances of a successful appeal, you must carefully reconstruct the reasons why you lost the case. You must also decide whether to hire your present lawyer or to hire a specialist in appeal matters. Although your lawyer is quite familiar with your case, there is much to be said for hiring a lawyer who makes his living writing briefs and arguing appeals (it is an art).

Be certain you know how much the appeal will cost. Always sign a retainer agreement similar to the following which clearly spells out lawyer fees, costs, and disbursements.

(Date)

Name of Client
650 Linda Lane
Anyplace, U.S.A.

Re: Retainer Agreement
Regarding Appeal

Dear (Name):

This letter confirms that you have retained me as your attorney to represent you in the prosecution of an appeal of a judgment granted by Justice Mitchell on September 16, 1984, in the State Supreme Court, and entered on September 17, 1984, in the office of the Clerk. The appeal will be taken to the Appellate Division.

You have agreed to pay to me promptly a fee of $2,500 for my legal services and to pay for all disbursements in addition to my fee upon my request. Disbursements include but are not limited to the cost of the transcript of the trial (which the court reporter has estimated at about $800), the cost of the appellate printer to print the record on appeal and the briefs which we submit, and to cover the costs for serving the papers on appeal (which is estimated at about $1,200). The actual disbursements may vary from the estimates, which are only approximate.

You are aware of the hazards of litigation and that despite my efforts on your behalf there is no assurance or guarantee of the outcome of this appeal.

Kindly indicate your understanding and acceptance of the above by signing this letter below where indicated. I look forward to serving you.

Very truly yours,

I have read and understand the above letter, have received a copy, and accept all of its terms:

_____

George Smith

No matter who serves you, obviously you are in a better position when you win your case the first time, since appeals are uphill battles. Remember, appeals are generally costly, time-consuming, and frequently do not produce anticipated results.

Summary of Steps to Use Your Lawyer Effectively

1. Speak to a lawyer before action is contemplated to determine if one is needed

2. Schedule an interview, if necessary; inquire if you will be charged for it

3. Bring relevant documents to the interview

4. Ask for an opinion letter

5. Do not be overly impressed by plush surroundings

6. Be sure the lawyer of your choice will be handling your matter

7. Hire an experienced practitioner who devotes at least 30 percent of his working time to your type of problem

8. Look for honesty and integrity in a lawyer

9. Insist on signing a retainer agreement to reduce misunderstandings

10. Have the agreement read and explained to you before signing, and save a copy for your files

11. If the lawyer cannot tell you exactly how much you will be charged, get minimum and maximum estimates. Include this in the agreement

12. Be certain you understand how additional costs are calculated, and who will pay for them

13. If an hourly rate is agreed upon, negotiate that you will not be charged for telephone calls to your lawyer

14. If you pay the fee in cash, get a receipt. Inquire if you can pay your bill by credit card

15. Structure the fee arrangement to maximize your tax deduction

16. Insist on receiving copies of incoming and outgoing correspondence, and monthly, detailed, time records

17. Be sure the lawyer will be available, that he will immediately commence work on your matter, and that there are no potential conflicts of interest

18. Insist that all funds received by you be deposited in interest-paying escrow accounts. Don't forget to ask for the interest later on

19. Never allow your lawyer to pressure you into settling a case

20. Always consult another lawyer before deciding to fire your present one, file a complaint with the grievance committee, or commence a malpractice lawsuit

21. Be wary of conducting business with your lawyer

22. Do not expect miracles

7

Making
Small Claims Court
Work for You

- **Introduction** 260
- **Who May Be Sued?** 262
- **Do You Have a Valid Claim?** 262
- **Where to Sue** 263
- **What Can You Sue For?** 263
- **Starting the Lawsuit** 264
- **The Defendant's Response** 266
- **Your Duties as the Moving Party** 267
- **Preparing for Trial** 268
- **The Trial** 269
- **Obtaining Judgment** 271
- **Some Minor Procedural Points** 272
- **Strategies if You Are Sued in Small Claims Court** 273
- **Strategies to Help You Win Your Case** 274
  - Automobile Accident Negligence Cases 275
  - Consumer Product Purchase Cases 276
  - Improper Work, Labor and Service Cases 278
  - Wrongful Taking and Bailment Cases 279
  - Insurance Policy Cases 281
  - Goods Sold and Delivered Cases 282
  - Loan Cases 283
  - Assault and Battery Cases 283
- **Summary of Steps to Increase Your Success in Small Claims Court** 284

Introduction

Small Claims Courts are busier than ever. Over 3.5 million cases are heard each year—an increase of 25 percent over the past fifteen years. Most people, however, do not know how to use Small Claims Court effectively.

Small Claims Courts help you collect money in an informal and inexpensive manner *without* hiring a lawyer. They can be used in many different situations. For example, you may wish to sue for money damages when:

- Your employer fails to pay you
- Someone carelessly damages your property and refuses to pay for repairs
- A car dealer refuses to return a refundable deposit when you cancel the deal
- You purchase merchandise which is damaged during delivery and the store refuses to replace it or refund your money
- You want to recover money you paid to a garage mechanic after receiving shoddy workmanship or service
- You are a victim of a business's misleading advertising
- A dry cleaning establishment damages your clothing

In all of these cases, and countless more, you should consider suing in Small Claims Court to recover your loss.

Critics of the system attack Small Claims Courts as ineffective. They state that Small Claims Courts are supposed to make justice accessible to working people, but many do not convene at night or on Saturdays. This causes people to lose valuable work time and pay. Critics also claim that litigants often have trouble collecting after winning their case, and that some states allow lawyers to represent the parties. Thus, people who choose to argue their own cases in these states often risk being outmaneuvered.

Despite these criticisms, Small Claims Courts work. The backlog of cases has been reduced. Night sessions are becoming more common. Matters are resolved quickly, usually within a month from the time an action is filed. The maximum amount of money you can recover has been raised in many states from $300 to $1,500 or more. Judges are employing the services of arbitrators, mediators, and private organizations to resolve disputes, and are sympathetic to litigants who oppose adversaries represented by lawyers.

The following information is designed to clarify areas of confusion, reduce your anxieties, and to improve your chances of success. The material will explain, step by step, how to start an action, prepare your case, successfully argue it in court, and enforce your judgment. It will also discuss how to defend yourself properly if you are sued in Small Claims Court.

AUTHOR'S NOTE: The following material describes the procedures of a typical Small Claims Court. However, the rules vary in each city and state. Thus, before you contemplate starting a lawsuit in a particular Small Claims Court, it is wise to call the clerk of that court and ask for a written copy and explanation of the specific procedural rules to be followed.

(NOTE: Small Claims Courts are often listed in telephone directories as Justice Courts, District Courts, Municipal Courts, or Justice of the Peace Courts, so don't be confused.)

The most important thing to remember is that you should not be afraid to use Small Claims Court if you feel you have been wronged. By using the following information as a guide, you *can* benefit both financially and emotionally from your efforts.

Who May Be Sued?

Small Claims Court may be used to sue any person, business, partnership, corporation, or government body owing you money. However, Small Claims Courts limit the amount of money for which you can sue and which you can recover if you are successful. This figure usually ranges from $300 to $1,500. If you sue in Small Claims Court and recover a judgment, you are precluded from suing again to recover any additional money owed to you. Thus, if you feel your claim greatly exceeds the maximum amount of money that might be awarded in Small Claims Court, you should consider instituting suit in a higher court (e.g., District Court). In this event, you will need a lawyer to start the action and represent you.

Do You Have a Valid Claim?

In order to be successful, you must have a valid claim. This means that you must be able to:

1. Identify the person or business who damaged or caused you harm

2. Calculate the amount of damages you suffered

3. Ascertain whether there is some basis in law to have a court award you damages

4. Determine that you will not be precluded from obtaining a judgment because of legal or procedural grounds (i.e., that you were the main cause of your own harm, that you waited too long to start the action and are barred by a legal principle called The Statute of Limitations, or that you signed a written release)

The section at the end of this chapter, "Strategies to Help You Win Your Case," will clarify whether you have a valid claim and what you must prove at the trial to be successful.

Where to Sue

Call your local bar association, City Hall, or the county courthouse to discover where the nearest Small Claims Court is located. You cannot start the action wherever you desire. In most states, suit can only be brought in the county in which the person or business you are suing lives or does business.

Confirm this with the Small Claims Court clerk and ask what days and hours the court is in session. Also, find out the maximum amount of money you can sue for, what documents are needed to file a complaint, the filing fee, and whether this can be paid by cash, check, or money order.

What Can You Sue For?

You can only sue to collect *money* in Small Claims Court. If, for example, you purchased a defective dishwasher and seek another replacement, the court does not have the power to order the store to give you another dishwasher. Rather, if you win your case, you will be awarded money to buy another one. Thus, before you begin to sue in Small Claims Court, you must always estimate the loss in money you wish to collect.

Sometimes you need not have spent money before starting an action. For example, you can sue in Small Claims Court when a car dealer refuses to honor his warranty, and this will force you to spend money to have your car repaired. However, before you sue the dealer, you should obtain written estimates from local merchants *to prove your claim.* Or, you may have been promised that a new stereo system would be delivered to your house the day before an important party and the unit never arrived. In this situation, you would be required to calculate a monetary figure for the damage you sustained as a result of the nondelivery.

When calculating the amount of your claim, do not forget to include all incurred expenses, including gasoline bills, tolls, telephone costs, losses due to time missed from work, etc. Don't overlook items such as sales tax and interest, if applicable. Save all your receipts for this purpose.

Starting the Lawsuit

You begin the lawsuit by paying a small fee (about $4) and either going down to the Court in person or mailing in a complaint which states the following information:

1. Your name and address
2. The complete name and address of the person, business, or corporation you are suing
3. The amount of money you believe you are owed
4. The facts
5. The reasons why you (the plaintiff) are seeking redress

If you are filing a claim on behalf of an individually owned business, you must list the name of the owner in addition to the name of the business. If you are filing a claim on behalf of a partnership, you must list the name of the partnership as the plaintiff. Also, be aware that some states do not allow a corporation to sue someone in Small Claims Court. Investigate this with the clerk.

Be sure to write the accurate and complete name and address of the defendant (the person or entity you are suing) on the complaint. This will avoid problems obtaining the money if you are awarded a judgment. Write the corporation's formal name, rather than its "doing business" (d/b/a) name. Thus, if you are suing a corporation, always contact the County Clerk's office in the county where the corporation does business to obtain its proper name and address. Better still, it may be wise to call the Department of Corporations in your state to obtain such information.

When you are suing more than one person, for example, a husband and wife, be sure you sue each one separately in the complaint. Sue a woman in her full name, rather than her married name (e.g., Mrs. Allison Kane, not Mrs. Mark Kane).

If your problem is consumer-oriented, state how you were mistreated. For example, if you personally demanded satisfaction, or sent a certified letter, specify when and whom you contacted. You might also write, if applicable, that the defendant failed to make you a reasonable offer of settlement after becoming aware of your problem.

(NOTE: Some states require you to send a demand letter before suing in Small Claims Court. Investigate this with the clerk.)

The following is an example of a simple complaint:

> On February 6, 1984, I purchased a Sonic Dishwasher, style #1401B, from Bernard's Bargain Store in Great Neck, New York. After it was installed by employees from Bernard's Store, the following day, the appliance malfunctioned, causing a small electrical fire and damage to my utility room wall. Based upon written estimates, the approximate cost of repair to my home totals $972.50. Additionally, I am seeking $488.89, which represents the purchase price and/or replacement value of another dishwasher. Demand for this amount was made repeatedly to Mr. Victor Tegeria, general manager of Bernard's Bargain Store, in person on February 9 and February 12, by telephone, and by two (2) certified letters dated February 9 and February 12. To date, my requests for reimbursement have been ignored.

At this time, you may also be required to prepare another form called a *summons* which notifies your opponent that you are suing him. Sometimes the clerk will do this. Ask the clerk whether the court will mail the summons by registered or first class mail, personally serve the defendant on your behalf, or whether you must hire a professional process server. *This is important.*

If a professional process server is required, ask the clerk to explain what is necessary to prove that service was accomplished. You may have to pay the process server an additional fee (between $10 and $30). However, you can recover this if you win your case by asking the judge to include the process server's fee in the award.

When the clerk gives you a hearing date, be sure that it is convenient and you have no other prior commitments. You are now on your way!

The Defendant's Response

When the person or company you are suing receives the summons, the defendant or his attorney can:

1. Deny your claim by mailing a written denial to the court
2. Deny your claim by personally appearing in court on the day of the hearing
3. Sue you for money you supposedly owe (this is called a *counterclaim*)
4. Contact you to resolve the matter by settlement

If an offer of payment is made, ask to be reimbursed for all filing and service costs. Notify the court that you are dismissing the action only *after* you receive payment in hand, never before. (If you are paid by check, wait until it clears.) Do not postpone the case. Tell your opponent that unless you are paid before the day of the trial, you are prepared to go to court and either commence with the trial or stipulate the offer of settlement to the judge. *This will protect you.*

If a written denial is mailed to the court, ask the clerk to read it to you over the phone, or else go to the court and read it yourself. This is your right and it may help you prepare for your opponent's defense.

The following is an example of a simple denial in an answer:

I deny each and every allegation in the face of the complaint.

With this kind of denial, you must now prove your allegations in court to recover your claim.

Your Duties as
the Moving Party

It is up to you to carefully follow the progress of your case. Call the clerk and refer to the docket number to discover whether the defendant received the complaint and whether it was answered. If you discover that the defendant did not receive the complaint by the day of the trial, request the clerk to issue a new complaint to be served by a sheriff or process server. However, go to court that day anyway, to be sure that the case is not dismissed because of your failure to appear.

Once the complaint is personally served and your opponent does not appear at the trial, he will be in default and you may be awarded a judgment automatically. In some states, you still have to prove your case in order to be successful. Also, be aware that defendants sometimes file motions (legal affidavits) requesting the court to remove the default judgment on the grounds that there was a valid reason why they could not attend the hearing. If this motion is granted, your trial will be rescheduled to a new date.

If you are unable to come to court on the day of the trial, you *must* send a registered letter to the clerk asking for a continuance. The letter should specify the reasons why you will be unable to appear. Include future dates when you will be able to come to court. *Send a copy of this letter to your opponent.* Once you receive a new date, send your opponent an additional letter by registered mail which informs him of the revised date.

Requests for continuances are sometimes *not* honored. Thus, call the clerk on the day of the old trial date to be sure that your request has been granted. Be prepared to send a friend or relative to court to ask for a continuance on your behalf if a continuance has not been obtained by the day of the trial.

Preparing for Trial

Subpoenas

You have several weeks to prepare for trial. Use the time wisely. First, be sure that your friendly witnesses, if any, will attend the trial and testify on your behalf. Select witnesses whom you think are believable, and who will not say things that will surprise you at the trial.

If necessary, you can ask the clerk to issue a subpoena to compel the attendance of important witnesses whom you believe may refuse to attend and testify. A subpoena is a document that orders a person to testify or produce books, papers, and other physical objects into court on a specified date. Once the subpoena is issued and the person refuses to appear, a judge can direct a sheriff to bring the witness into court, or even impose a jail sentence for a willful violation of the order.

On the date you come to court for your trial, check to see if the clerk received any subpoenaed documents. If such records are crucial to your case and have not been received, you can ask for an adjournment. If you have subpoenaed an individual and do not know what he looks like, ask the clerk to call out his name to determine if he is present so you can proceed with the trial.

(NOTE: In some states, you can present the judge with signed affidavits or statements of friends and witnesses who are unable to appear at the trial. Ask the clerk if this is allowed. If so, you might be able to save time and trouble. A few states also permit judges to hear testimony via conference telephones. *Investigate this.*)

Organizing the Facts

To maximize your chances of success, organize your case before the day of the trial. For example, you should gather and label all of your evidence so that you can produce the documents easily in court. You may also wish to speak with a lawyer or call a lawyer's referral service for legal advice. Many communities have such advisory organizations which are willing to inform you, without charge, about relevant cases and statutes. This may help you know what damages you are legally entitled to. You may cite these laws, if applicable, at the hearing.

You should also practice what you will say to the judge. This will put you at ease and help you organize the important facts. Better still, make a brief outline and refer to it while speaking. Prepare a list of questions that you would like to ask each witness and your opponent. You are allowed to ask questions from a piece of paper at the hearing. By doing so, you will not forget to ask important questions.

The Trial

On the day or evening of the trial, arrive early, locate the correct courtroom, find the name of your case on the court calendar, and check in with the clerk. You should also be properly attired, preferably in business clothes.

Come prepared with all relevant documents. These include:

1. Receipts and canceled checks
2. Correspondence
3. Contracts, leases, and bills of sale
4. Warranties, advertisements, written promises and statements made to you
5. Estimates
6. Signed affidavits or statements from friends and witnesses unable to appear at the hearing
7. Clear photographs and other evidence to prove your case
8. An employer's statement of lost wages, and a doctor's letter reflecting lost time from work
9. Medical bills and reports
10. Police and accident reports
11. Diagrams or charts
12. Copies of applicable statutes, cases, and regulations

(HINT: It is often effective to bring actual exhibits or products into court if possible. For example, if you bought a new part and a used part was installed in your car instead, you may wish to bring the used part into court if it can be easily removed and carried.)

Wait until your case is called. At that time, you and your opponent will be sworn in. The judge or a court-appointed arbitrator will conduct the hearing and ask you questions.

Be relaxed. Keep your presentation brief and to the point. Tell the judge why you are suing the defendant and what you are seeking in money damages. Show the judge your evidence. Bring along the short written summary of the case which you have prepared. You can refer to it during the trial and if the judge does not come to an immediate decision, he can use your outline for reference.

Talk directly to the judge and respond to his questions. Show respect for the judge. Always refer to him as "Your Honor" or "Judge." Listen to the judge's instructions and never argue with him. If the judge asks you a question while you are speaking, stop immediately. Then answer his question honestly and to the point.

Try to be diplomatic rather than emotional. This will score points. Also, avoid arguing with your opponent in court and *never* interrupt his presentation.

After both sides have finished speaking, you have the opportunity to refute what your opponent told the judge. Do not be afraid if he is accompanied by a lawyer. Some Small Claims Courts do not allow lawyers to participate, and others actively discourage their use. Simply inform the judge in a polite tone that you are not represented by counsel and are not familiar with Small Claims Court procedures. Ask the judge to intercede on your behalf if you feel that your opponent's attorney is treating you unfairly. Most judges will be sympathetic, since Small Claims Courts are specifically designed for you to present your case without an attorney.

Obtaining Judgment

Some Small Claims Court judges do not render oral decisions on the spot. Instead, they usually issue a decision in writing several days after the hearing. This gives them time to weigh the testimony and exhibits that have been presented at the trial. However, if your opponent failed to attend the hearing, judges usually render a judgment of default immediately after your presentation.

In most states, you are notified of the decision by mail. If you win the case, make sure you know how and when payment will be made. Check to see that all of your disbursements, including court costs, filing fees, service of process and applicable witness fees are added to the amount of your judgment.

Once you receive notice of a favorable decision, send a copy of the decision by certified mail to your opponent, together with a letter requesting payment. Some states require that payment first be made to the court. Others allow payment to be made directly to you.

Do not hesitate to act if you do not receive the money. Here's what to do. First, contact the clerk and file a *Petition for Notice to Show Cause*. This will be sent to the defendant ordering him to come into court and explain why he has not paid. You should also file an *Order of Execution* with the Sheriff's, Constable's, or Clerk's Office in the county where the defendant resides, works, or owns a business. By doing this, you can discover where the defendant-debtor has assets.

The sheriff or other enforcement agent has the power to go out and collect the judgment either by seizing personal property belonging to the debtor, freezing his bank account, placing a lien on any real estate owned by him, or even garnishing his salary. The clerk of your Small Claims Court will tell you exactly what to do to collect your judgment. *Don't be discouraged.* Chances are you will eventually be paid if you win your case and know where to locate the defendant or his property.

Some Minor Procedural Points

Once you proceed in Small Claims Court, you usually waive your rights to a trial by jury. However, the defendant can surprise you. Some states allow defendants to move a Small Claims Court case to a higher court and/or obtain a trial by jury. If this occurs, you will need a lawyer to represent you and his services could conceivably cost as much as your claim in the dispute.

In addition, people often wonder if it is wise to appeal an unfavorable Small Claims decision. The answer is generally no. Some states don't allow losing plaintiffs to appeal. Also, in all courts, an appeals court will not overturn the decision of a Small Claims judge, except for strong proof that the judge was unfairly biased or dishonest. This is very difficult to prove. *So, it is best to prepare your case properly the first time and walk away if you lose.*

Strategies if You Are Sued in Small Claims Court

Up to now, this chapter discussed how to successfully sue someone in Small Claims Court. However, the following material will explain how to defend yourself properly if you are sued.

The first time you will become aware that someone is suing you or your business in Small Claims Court is usually when you receive the summons and complaint. *Don't panic when you get it.* Remember, this is only a piece of paper requesting you to come into court on a specified day and tell your side of the story. *Never ignore the summons.* If you do, it's likely that a default judgment will be obtained against you.

Thus, it's best to respond without delay in one of the following ways:

1. *Contact the plaintiff to negotiate a settlement.* If you elect this route, offer to pay less money in compromise or seek a pay-out arrangement over an extended period of time.

2. *Send the court a denial by mail.* If you believe no money is owed, if you feel you have a valid defense, if a third party was responsible for the loss, or if your settlement offer was refused, mail your denial to the court.

3. *Countersue the plaintiff for damages.* If you believe that the plaintiff owes you money, include a *counterclaim* for that amount. Call the clerk for advice on how this should be done.

Strategies to Help
You Win Your Case

To maximize the chances of success when suing someone, you must:

- Determine if you have a valid claim
- Prove that claim in court
- Foresee points which your opponent might make to defeat you

The fact that you have been damaged physically or monetarily does not mean that you will automatically recover money damages in Small Claims Court for your loss.

For example, suppose you were assaulted after striking someone, or were involved in an automobile accident that you could have avoided, or were given a check that bounced after you failed to deliver goods as promised. Chances are you would not be able to recover money for your loss in any of these cases.

The following material will acquaint you with the elements that must be proved in court to win your Small Claims case. It will also help you anticipate what your opponent may do to defeat your claim. These charts include some of the more common complaints heard in Small Claims Court. Study the information carefully before filing a complaint or defending yourself. It may save you time, money, and aggravation.

If you are a defendant, follow the same procedures as the plaintiff to maximize your chances of success. Prepare your testimony. Contact your witnesses to be sure that they will appear at the trial and testify on your behalf. Collect your exhibits and documents.

Arrive early on the day of the trial and check in with the clerk. If you have any doubts, try to settle the case with the plaintiff before the judge hears the case. Regardless of whether or not a settlement is reached, show the judge respect when your case is called.

Request that the case be dismissed if your opponent fails to appear. Your adversary will speak first if he does appear. Wait until he is finished speaking before telling the judge your side of the story. Conclude your remarks by highlighting the important aspects of your case. Don't forget to point out any inconsistencies or flaws in your opponent's story.

Automobile Accident Negligence Cases

EXAMPLE: You are involved in an automobile accident which was not your fault.

WHAT YOU MUST PROVE AT THE TRIAL	HOW TO PROVE IT
1. Time, place, and date of accident	1. Police report, accident report, your testimony, other witnesses
2. Facts describing your conduct	2. Your testimony, other witnesses, diagrams, sketches of street, etc.
3. Facts describing the negligent conduct of your opponent	3. Your testimony, other witnesses, diagrams, sketches of street, etc.
4. Damages you suffered (a) To your automobile	(a) Title or registration, photographs, mechanics' estimates, your testimony, other witnesses, itemized repair bills
(b) To you or your passengers	(b) Medical bills, employer report showing lost wages, time from work, doctor's report, accident report, police report, your testimony, other witnesses

DEFENSES:

1. That you were contributorily negligent
2. That you were the main cause of the accident

Consumer Product Purchase Cases

EXAMPLE: You purchase goods from an individual, store, or business which:

1. Are defective
2. Do not function or perform as promised
3. Are not what you ordered

WHAT YOU MUST PROVE AT THE TRIAL	HOW TO PROVE IT
1. The date and place of purchase	1. Your testimony
2. What you bought	2. Contract of sale, sales receipt
3. That you paid for it	3. Canceled check, sales receipt
4. (a) That the product is defective	4. (a) Your testimony, other witnesses, estimates of repair
(b) That the product did not perform as promised by (literature, salesperson, etc.)	(b) Warranties in your contract, written advertisements, statements made to you
(c) That the product was not what you ordered	(c) Contract of sale, sales receipt, your testimony, other witnesses

DEFENSES:

1. That the product was used recklessly, carelessly, or in an abnormal manner

2. That specific promises about the capabilities of the product were never given, that the warranties do not apply, that there is a disclaimer in the contract of sale

3. That the store or business was never notified of the problem and given an opportunity to correct it

(HELPFUL HINTS: To increase the chances of success in a case involving a retail store or business, always contact the seller by mail to document your protest. A "thirty-day demand letter" should be sent by certified mail, return receipt requested. Keep a copy for your own files and staple the mail receipt to your copy.

Once this letter is sent, you may be in the position of informing the judge that your demands were ignored. Or, if the letter is answered and the store or business refuses to pay, you may learn what position they intend to take at the trial. This information will help prepare you for the hearing, since you will be aware of your opponent's story.)

The following is a sample of what should be included in your demand letter. Remember, some states require this before filing an action in Small Claims Court.

(Your Address)
(Telephone Number)
(Date)

(Seller or Business)
(Address)

Dear (Seller or Business):

Under the laws of (state), I hereby make this written demand for relief as outlined in the statutes.

On or about (date), (describe what happened, including details on what was purchased or leased).

As a result, I have suffered the following injury: (describe the money and/or property loss). Moreover, I believe this behavior constitutes (an) unfair or deceptive act(s) or practice(s).

Therefore, I demand (indicate what you want the seller or business to do to remedy the situation, e.g., refund, replacement, repair, and any other compensation).

You have the opportunity to make a good faith response to this letter within thirty (30) days. Your failure to do so could subject you to treble damages, attorney's fees, and costs if I decide to institute legal action.

Sincerely,

P.S. I am taking the liberty of sending copies of this letter to the Attorney General's Office as well as the local Consumer Protection Agency and Better Business Bureau.

(Send certified mail, return receipt requested.)

Improper Work, Labor, and Services Cases

EXAMPLE: You pay a person or business to perform work, labor or services and you:

1. Do not receive service
2. Receive inferior workmanship
3. Receive the wrong service
4. Perform work, labor, or services and are not paid

WHAT YOU MUST PROVE AT THE TRIAL	HOW TO PROVE IT
1. The person, company, or business who agreed to perform services	1. Your testimony
2. What work was promised	2. Written contract, notes, correspondence, sketches, promotional material given to you by defendant

WHAT YOU MUST PROVE AT THE TRIAL	HOW TO PROVE IT
3. What was paid	3. Canceled check, receipt
4. a. Service was not performed	4. a. Photographs, your testimony, other witnesses
b. Inferior workmanship	b. Photographs, your testimony, other witnesses, mechanics, estimates of repair
c. Wrong services performed	c. Your testimony, other witnesses
d. You performed work competently, for a fee; the defendant accepted the work performed but won't pay as agreed	d. Photographs, your testimony, other witnesses, written contract, notes, partial payment by canceled check, receipt

DEFENSES:

1. Services were properly performed
2. Payment was not made as agreed
3. You were unreasonable (kept changing work plans, etc.)

Wrongful Taking and Bailment Cases

EXAMPLE: A guest in your home borrows your luggage, you check your coat in a restaurant, you hire a company to store your furs or deliver goods which you purchased and:

1. The item(s) is damaged
2. The item(s) is misplaced or lost
3. The item(s) is stolen
4. The item(s) is not returned

WHAT YOU MUST PROVE AT THE TRIAL	HOW TO PROVE IT
1. Time, place, and delivery of the goods to a person, business, or company	1. Contract, receipt, canceled check
2. Description of the property and proof of ownership	2. Original bill of sale, your testimony, other witnesses
3. Value of property when originally purchased or acquired, current and replacement value	3. Sales receipt, canceled check, report of appraiser
4. a. Item returned damaged	4. a. Photographs, estimate of repair, your testimony, other witnesses
b. Item is lost	b. Your testimony, other witnesses, police report, insurance report
c. Item is reported stolen	c. Your testimony, other witnesses, police report, insurance report
5. That you demanded return of your property	5. Demand letter (sent certified or registered mail), your testimony, other witnesses
6. Damages	6. Cost or replacement value, canceled check, appraiser's report, sales receipt

DEFENSES:

1. Never notified of demand for return
2. Goods held longer than required (disclaimer in contract)
3. Plaintiff cannot prove that he/she owns the goods (no ticket)
4. Storage bill not paid
5. Other money owed

Insurance Policy Cases

EXAMPLE: You purchase a burglary, accident, fire, or marine insurance policy and the company:

1. Refuses to pay
2. Agrees only to pay less than you are willing to accept

WHAT YOU MUST PROVE AT THE TRIAL	HOW TO PROVE IT
1. That a contract of insurance existed at the time the claim was made	1. Insurance policy, insurance binder, representations made by insurance agent
2. That the policy was in effect at the time the claim was made	2. Insurance policy, correspondence, premium notice, canceled check
3. That you are the owner or beneficiary of the policy	3. Insurance policy, your testimony, other witnesses
4. That a loss occurred	4. Your testimony, other witnesses, photographs
5. That you properly notified the company	5. Demand letter (sent certified or registered mail), your testimony, witnesses
6. Damages	6. Your testimony, other witnesses, photographs, report of appraiser

DEFENSES:

1. Nonpayment of premium
2. Failure to perform specified duties according to the insurance policy
3. Failure to make timely demand as specified in the policy
4. Fraudulent intent to collect

Goods Sold and Delivered Cases

EXAMPLE: You, your business, or company sells and delivers goods to a person, business, or company, and those goods:

1. Are returned for no valid reason
2. Are accepted, used, and not paid for

WHAT YOU MUST PROVE AT THE TRIAL	HOW TO PROVE IT
1. Date, time, and person you agreed to sell and deliver goods	1. Contract of sale, memorandum of agreement, your testimony, other witnesses
2. That the agreement to sell and deliver was made at the request and acceptance of defendant	2. Your testimony, other witnesses, agreement, contract of sale, partial payment via canceled check, receipt
3. Date, place, quantity, and description of goods delivered	3. Your testimony, other witnesses, delivery receipt
4. Demand for payment	4. Your testimony, other witnesses, demand letter (sent certified or registered mail)
5. Damages	5. Contract price (contract of sale, memorandum letter of agreement); amount of money you lost upon resale (canceled check, receipt)

DEFENSES:

1. Goods were not of ordered quality
2. Goods were defective
3. Goods were shipped late
4. Goods were never received

Loan Cases

EXAMPLE: You loan money to someone which is not repaid in a timely fashion.

WHAT YOU MUST PROVE AT THE TRIAL	HOW TO PROVE IT
1. The date and place you loaned the money	1. Your testimony, other witnesses
2. Who you agreed to loan the money to	2. Your testimony, other witnesses, loan agreement, note of indebtedness
3. The amount of money loaned	3. Loan agreement, note, canceled check, your testimony, other witnesses
4. The amount and time intervals of repayment	4. Loan agreement, your testimony, other witnesses
5. That timely demand was made	5. Demand letter (sent certified or registered mail), your testimony, other witnesses
6. That the amount has not been repaid	6. Your testimony, other witnesses

DEFENSES:

1. That the amount of interest charged was usurious
2. That the loan was really a gift
3. That the loan was forgiven
4. That the loan was repaid

Assault and Battery Cases

EXAMPLE: You are threatened or injured by a person, or are bitten by a pet.

WHAT YOU MUST PROVE AT THE TRIAL	HOW TO PROVE IT
1. The time and place of the incident	1. Your testimony, witnesses
2. Facts showing the act was intentional	2. Your testimony, witnesses
3. If a dog bite, show owner, describe dog, place of incident, what you were doing at the time	3. Your testimony, witnesses
4. Injuries you sustained	4. Photographs (preferably color and taken as soon after injury as possible), police report, medical bills, employer's statement of lost wages, letter from doctor showing lost time from work

DEFENSES:

1. Provocation/self-defense
2. Reasonable force was used to remove a trespasser from the premises

Summary of Steps to Increase Your Success in Small Claims Court

1. Determine if you have a legally valid claim
   a. Call a lawyer or lawyer's referral service for advice
2. Locate the Small Claims Court in the county where the defendant lives or does business
3. Call the clerk and ask for assistance
4. File the summons and complaint; obtain a hearing date

5. Be sure the summons and complaint has been served on the defendant

6. Prepare for the trial:
   a. Gather your witnesses and evidence
   b. Practice what you will say
   c. Write your outline

7. Arrive in court on the day of the hearing
   a. Locate the correct courtroom
   b. Find your name on the calendar; check in with the clerk

8. Present your case
   a. Be relaxed and diplomatic
   b. Submit your evidence
   c. Show the judge respect
   d. Ask for reimbursement of filing costs, etc.

9. Collect your judgment
   a. Receive notification of the decision
   b. Make arrangements with the clerk for payment
   c. Send a copy of the decision and a letter requesting payment to the defendant-debtor.
   d. Don't delay—contact the clerk if you are having a problem collecting
   e. File an execution order with the sheriff

8

All about
Arbitration

- **Introduction** 287
- **How to Obtain Arbitration** 287
- **Summary of Steps Leading to the Hearing** 291
- **The Hearing** 295
- **How to Increase Your Chances of Success in Arbitration** 298
- **What to Do after Obtaining a Judgment** 300
- **A Word about Mediation** 300

Introduction

Litigants often settle disputes informally through arbitration. This process is used in a variety of areas to resolve employment and labor misunderstandings, recover uninsured motorist and no-fault insurance claims, settle disagreements between businesspeople, clarify property distribution clauses in divorce cases, and enforce consumer purchases and contracts. Cases are heard by arbitrators rather than judges, and their decisions are legally binding.

Despite the usefulness of arbitration, however, many people are unaware of its existence. This chapter will tell you what you should know about arbitration. You will learn how it is obtained, how the hearing is conducted, and its advantages and disadvantages. You will also become familiar with an alternative legal proceeding called mediation. All of this information will assist you to better manage business controversies and help you select the most favorable legal forum for your particular problem.

How to Obtain Arbitration

Individuals cannot initiate arbitration hearings merely because they have a dispute which requires legel intervention. In order to obtain a hearing, both parties must agree in writing that the controversy will be submitted to binding arbitration.

Oral agreements to arbitrate disputes are *not* enforceable. This is because arbitration works differently than litigation. Arbitrators have broader powers than judges, and are not limited by strict rules of evidence. They can hear all relevant testimony when making an award, including some forms of evidence (e.g., hearsay, questionable copies of documents, etc.) that would be excluded in a regular court. Arbitrators have the authority to hear witnesses out of order. Their decision is usually *final and unappealable.* Thus, the law requires both parties to agree to the arbitration process *beforehand in writing* to avoid claims of unfairness by the losing side.

The right to proceed to arbitration is usually accomplished by including the following type of clause in an employment contract, lease, loan agreement, or other document.

> Any controversy or claim arising out of or relating to this agreement, or the breach thereof, shall be settled by arbitration in accordance with the Rules of the American Arbitration Association and judgment upon the award rendered by the arbitrator(s) may be entered in any court having jurisdiction thereof.

Once an agreement containing such a provision is signed, both parties waive their right to sue in court and agree to submit future disputes to the binding decision of arbitrators.

Hearings can be obtained another way. The parties are free any time to sign a document called a *submission agreement.* Submission agreements are usually prepared after a dispute has arisen and the parties agree it is better to arbitrate, rather than face the expense, time delay, and inconvenience of litigation.

To be valid, the submission agreement must disclose the identity of the parties, the nature of the controversy, and the manner of arbitrator selection. The following is an example:

> We, the undersigned parties, hereto submit to arbitration under the Commercial Arbitration Rules of the American Arbitration Association the following controversy (cite briefly). We further agree that the above controversy be submitted to (one) (three) Arbitrators selected from the

panels of arbitrators of the American Arbitration Association. We further agree that we will faithfully observe this agreement and the Rules and that we will abide by and perform any award.

Both a signed agreement containing an arbitration clause and a submission agreement will bind the parties to the arbitration process in the forty-two states that have enacted modern arbitration statutes, as well as in cases governed by the United States Arbitration Act. A list of the various state arbitration statutes is produced at the end of this chapter.

The following information summarizes the major advantages and disadvantages of arbitration:

Pros

1. *Expense.* Substantial savings are achieved through arbitration. Attorney fees are reduced because the average hearing is shorter than the average trial (i.e., typically less than a day, versus several days). Time-consuming and expensive pre-trial procedures, including depositions, interrogatories, and motions are usually eliminated. And, out-of-pocket expenses are reduced because stenographic fees, transcripts, and other items are not required.

2. *Time.* Arbitration hearings and final awards are obtained quickly; cases are usually decided in a matter of months, compared to several years in formal litigation.

3. *Privacy.* The arbitration hearing is held in a private conference room, rather than a courtroom. Unlike a trial, the hearing cannot be attended by the general public. Thus, unwanted publicity is often avoided.

4. *Expertise of arbitrators.* Arbitrators usually have special training in the area of the case. In a textile dispute, for example, arbitrators serving on the panel are probably respected merchants, lawyers, or other professionals with significant experience in the textile industry. Their knowledge

of trade customs helps them identify and understand a problem quicker than a judge or jury.

5. *Increase the odds of obtaining an award.* Many lawyers believe that arbitrators are more likely than judges to *split close cases down the middle.* The theory is that arbitrators bend over backwards to satisfy both parties to some degree since their rulings are final and binding. This tendency to compromise, if true, *benefits claimants with weaker cases.* In a recent survey conducted by the American Arbitration Association, however, the results indicated that in 56.9 percent of the cases, the arbitrators either awarded the full amount claimed, or denied the claim in its entirety. In only 2.3 percent of the cases did the arbitrators award about half of the amount claimed.

Cons

1. *Finality.* Arbitrators, unlike judges, need not give formal reasons for their decisons. They are not required to maintain a formal record of the proceedings. The arbitrator's decision is binding. This means that an appeal *cannot* be taken if you lose the case or disagree with the size of the award except in a few extraordinary circumstances where arbitrator misconduct, dishonesty, or bias can be proved.

2. *Arbitrator selection.* The parties sometimes agree that each will select his own arbitrator. Here, it is assumed that the selected arbitrators are more sympathetic to one side than the other. However, arbitrators are usually selected from a list of neutral names supplied by the AAA. This method all but eliminates bias.

3. *Loss of sympathetic juries.* Some knowledgeable lawyers believe that juries tend to empathize more with certain kinds of people. Their view is that salespeople, fired employees, automobile accident victims, destitute wives, and older individuals are better off seeking damages before a jury rather than a panel of arbitrators. Arbitrators are usually successful lawyers, professionals, and businesspeople who

are not easily swayed by a talented lawyer's courtroom style. Their philosophical orientation sometimes leans closer toward companies rather than individuals. *Be aware of this.* Conversely, use this to your advantage, if appropriate.

4. *Loss of discovery devices.* Some claimants must rely upon an adversary's documents and records to prove their case. For example, independent sales agents, songwriters, authors, patent holders, and others often depend upon their company's (or licensee's) sales figures and accurate record-keeping to determine how much commission and royalties they are owed. The same is true for minority shareholders who seek a proper assessment of a company's profit picture.

These people may be disadvantaged by the arbitration process. The reason is that lawyers have ample opportunity to view the private books and records of an adversary long before the day of the trial. This is accomplished by pre-trial discovery devices which include interrogatories, depositions, and notices to produce documents for inspection and copying. However, these devices are *not* as readily available to litigants in arbitration. In many instances, records are not viewed until the day of the arbitration hearing. This makes it difficult to detect whether they are accurate and complete. And, it is often up to the arbitrator's discretion whether to grant an *adjournment* for the purposes of reviewing such records. These requests can be refused.

Thus, consider all your particular needs before agreeing to resolve disputes by arbitration. Generally, the process works well to your advantage. However, there may be "landmines," so proceed carefully.

Summary of Steps Leading to the Hearing

Commencing the hearing is a relatively simple matter once arbitration has been selected as the method of resolving a dispute. Either you or your lawyer sends a notice called a

Demand for Arbitration to the adversary. Copies of the Demand are sent to the American Arbitration Association, along with the appropriate administrative fee.

The AAA is most often selected to arbitrate disputes. It is a public service nonprofit organization which offers dispute settlement services to business executives, individual employees, trade associations, unions, management, consumers, farmers, families, communities, and all levels of government. Services are available through the national office in New York City and through twenty-five regional offices in major cities throughout the United States.

The notice briefly describes the controversy. It specifies the kind of relief sought, including the amount of money damages requested.

On the facing page is an example of a Demand for Arbitration.

A reply is then sent by the opposing party, usually within seven days. The reply responds to the charges. It may also allege a *counterclaim for damages*. Either party can add or change claims in writing until the arbitrator is appointed. Once this occurs, changes and additional claims can only be made with an arbitrator's consent.

After the AAA receives the Demand for Arbitration and reply, an AAA administrator usually supplies the parties with a list of potential arbitrators. The list contains the arbitrator's name, current occupation, place of employment, and appropriate background information. On page 294 is an example of the kind of list that is submitted to the parties.

The parties mutually agree to nominees from this list. Potential arbitrators are obligated to notify the AAA immediately of any facts likely to affect their impartiality (e.g., prior dealings with one of the litigants), and disqualify themselves where appropriate.

(NOTE: If the parties do not agree beforehand to the number of arbitrators, the dispute is decided by one arbitrator, unless the AAA determines that three arbitrators is appropriate.)

Once the arbitrator is selected, the AAA administrator schedules a convenient hearing date and location. There is

AMERICAN ARBITRATION ASSOCIATION

COMMERCIAL ARBITRATION RULES
DEMAND FOR ARBITRATION

DATE: November 2, 1984

TO: (Name) _____ ACME IMPORTING COMPANY _____
(of party upon whom the Demand is made)

(Address) _____ 4071 West Street _____

(City and State) Chicago, Illinois _____ (Zip Code) 60601

(Telephone) _____

Named claimant, a party to an arbitration agreement contained in a written contract,

dated _____ November 17, 1983 _____, providing for arbitration, hereby
demands arbitration thereunder.
(attach arbitration clause or quote hereunder)

Any controversy or claim arising out of or relating to this contract, or any breach thereof, shall be settled in accordance with the Rules of the American Arbitration Association, and judgment upon the award may be entered in any court having jurisdiction thereof.

NATURE OF DISPUTE:

Claimant alleges breach of contract on the part of Acme Importing Company in that shipment of 407 bales of jute was not of first grade quality, as required by the contract dated November 17, 1983.

CLAIM OR RELIEF SOUGHT: (amount, if any)

An allowance of $60 per bale is demanded, to a total of $24,420.

TYPE OF BUSINESS:

Claimant _Burlap manufacturer_ Respondent _Importer_

HEARING LOCALE REQUESTED: _____ Chicago, Illinois _____
(City and State)

You are hereby notified that copies of our arbitration agreement and of this demand are being filed with the American Arbitration Association at its __Chicago__ Regional Office, with the request that it commence the administration of the arbitration. Under Section 7 of the Commercial Arbitration Rules, you may file an answering statement within seven days after notice from the Administrator.

Signed __John Jones__ _John Jones_ Title__ President__
(May Be Signed by Attorney)

Name of Claimant__ABC Company__

Home or Business Address of Claimant__Any Place, U.S.A.__

City and State_____ Zip Code _____

Telephone_____

Name of Attorney__Larry Lawyer__

Attorney's Address_____

City and State_____ Zip Code _____

Telephone_____

To institute proceedings, please send three copies of this Demand with the administrative fee, as provided in Section 48 of the Rules, to the AAA. Send original Demand to Respondent.

FORM C2-AAA-3/82

American Arbitration Association

COMMERCIAL ARBITRATION RULES

In the Matter of the Arbitration between

ABC Company

–and–

DEF Company

CASE NUMBER: 000-000-000

LIST SUBMITTED TO THE PARTIES

To: ABC Company

Please indicate by number your order of preference upon this list of proposed Arbitrators. You may strike out names that are not acceptable but please leave as many names as possible.

Frank Jones......................Sales Manager, Acme Duplicating Company.

Morris Smith.....................Attorney; former President, Metropolitan Board of Trade.

James O'Neill....................President, Industrial Products, Inc.

Jonathan Sack....................Senior Partner, Sack & Sack, public accountants; former purchasing agent, Standard Textiles, Inc.

Fred C. Wilkens..................Professor, State School of Business Administration.

Randall Wilson...................Attorney, Board of Trade.

DATED: _____   Signed _____

NOTICE: _____   On behalf of _____

1. This List is returnable to the Tribunal Administrator on or before _____

2. Unless this List is received by the Tribunal Administrator within the time specified, all persons named herein shall be deemed acceptable.

3. If the Parties fail to agree upon any of the names, or if those named decline or are unable to act, or if for any other reason the appointment cannot be made from the submitted List, the Administrator is authorized to make the appointment from other members of the Panels.

FORM C4-AAA

no direct communication between the parties and the arbitrator until the hearing date; all requests, inquiries, etc., are received by the administrator and relayed to the arbitrator. This avoids the appearance of impropriety. The parties are free to request a pre-hearing conference to exchange documents and resolve certain issues. Typically, however, the parties, administrator, lawyers, and arbitrator meet face-to-face for the first time at the actual hearing.

The Hearing

Most hearings are conducted in a conference room at an AAA regional office. A stenographer is present, if requested.
(NOTE: The requesting party bears the cost.)
The arbitrator introduces the parties and usually asks each side to:

1. Briefly summarize its version of the dispute
2. State what each intends to prove at the hearing

The complainant goes first to present his case. Witnesses are called to give testimony (usually under oath). After a witness has finished speaking, he is usually cross-examined by the opposing party's lawyer. He may also be questioned by the arbitrator. The complaining party continues to introduce other witnesses, documents, and affidavits until he has finished presenting his side of the case.

The opposing party then introduces his witnesses, documents, etc., to defend his case and/or prove damages. His witnesses are cross-examined by the opposing party's lawyer and the arbitrator. After he has concluded his case, both sides are usually requested to briefly summarize the facts— i.e., what they felt was proved at the hearing. The arbitrator then concludes the hearing.

(NOTE: Sometimes the arbitrator may request that legal briefs be submitted which summarize the respective position of the parties, before rendering a final decision.)

Arbitrators are generally required to render written decisions within thirty days, unless the parties agree to some other time period. When there is more than one arbitrator, a majority decision is required. The arbitrator can make any award that is equitable. He can order the losing party to pay additional costs, including AAA filing fees, and arbitrator fees.

(NOTE: For disputes under $20,000, it costs about $200 to commence a hearing; the figure increases proportionally with the amount at stake, e.g., $1,000 for disputes up to $40,000 and $1,400 for disputes up to $80,000.) Legal fees may be awarded if the arbitration clause so provides.

Arbitrators volunteer their time for hearings lasting under two full days; they are paid a reasonable per diem rate for additional hearings. If the parties settle their dispute prior to a decision, the parties may request that the terms of the settlement be embodied in a consent award.

Arbitrators have no contact with the parties after the hearing has concluded. The parties are notified in writing by the AAA administrator, and are sent a copy of the award. The decision in a typical commercial case is brief—usually no formal reasons are given to explain why a particular award was rendered or the basis on which damages were calculated. The following illustrates how a typical award is reported:

AMERICAN ARBITRATION ASSOCIATION, Administrator
  Commercial Arbitration Tribunal

In the Matter of the Arbitration between   *
*
SMITH SUPPLY COMPANY   *
*
AND   *   AWARD OF
*   ARBITRATOR
DOE CORPORATION, INC.   *
*
CASE NUMBER: 1310-9966-82   *

I, THE UNDERSIGNED ARBITRATOR, having been designated in accordance with the Arbitration Agreement entered into by the above named Parties, and dated May 1, 1980, and having been duly sworn and having duly heard the proofs and allegations of the Parties, AWARD, as follows:

1. Within ten (10) days of the date of this Award, DOE CORPORATION, INC., hereinafter referred to as DOE, shall pay to SMITH SUPPLY COMPANY, the sum of FIFTEEN THOUSAND ONE HUNDRED EIGHTY TWO DOLLARS AND TWENTY CENTS ($15,182.20), plus interest in the amount of ONE THOUSAND THREE HUNDRED DOLLARS ($1,300), for goods sold and delivered.

2. The counterclaim of DOE against SMITH is hereby denied in its entirety.

3. The administrative fees of the American Arbitration Association totaling FOUR HUNDRED DOLLARS ($400) shall be borne entirely by DOE. Therefore, DOE shall pay to SMITH the sum of TWO HUNDRED DOLLARS ($200) representing that portion of the fees previously advanced by SMITH to said Association.

4. This AWARD is in full settlement of all claims and counterclaims submitted in this arbitration.

Signature of Arbitrator

It is practically impossible to appeal a losing case. The arbitrator has no power once the case is decided. The matter can only be reviewed by a judge, and judges cannot overturn the award on the grounds of insufficient evidence. The only ways a case can be overturned on review are:

1. For arbitrator dishonesty, partiality, or bias
2. When no valid agreement was entered which authorized the arbitration process
3. When issue was ruled upon which the arbitrator was not authorized to decide

In addition, awards are modifiable only if there was a miscalculation of figures, or a mistake in the description of the person, property, or thing referred to in the award.

How to Increase Your Chances of Success in Arbitration

Since the arbitrator's award is final and binding, it is essential to prepare and present your case properly the first time, *because you won't get a second chance.* The following strategies will help you increase your chances of success:

1. *Hire a lawyer.* You have the right to appear yourself (pro se), but it's best to have a lawyer represent you at the hearing, particularly if the dispute involves a large amount of money or complicated legal question. The familiar expression, "He who represents himself has a fool for a client," is certainly applicable in arbitration.

Always seek the services of an experienced lawyer who is familiar with the intricacies of the arbitration process. This can be discovered by asking the lawyer how many times he has represented clients in arbitration within the past several years. If the answer is "never" or "only a few times," look elsewhere for representation.

2. *Prepare for the hearing.* It is important that both you and your lawyer carefully prepare for the hearing. Your goal is to submit evidence that will prove your case. The following material may help you effectuate this. Some of the strategies were written by Robert Coulson, President of the American Arbitration Association, in his book, *Business Arbitration: What You Need to Know.*

    a. *Organize the facts.* Gather and label all documents you will need at the hearing. This should be done so you will be able to produce your evidence in an orderly fashion when presenting your case. Prepare a checklist of your documents and exhibits for this purpose.

Make copies for the arbitrators and your adversary. If some of the documents you need are in the possession of the other party, ask that they be brought to the hearing. Under some state arbitration laws, the arbitrator or an attorney of record has the authority to subpoena documents and records. Be aware of this.

b. *Interview witnesses.* You will have plenty of time to prepare for the hearing—use the time wisely. Interview all of your witnesses. Be sure that friendly witnesses, if any, will attend and testify on your behalf. If there is the possibility that additional witnesses may have to appear, alert them to be available on call without delay.

Be sure the witnesses understand the case and the importance of their testimony. Select witnesses who you think are believable, and who will not say things at the hearing that will surprise you. Coordinate the witnesses' testimony so that your case will seem consistent and credible. Prepare them for the rigors of cross-examination. If one of your witnesses requires a translator, make arrangements in advance.

You may also wish to prepare a written summary of what each witness will hopefully prove and can refer to it at the hearing.

c. *Consider your opponent's case.* Never overlook your opponent's case; study the controversy from his point of view. Anticipate what your opponent will say to defeat your claim. Be prepared to refute his evidence.

d. *Make appropriate arrangements.* For example, if it is necessary for the arbitrator to visit a building for an inspection, plan this in advance. The arbitrator must be accompanied by representatives of both sides unless the parties permit the arbitrator to conduct the investigation without them.

e. *Practice your story.* Practicing what you will say will put you at ease and help you organize important facts. You also should prepare a list of questions you want your lawyer to ask your opponent at the hearing.

f. *Dress appropriately.* Men and women should wear conservative business attire at the hearing.

g. *Act professional.* Show your respect for the arbitrators. Listen to their questions and instructions. Never argue with them. If an arbitrator asks you a question while you are speaking, stop talking immediately. Answer his question honestly and to the point. Try to be diplomatic, rather than emotional. Avoid arguing with your opponent at the hearing. Interrupt his presentation only where absolutely necessary.

What to Do after Obtaining a Judgment

Most losing parties voluntarily comply with the terms of an unfavorable award. However, if you obtain a judgment and your opponent decides not to pay, you can enforce the judgment in a regular court. This is usually done by your lawyer.

A Word about Mediation

Mediation is an alternative to arbitration and formal litigation. It is a voluntary dispute resolution process whereby a neutral third party tries to help contesting parties settle their differences.

The use of mediation and court-related counseling services is increasing, particularly in matrimonial disputes. A growing number of separating spouses, legal, and mental health professionals believe the process works better than a traditional adversarial divorce. In an atmosphere of cooperation (rather than confrontation), couples try to negotiate a satisfactory settlement with the assistance of a trained mediator.

Mediation is cheap. The typical cost is under $1,500 versus $3,000–$30,000 for a contested divorce. However, it differs from arbitration and litigation in one significant respect: *the mediator's decision is not final and binding.* Thus, the parties are free to stop mediation at any time and litigate the dispute if they choose. This frequently happens where one of the parties is not pleased with the progress.

If you are interested in learning more about mediation or desire to use this process to resolve a problem, contact your local bar association or nearest American Arbitration Association regional office for further details. The following is a list of AAA regional offices:

AMERICAN ARBITRATION ASSOCIATION
REGIONAL OFFICES

ATLANTA (30303) • **India Johnson**
100 Peachtree Street, N.W. • (404) 688-4151

BOSTON (02114) • **Richard M. Reilly**
60 Staniford Street • (617) 367-6800

CHARLOTTE (28218) • **Mark E. Sholander**
P.O. Box 18591, 3717 Latrobe Drive • (704) 366-4546

CHICAGO (60606) • **LaVerne Rollé**
205 West Wacker Drive • (312) 346-2282

CINCINNATI (45202) • **Phillip S. Thompson**
2308 Carew Tower • (513) 241-8434

CLEVELAND (44115) • **Earle C. Brown**
1127 Euclid Avenue • (216) 241-4741

DALLAS (75201) • **Helmut O. Wolff**
1607 Main Street • (214) 748-4979

DENVER (80203) • **Mark Appel**
789 Sherman Street • (303) 831-0823

DETROIT (48226) • Mary A. Bedikian
615 Griswold Street • (313) 964-2525

GARDEN CITY, N.Y. (11530) • Mark A. Resnick
585 Stewart Avenue • (516) 222-1660

HARTFORD (06106) • Karen M. Barrington
2 Hartford Square West • (203) 278-5000

LOS ANGELES (90020) • Jerrold L. Murase
443 Shatto Place (213) 383-6516

MIAMI (33129) • René Grafals
2250 S.W. 3rd Avenue • (305) 854-1616

MINNEAPOLIS (55402) • James R. Deye
510 Foshay Tower • (612) 332-6545

NEW JERSEY (SOMMERSET 08873) • Richard Naimark
1 Executive Drive • (201) 560-9560

NEW YORK (10020) • George H. Friedman
140 West 51st Street • (212) 484-4150

PHILADELPHIA (19102) • Arthur R. Mehr
1520 Locust Street • (215) 732-5260

PHOENIX (85012) • Deborah A. Krell
77 East Columbus, #201 • (602) 234-0950

PITTSBURGH (15222) • John F. Schano
221 Gateway Four • (412) 261-3617

SAN DIEGO (92101) • Shelagh Hurley
530 Broadway • (714) 239-3051

SAN FRANCISCO (94108) • Charles A. Cooper
445 Bush Street • (415) 981-3901

SEATTLE (98104) • Neal M. Blacker
811 First Avenue • (206) 622-6435

SYRACUSE (13202) • Deborah A. Brown
720 State Tower Building • (315) 472-5483

WASHINGTON, D.C. (20036) • Garylee Cox
1730 Rhode Island Avenue, N.W. • (202) 296-8510

WHITE PLAINS, N.Y. (10601) • Marion J. Zinman
34 South Broadway • (914) 946-1119

NATIONAL HEADQUARTERS
American Arbitration Association
New York (10020) · 140 West 51st Street (212) 848-4000

United States Arbitration Act, 9 U.S.C.A. §1 et seq.

Alaska Stat. §09.43.010 et seq.* (4).

Ariz. Rev. Stat. §12-1501 et seq.* (4).

Ark. Stat. Ann. §34-511 et seq.* (2, 4, 7).

Cal. Code Civ. Proc. §1280 et seq.

Colo. Rev. Stat. §13-22-201 et seq.*

Conn. Gen. Stat. Ann. §52-408 et seq.

Del. Code Ann. Title 10, §5701 et seq.* (4).

D.C. Law 1-117.*

Fla. Stat. Ann. §682.01 et seq.

Ga. Code Ann. §7-301 et seq.

Haw. Rev. Stat. §658-1 et seq.

Idaho Code §7-901 et seq.* (4).

Ill. Rev. Stat. Chap. 10, §101 et seq.*

Ind. Code Ann. §34-4-2-1 et seq. * (3, 5, 6).

Iowa Acts, Chap. 202* (4).

Kan. Stat. §5-401 et seq.* (2, 4, 7).

La. Rev. Stat. §9:4201 et seq.* (4).

Me. Rev. Stat. Ann. Title 14, §5927 et seq.* (8).

Md. Cts. & Jud. Proc. Code Ann. §3–201 et seq.* (4).

Mass. Ann. Laws Chap. 251, §1 et seq.* (4).

Mich. Comp. Laws §600.5001 et seq.

Minn. Stat. Ann §572.08 et seq.*

Miss. Laws, Chap. 495.

Mo. Ann. Stat. §435.350 et seq.* (2).

Nev. Rev. Stat. §38.015 et seq.*

N.H. Rev. Stat. Ann. §542:1 et seq.

N.J. Stat. Ann. §2A:24-1 et seq.

N.M. Stat. Ann. §22-3-9 et seq.*

N.Y. Civ. Prac. Law §7501 et seq.

N.C. Gen. Stat. §1-567.1 et seq.* (4).

Ohio Rev. Code Ann. §2711.01 et seq.

Okla. Stat. Ann. Title 15, §801 et seq.* (2, 4).

Or. Rev. Stat. §33.210 et seq.

Pa. Stat. Ann. Title 42, Chap. 73 §7301-7320.*

R.I. Gen. Laws §10-3-1 et seq.

S.C. Code §15-48-10 et seq.* (2, 4, 7, 9).

S.D. Codified Laws §21-25A-1 et seq.* (2).

Tex. Rev. Civ. Stat. Ann. Title 10, Art. 224 et seq.* (1, 2, 4).

Utah Code Ann. §78-31-1 et seq.

Va. Code Ann. §8.01-577 et seq.

Wash. Rev. Code Ann §7.04.010 et seq.

Wis. Stat. Ann. §298.01 et seq.

Wyo. Stat. §1-36-101 et seq.*

See also, Laws of Puerto Rico Ann. Title 32, §3201 et seq.

---

1) Modern statutes are those enforcing agreements to arbitrate existing controversies and any arising in the future. Other state arbitration statutes (for example, Alabama) apply to existing controversies only. (Code of Alabama, Chap. 19.)
* Referred to as Uniform Arbitration Act. Numbers following the asterisk indicate statute exclusions as to: (1) Construction, (2) Insurance, (3) Leases, (4) Labor Contracts, (5) Loans, (6) Sales, (7) Torts, (8) Uninsured Motorists, (9) Doctors, Lawyers.

9

Avoiding
Collection Agency
Harassment

* **Introduction** 305
* **When Does the Law Apply?** 307
* **What Collectors Cannot Do** 308
* **Collection Agency Efforts to Find You** 309
* **What to Do when You Are Contacted** 310
* **Getting the Collection Agency off of Your Back** 312
* **How to Remedy Abuses** 313
* **Summary of Steps to Limit Collection Abuse** 315

Introduction

Retail establishments employ various tactics to collect arrears from people who buy on credit and cannot pay. The method used depends on the store's size and business policy. Usually, a store will first attempt to collect the debt either directly or through an attorney. Many stores, however, utilize the services of collection agencies. The majority of personal abuses occur in the collection efforts of these organizations.

Abuses arise in a variety of ways. Persistent, collect telephone calls are received at home during inconvenient hours. Threatening letters and telegrams, including phony legal subpoenas, are sent. Collectors frequently pretend that they are collection reporting services, as well as collection agencies, and say that they can list unpaid accounts with various merchant credit retail associations. Thus, people are unfairly led to believe that their credit rating will be seriously affected unless the bill is promptly paid. Also, some agencies illegally tack on collection charges to the debt.

Although the majority of collection agencies stay within bounds of the law by following acceptable collection practices, consumers are constantly subjected to a variety of harassing forms of conduct. According to a recent Federal Trade Commission Report to Congress, the debt collection area continues to be a principle source of consumer complaints. The problem stems from the fact that there are more than 5,000 debt collection firms in the United States. Entry into this market is relatively easy, with minimal licensing restrictions in most states. According to the report, the use of WATS lines makes it possible for a small firm to have nationwide impact. Computerized mailing and billing systems also make it possible for a small firm to contact large numbers of consumers.

Actual cases reveal how low collectors sometimes stoop. One man from Michigan was threatened by a collector that his house would be bombed if he did not pay his debt. A woman in Atlanta, Georgia, was told to perform sexual favors. In another reported case, the mother of a debtor received a telephone call at her Conventry, Rhode Island, home from a collector who identified herself as a hospital employee. The woman was informed that her grandchildren had been involved in a serious automobile accident. This was done merely to obtain her son's home address and telephone number!

For years, people endured these and similar practices, and in the vast majority of instances were unable to obtain relief. Until recently, harassed people were forced to sue collection agencies using various common law tort theories including defamation (harm to one's reputation), intentional infliction of emotional distress, and invasion of privacy. These suits were often quite expensive, damages were hard to prove, and consumers experienced only minimal degrees of success.

However, Congress has expanded the rights of consumers by creating the 1978 Fair Debt Collection Practices Act. This law now enables you to sue debt collectors who employ false representations, unfair practices, and abuse while trying to enforce a debt. *Most people are unaware of this law.* Now, any collection agency that fails to comply with the Act's provisions is liable for actual damages, statutory damages up to $1,000, and attorney fee costs. No longer are you dependent upon state or federal prosecution or proving your case under the common law to obtain a remedy.

Though not perfect, the law is a substantial step in the right direction. Collection agencies are forbidden from calling you at home repeatedly, or sending you threatening letters. Nor are they allowed to continuously contact your neighbors, relatives, and employers.

The following material will tell you how to protect yourself if you have trouble paying for the products you purchase. You will learn what collection agency acts are improper, how to stop harassment, and how to limit further contact with the debt collector. For example, you will know what to do when:

- You are having company at your house on Sunday and a collection agency employee knocks on your door
- Your boss summons you into his office to inform you that you are living beyond your means
- A neighbor calls you to tell you that a collection agency has been trying to get in touch

(NOTE: The term "debtor" refers to a person who has purchased a product and is now unable or unwilling to pay for it. The term "creditor" denotes the person, store, establishment or business from whom the purchase was made.)

When Does the Law Apply?

The law protects you against abusive practices of private collection agencies, i.e., professional collectors in the business of collecting debts for others (banks and companies who service mortgage loans are included). It does *not* apply to attorneys, federal employees, and in-house collectors. However, there are several exceptions. For example, if you buy a television set from Bad Bernie's (BB) Appliance Store on credit, and BB has its own credit department to collect payments, that department is an in-house collector and cannot be sued under the Fair Debt Collection Practices Act. However, BB *can* be sued if:

1. BB's credit department collects money for BB's Appliance Store under a different name
2. BB employees mail collection letters on the personal stationary of an attorney who plays only a small role in the collection process

3. BB's Appliance Store purchases notices from a collection agency and sends out the letters on the agency's letterhead, even though the letter states that all payments are to be sent directly to BB's

What Collectors Cannot Do

Debt collectors cannot speak obscene language or publish "shame" lists of people who allegedly refuse to pay their debts. Collectors cannot misrepresent themselves as attorneys and/or say that they are associated with a government or law enforcement agency. Nor can they threaten to use force to harm you, your property, or your reputation. For example, letters stating "It may be necessary for our agent to call on you personally" or "A copy of this letter is being sent to an attorney, instructing him to bring you in for an oral examination and attach your personal property" are forbidden. Additionally, threats of arrest or wage garnishment for nonpayment (when not allowed by local law), or threats to take legal action which collectors never intend to pursue, gives you a legal basis to sue.

A favorite collection tactic that agencies often use is to send ornamented collection letters with official-looking seals. These convey the impression that they are legal documents issued by a court. A popular version states "The Within Named Creditor under State Statutes and Provisions hereby makes final demand for nonpayment of indebtedness." Letters of this sort and those which pretend to offer legal advice (for example, by stating "In our judgment") are not allowed. So, too, are notices which demand the debtor to appear at collection agency offices.

Collectors sometimes charge telegram fees and reverse telephone charges by calling collect before revealing the purpose of the communication. The new law protects people from these unfair practices. In addition, late charges, interest, collection fees, and expenses cannot be added to the amount of money owed unless this is permitted under state law and you originally agreed *in writing* to such an arrangement before a purchase was made.

The law also restricts the frequency and time of day when a person can be contacted. No communication to you or your family is allowed before 8:00 A.M. or after 9:00 P.M. A debtor cannot be called at work if the collector is told that the employer forbids personal phone calls. Letters can no longer be sent to an employer asking him to discuss the debt with you. In addition, once a lawyer is hired, contact can only be made through the lawyer, unless he allows the collection agency to communicate with you.

Collection Agency Efforts to Find You

Collection agencies may ask third persons where debtors can be located, provided that the information sought includes only a home address, telephone number, or business address. Relatives and neighbors have been the target of ingenious ploys to obtain this information. Prizes, gifts, and rewards have been offered but never given. Such practices are now illegal. Although communications can be made by mail, telephone, or personal visits, a debt collector must:

1. Always identify himself and say that he is seeking to acquire or confirm location information. He must give the true name of his collection agency upon request

2. Contact the party only once unless the information which he received is incorrect, or he is given permission to call back for more complete information

3. *Never state that he works for a collection agency, or that he is making this communication because a debt is owed*

These rules are quite strict. The Federal Trade Commission, whose responsibilities include enforcing the Fair Debt Collection Practices Act, forbids the suggestion of collection conveyed to the public through the mail. For example, the mere use of language on a postcard or letter indicating debt collection, such as the name General Credit Control, Inc., on the return address, or on the back of an envelope, violates the law. This ensures that the debtor's relatives and neighbors do not learn of his financial condition.

The same rules also apply to communications with an employer. Collectors can only contact employers *once* to obtain location information. Collectors cannot reveal directly or by implication that a debt is owed. This is to ensure that harassment will not take place, and that your privacy will not be invaded.

What to Do When You Are Contacted

Many people are willing to pay their debts, but need additional time to do so. The new law solves this problem for you. Once you are contacted by a collection agency, you should request verification of the debt. The agency is then required to convey information which includes the amount of the debt, the name, and the address of the original creditor. After this is received, you then have the right to dispute the debt. If a dispute is made, *all collection agency activity must stop* until:

1. The agency contacts the creditor to determine if the debt is correct

2. The agency then sends written notification about the debt to you

(STRATEGY: If you are a debtor who needs more time to ready your finances, and the collection agency threatens to sue unless payment is made immediately, send a letter by certified mail to the agency requesting written verification of the disputed debt. This will effectively stall agency action for some time.) The following is an example of what the letter should say:

(Name)
(Address)
(Date)

Mr. Charles Smith
(Title)
ABC Collection Agency
(Address)

Re: Request for Written Verification of My Disputed
Debt with (Name of Creditor)

Dear Mr. Smith:

On (date), you contacted me by (letter, phone, telegram, in person) concerning a purported debt I owe to (name of creditor).

I do not own such a debt because (billing error, purchase returned, purchased damaged, purchase unsatisfactory).

I shall be contacting (name of creditor) in an effort to resolve this matter. However, in the meantime, pursuant to the Fair Debt Collection Practices Act, I demand that you:

1. Verify the amount of the alleged debt with (name of creditor)
2. Send me a copy of the written verification
3. Stop all collection efforts until I receive a copy of this written verification

Be aware that I will assert all remedies under the law, including filing a complaint with the Federal Trade Commission, in the event that my requests are not honored.

Thank you for your cooperation in this matter.

Very truly yours,

cc: (Name of creditor)

(Send certified mail, return receipt requested.)

Getting the Collection Agency off of Your Back

One of the most important features of the Fair Debt Collection Practices Act is that it protects your right to be left alone. Even if you legitimately owe a debt, you can notify the agency in writing to stop all further contact and *this request must be honored.*

This is your right, and it can be exercised before or after you send a letter by certified mail to the agency requesting written verification of the debt.

For example,

> Judith owes $130 to Bob's Department Store. She refuses to pay the bill (e.g., she is dissatisfied with the item she purchased, and the store refuses to refund it, there has been a billing mistake, or she is broke). The store retains DEF Credit Corporation to collect the debt. Judith receives a collection letter from DEF Credit Corporation. She sends a letter by certified mail, requesting written verification of the debt. She is sent the necessary information. Now she sends a letter similar to the following, forbidding DEF Credit Corporation from contacting her again:

(Name)
(Address)
(Date)

Mr. Robert Scott
(Title)
DEF Credit Corporation
(Address)

Re: Demand to Stop All Collection Efforts

Dear Mr. Scott:

I hereby demand you to stop contacting me regarding my alleged debt with (name of creditor).

You realize that under the Federal Fair Debt Collection Practices Act, your failure to comply with this request will subject you to statutory damages and other sanctions that may be imposed by the Federal Trade Commission.

Thank you for your cooperation in this matter.

Very truly yours,

cc: (Name of creditor—Bob's Department Store)
(Send certified mail, return receipt requested.)

Now the agency can no longer contact Judith, except by letter stating:

1. That all collection efforts are being stopped
2. That specific legal action to recover the debt has been started

It is that simple. DEF's Credit Corporation's only alternative may be litigation. However, commentators have suggested that as a result of the law, persons with small debts such as Judith, who forbid collection agencies from contacting them, will have their debts "wiped out" since the amount of money owed will not justify the time and expense of a lawsuit.

How to Remedy Abuses

Although creditors have the right to receive payment for the goods and services they furnish, this should always be done in a courteous and polite manner. Outrageous means of collection should never be used. If so, you must fight back.

Now that you are aware of illegal practices, several strategies are available to you. First, you must remember that although the new law provides a means of recourse, all abuses must be proved in court. Thus, save all letters, telegrams, and other written documents. Sworn affidavits from friends, neighbors, and employers should be collected. If you are unable to sleep, or suffer a physical ailment (such as nausea or weight loss) as a result of harassment, document all doctor visits, medical reports, bills, and prescription purchases. Some people even tape abusive phone conversations in order to obtain documented proof of wrongful acts.

(NOTE: If you wish to do this, consult a lawyer.)

Speak to a lawyer after collecting your information. The lawyer will decide whether to sue the collection agency under state law, the Fair Debt Collection Practices Act, or contact the Federal Trade Commission. If suit is brought under the Fair Debt Collection Act, it must be filed within one year. Thus, it is important to contact a lawyer immediately after the incident(s).

If you prove your case, the court will order the collection agency to reimburse you for legal fees and court costs. Be aware that a court may award money for mental anguish caused by repetitious phone calls placed during early morning hours. You can also recover money spent for medical treatment, as well as lost wages, provided the collector's calls caused this condition. Punitive damages for vindictive behavior may also be awarded.

The law in your state should be consulted to determine whether the state imposes stronger penalties than federal law. If so, a lawsuit should be commenced in state court.

There is another alternative. A violation of the Fair Debt Collection Practices Act is considered an unfair and deceptive act. Thus, contact the Federal Trade Commission if you believe you are the victim of harassment. The FTC can impose a variety of sanctions on a collection agency. These include the return of money or property, fines, and a public announcement of wrongdoing. Recently, the Commission entered into a consent judgment with a large collection agency accused of telephone harassment, illegal third party contacts, and false threats of civil and criminal process. The agency agreed to pay $90,000 in civil penalties and equitable relief. Another $65,000 penalty was obtained from a firm that overcharged debtors (The money was used to refund these overcharges). Thus, contact the FTC where appropriate.

**Summary of Steps to
Limit Collection Abuse**

The following suggestion will prove helpful in preventing collection agency abuses.

NEVER:

1. Disclose an unlisted telephone number on a credit application

2. Sign retail establishment contracts which authorize additional charges, and which permit collectors to contact whomever they wish about the debt

3. Accept collect calls from collection agencies

4. Volunteer personal information about your finances

5. Sign postdated checks to demonstrate good faith, no matter what the collector promises. Collectors often deposit these checks prematurely and sue you for fraud and/or conversion when they bounce

6. Be intimidated when collectors state that you risk losing your "credit name" if a debt remains unpaid. Most collectors are *not* associated with credit reporting bureaus, and those who are must furnish truthful information—for example, that an unpaid debt is disputed

ALWAYS:

1. Assert your rights. Inform the collector in writing that your debt will be disputed, that you wish written verification of the debt, or that all further contact must stop immediately

2. Send all correspondence by registered or certified mail; this will insure that the collector receives your letters and you will have proof

3. Contact the Federal Trade Commission, the Attorney General's Office, or a local Consumer Protection Agency for advice if you are being harassed

4. Inquire whether interest and collection charges have illegally been added to the principal debt

5. Instruct collectors not to call at work since your employer forbids personal phone calls

6. Instruct the collector to apply payment to a *specific* debt if more than one debt is owed

7. Attempt to resolve debts since some judges may not award damages for abusive conduct if a person fails to take positive steps toward settlement

In the event that you wish to register a complaint with the Federal Trade Commission regarding an unfair collection agency practice, the following letter will be helpful:

(Name)
(Address)
(Date)

Director
Regional Office
Federal Trade Commission
(Address)

Re: Violation by (Name of Agency) of the Fair Debt Collection Practices Act

Dear (Name of Director):

I am writing to you regarding the unfair practices of (name of agency) located at (address).

On (name, dates) I was harassed by said agency (explain how). This arose out of a disputed debt with (name of creditor).

I (state what you told the agency, who you spoke with, and why your requests have not been honored).

I enclose copies of correspondence with (name of agency). I would appreciate it if you would look into this matter for the purpose of eliminating such outrageous conduct for myself and other debtors.

I am available to assist you at your convenience. Kindly notify me of all developments in this matter.

Thank you for your cooperation.

Very truly yours,

cc: Copies sent certified mail, return receipt requested to collection agency and home of creditor

Glossary

You can reduce the chances of being exploited in your personal business dealings by understanding the meaning of the words in this glossary. In addition, you will be able to communicate better with your lawyer because these terms are commonly used in legal proceedings.

Abuse of process   A cause of action which arises when one party willfully misuses the legal process to injure another

Accord and satisfaction   An agreement between two parties to settle a dispute by compromise

Action in accounting   A type of lawsuit where one party seeks a determination of the amount of money owed by another

Admissable   Capable of being introduced in court as evidence

Advance   A sum of money which is usually applied against money to be earned; sometimes referred to as "draw"

Affidavit   A written statement signed under oath

Allegations   Charges one party expects to prove in a lawsuit

Answer   The defendant's reply to the plaintiff's charges in a civil lawsuit

Appeal   A proceeding whereby the losing party in a lawsuit applies to a higher court to determine the correctness of that decision

Arbitration   A proceeding where both sides submit their dispute to the binding decision of arbitrators rather than judges

Assault and battery   A harmful, offensive, unpermitted touching of one person by another

Assignment   The transfer of a right or interest by one party to another

Attorney in fact   A person appointed by another to transact business on his behalf; the person does not have to be a lawyer

Award   A decision made by a judicial body to compensate the winning party for losses or injuries caused by another

Bail bondsman   A person who posts money for a fee to spring an incarcerated individual

Bailment   A legal relationship created when one person delivers property to another

Bill of particulars   A document used in a lawsuit which adds information contained in the plaintiff's complaint

Bonus   A sum of money paid by an employer to an employee

Breach of contract   The unjustified failure of a party to perform a duty or obligation specified in a contract

Breach of warranty   A legal cause of action often arising when a seller makes false representations regarding his product or service

Burden of proof   The responsibility for a party in a lawsuit to provide sufficient evidence to prove its claims

Business deduction   A legitimate expense which can be used to decrease the amount of reportable income subject to tax

Business slander   A legal wrong committed when a party orally makes false statements which impune the business reputation of another (e.g., imply that the person is dishonest, incompetent, or financially unreliable)

Calendar   A list of cases to be heard each day in court

Cause of action   Legal theories which the plaintiff alleges in a complaint to recover damages from his opponent

Caveat emptor   A Latin expression frequently applied to consumer transactions; translated as "Let the buyer beware"

Certificate of incorporation   A document creating a corporation

Check   A negotiable instrument; the depositor's written order requesting his bank to pay a definite sum of money to a named individual or business

Civil court   Generally, any court which presides over non-criminal matters

Claims court   A particular court which hears tax disputes

Clerk of the court A person who determines whether court papers are properly filed and court procedures followed

Common carrier An entity which transports persons and property for a fee

Common law Law which evolves from reported case decisions which are relied upon for their precedential value

Compensatory damages A sum of money awarded to a party by a court or jury representing the actual harm or loss suffered

Complaint A legal document which starts a lawsuit; the complaint alleges facts and causes of action which the plaintiff relies upon to collect damages

Computer consultant A person hired to match his client's needs with appropriate computer hardware and software equipment

Conflict of interest The ethical inability of a lawyer to represent a client because of competing loyalties

Consideration An essential element of an enforceable contract; something of value given or promised by one party in exchange for an act or promise of another

Contempt A legal sanction imposed when a rule or order of a judicial body is disobeyed

Contingency fee A type of fee arrangement where the lawyer is paid a percentage of the money recovered

Continuance The postponement of a legal proceeding to another date

Contract An enforceable agreement, either in writing, oral, or implied

Contract modification The alteration of contract terms

Counterclaim A claim asserted by the defendant in a lawsuit

Covenant A promise

Credibility The believability of a witness in the minds of a judge or jury

Creditor The party to whom money is owed

Cross-examination The questioning of a witness by the opposing lawyer

Damages An award, usually money, given to the winning party in a lawsuit as compensation for the wrongful acts of another

Debtor The party who owes money

Decision   The determination of a case or matter by a judicial body

Deductible premium   The unrecoverable portion of insurance proceeds

Defamation   An oral or written statement communicated to a third party which impunes a person's reputation in the community

Default judgment   An award rendered after one party fails to appear in a lawsuit

Defendant   The person or business who is sued in a lawsuit

Defense   The defendant's justification for relieving him of fault

Definite term of employment   Employment for a fixed period of time

Deposition   A pre-trial proceeding where one party is questioned, usually under oath, by the opposing party's lawyer

Disclaimer   A clause in a sales, service, or other contract which attempts to limit or exonerate one party from liability in the event of a lawsuit

Discovery   A general term used to describe several pre-trial devices (e.g., depositions, interrogatories, etc.), which enable lawyers to elicit information from the opposing side

District Court   A particular court that hears tax disputes

Dual capacity   A legal theory used to circumvent Workers' Compensation laws and allow an injured employee to sue his employer directly in court

Due process   Constitutional protections which guarantee that a person's life, liberty, or property cannot be taken away without the opportunity to be heard in a judicial proceeding

Duress   Unlawful threats, pressure, or force which induce a person to act contrary to his intentions; duress, if proved, will allow a party to disavow a contract

Employee   A person who works and is subject to an employer's scope, direction, and control

Employment at will   Employment which does not provide an employee with job security, since the person can be fired on a moment's notice with or without cause

Employment discrimination   Conduct directed at employees and job applicants that is prohibited by law

Equity   Fairness; the term is usually applied when a judicial body awards a suitable remedy other than money to a party (e.g., an injunction)

Escrow account   A separate fund where lawyers are obligated to deposit money received from or on behalf of a client

Evidence   Information in the form of oral testimony, exhibits, affidavits, etc., used to prove a party's claim

Examination before trial   A pre-trial legal device; also called a deposition

Exempt from execution   Property or assets which cannot be seized to satisfy a judgment

Exhibits   Tangible evidence used to prove a party's claims

Exit agreements   Agreements sometimes signed between employers and employees upon termination or resignation of an employee's services

False arrest   The unlawful detention of one person by another who claims to have sufficient legal authority

False imprisonment   The unlawful detention of a person who is held against his will without authority or justification

Field examination   An audit conducted by IRS agents at a taxpayer's home or business

Filing fee   Money paid to start a lawsuit

Financial statement   A document usually prepared by an accountant which reflects a business's assets, liabilities, and financial condition

Flat fee   A sum of money paid to a lawyer as compensation for his services

Flat fee plus time   A form of payment where a lawyer receives one sum for his services, and then receives additional money which is calculated on an hourly basis

Fraud   False statements of an existing fact relied upon and causing damages to the defrauded party

General denial   A reply contained in the defendant's answer

Guaranty   A contract where one party agrees to answer for or satisfy the debt of another

Hardware   A computer unit

Hearsay evidence   Unsubstantiated evidence which is often excluded by a court

Hourly fee   Money paid to a lawyer for his services which is computed on an hourly basis

Independent contractor   A worker not subject to an employer's scope, direction, and control, and who pays his own social security, withholding tax, and unemployment insurance

Infliction of emotional distress   A legal cause of action where one party seeks to recover damages for mental pain and suffering caused by another

Injunction   A court order restraining one party from doing or refusing to do an act

Interrogatories   A pre-trial device used to elicit information; written questions are sent to an opponent to be answered under oath

Invasion of privacy   The violation of a person's constitutionally protected right to privacy

Judgment   A verdict rendered by a judicial body; if money is awarded, the winning party is called the judgment creditor, and the losing party is called the judgment debtor

Jurisdiction   The authority of a court to hear a particular matter

Legal duty   The responsibility of a party to perform a certain act

Letter agreement   An enforceable contract in the form of a letter

Letter of protest   A letter sent to document a party's dissatisfaction

Liable   Legally in the wrong

Lien   A claim asserted against another party's property to satisfy a judgment

Lifetime contract   An employment agreement of an infinite duration which is often unenforceable

Limited partnership   A type of partnership with general partners and limited partners. Limited partners are only liable to the extent of money invested in the partnership

Liquidated damages   An amount of money agreed upon in advance by parties to a contract to be paid in the event of a breach or dispute

Malicious interference with contract rights   A legal cause of action where one party seeks to recover damages against another who induces or causes a party to terminate a valid contract

Malicious prosecution   A legal cause of action where one party seeks to recover damages after another party instigates or institutes a phony judicial proceeding (usually criminal) which is dismissed

Malpractice   The failure of a professional to render work, labor, services, or skill of suitable competence

Mediation   A voluntary dispute resolution process where both sides attempt to settle their differences without resorting to formal litigation

Medical malpractice   A legal cause of action where one party seeks to recover damages against a doctor for his failure to render services or skill of suitable competence

Misappropriation   The unlawful taking of another party's personal property

Misrepresentation   A legal cause of action which arises when one party makes untrue statements of fact which induce another party to act and be damaged as a result

Mitigation of damages   A legal principle which requires a party seeking damages to make reasonable efforts to reduce damages as much as possible; for example, to seek new employment after being unfairly discharged

Motion   A written request made to a court by one party during a lawsuit

Negligence   A party's failure to exercise sufficient degree of care owed to another by law

No-fault insurance   A system of compensation whereby a victim injured in an auto accident is paid regardless of fault

Nominal damages   A small sum of money awarded by a court

Noncompetition clause   A restrictive provision in a contract

Notary public   A person authorized under state law to administer an oath or verify a signature

Notice of deficiency   A letter sent by the IRS notifying a taxpayer of the amount of money owed

Notice to show cause   A written document in a lawsuit asking a court to rule on a matter

Objection   A formal protest made by a lawyer in a lawsuit

Offer   The presentment of terms, which, if accepted, may lead to the formation of a contract

Office examination   A tax audit conducted at a regional IRS office

Opinion letter   A written analysis of a client's case prepared by a lawyer

Option   An agreement giving one party the right to choose a certain course of action

Oral contract   An enforceable verbal agreement

Order of execution   A court order enabling a creditor to seize property of a debtor to satisfy a judgment

Pain and suffering   A form of compensable injury

Parol evidence   Oral evidence introduced at a trial to alter or explain the terms of a written contract

Partnership   A voluntary association between two or more competent persons engaged in a business as co-owners for profit

Party   A plaintiff or defendant in a lawsuit

Perjury   Committing false testimony while under oath

Plaintiff   A party who commences a lawsuit

Pleading   A written document which states facts or arguments of a party in a lawsuit

Power of attorney   A document executed by one party authorizing another to act on his behalf in specified situations

Pre-trial discovery   Legal procedures used to gather information of an opponent before the trial

Private letter ruling   An informal statement provided by the IRS at a taxpayer's request which reflects the IRS position on a particular issue

Process server   An individual who delivers the summons and/or complaint to the defendant

Product disparagement   False statements or depictions about the quality, condition, or capability of another's product

Product liability   A type of lawsuit arising when a person is injured by a defective product

Promissory note   A written acknowledgment of a debt whereby one party agrees to pay a specified sum on a specified date

Proof   Evidence presented at a trial which is used by a judge or jury to fashion an award

Punitive damages   Money awarded as punishment for a party's wrongful acts

Quantum meruit   A legal principle where a court awards reasonable compensation to a party who performs work, labor, or services at another party's request; also referred to as unjust enrichment

Reasonable reliance   One of the elements required to prove misrepresentation

Rebuttal   The opportunity for a lawyer at a trial to ask his client or witness additional questions to clarify points elicited by the opposing lawyer during cross-examination

Release   A written document which, when signed, relinquishes a party's rights to enforce a claim against another

Replevin   A type of lawsuit where one party attempts to recover personal property unlawfully held by another

Reply   A written document in a lawsuit which is the plaintiff's answer to the defendant's counterclaim

Restrictive covenant   A provision in a contract which forbids one party from doing a certain act; e.g., working for another or soliciting customers, etc.

Retainer   A sum of money paid to a lawyer for services to be rendered

Sales puffery   Statements of a general nature made by a salesperson which the customer is not expected to accept at face value

Service bureau   A company that processes data

Service letter statutes   Laws in some states that require an employer to furnish an employee with written reasons of his discharge

Sex harassment   Prohibited conduct of a sexual nature which occurs in the workplace

Slander   Oral defamation of a party's reputation

Small Claims Court   A particular court which presides over small disputes (e.g., not exceeding $1,500)

Software   A computer program

Sole proprietorship   An unincorporated business

Statement of fact   Remarks or comments of a specific nature that have a legal effect

Statute   A law created by an administrative body

Statute of frauds   A legal principle requiring certain contracts to be in writing to be enforceable

Statute of Limitations   A legal principle which requires a party to commence a lawsuit within a certain period of time

Stipulation   An agreement between lawyers

Subchapter S Corporation A hybrid corporation having attributes of both a corporation and a partnership

Submission agreement A signed agreement where both parties agree to submit a present dispute to binding arbitration

Subpoena A written order demanding a party or witness to appear at a legal proceeding; a subpoena *duces tacum* is a written order demanding a party to bring books and records to the legal proceeding

Summation The last part of a trial where both lawyers recap the respective positions of their clients

Summons A written document served upon the defendant which notifies him of a lawsuit

Surety A party who agrees to answer for the debt of another

Tax audit An IRS investigation of a party's affairs to determine the amount of tax due

Tax court A particular court which presides over tax disputes

Tax shelter An entity created to minimize taxes

Testimony Oral evidence presented by a witness under oath

Tort A civil wrong

Trespass A legal cause of action which arises when one party comes or remains on the property of another without permission

Time Is of the Essence A legal expression often included in agreements to specify the requirement of timeliness

Unfair and deceptive practice Illegal business and trade acts prohibited by various federal and state laws

Unfair discharge An employee's termination without legal justification

Verdict The decision of a judge or jury

Void Legally without merit

Waiver A written document which, when signed, relinquishes a party's rights

Warranty A factual statement made by a seller, either orally, in writing, by samples, models, etc., regarding the capabilities or qualities of a product or service

Whistleblowing Protected conduct where one party complains about the illegal acts of another

Witness A person who testifies at a judicial proceeding

Workers' Compensation A process where an employee receives compensation for his/her injuries

Bibliography

Coulson, Robert. *Business Arbitration—What You Need to Know.* New York: American Arbitration Association, 1980.

———. *The Termination Handbook.* New York: The Free Press, 1981.

Eagen, James. *How to Enforce Your Tenant's Rights without a Lawyer.* New York: Justin Publications, Inc., 1978.

Farmer, Robert A., et al. *How to Collect on Personal Injuries.* New York: Arco Publishing Company, Inc., 1967.

Gillers, Stephen. *The Rights of Lawyers and Clients.* New York: Avon Books, 1979.

Guinther, John. *Winning Your Personal Injury Suit.* Garden City, NY: Anchor Press/Doubleday, 1980.

Kass, Louis A. *Necessary Elements of Common Legal Actions.* Binghamton, NY: Gould Publications, 1978.

Larson, E. Richard. *Sue Your Boss.* New York: Farrar, Straus & Giroux, Inc., 1981.

Margolius, Sidney. *The Innocent Consumer* vs. *The Exploiters.* New York: Trident Press, 1967.

Marks, Burton and Gerald Goldfarb. *Winning with Your Lawyer.* New York: McGraw-Hill Book Company, 1980.

McCulloch, Kenneth. *Selecting Employees Safely under the Law.* Englewood Cliffs, NJ: Prentice-Hall, Inc., 1981.

Miller, Saul. *Super Traveler.* New York: Holt, Rinehart, & Winston, 1980.

Miller, Vernon X. *What Some People Ought to Know about Personal Injury Law.* New York: Vantage Press, 1978.

Morris, James E. *You Can Win Big in Small Claims Court.* New York: Rawson, Wade Publishers, Inc., 1981.

O'Neill, Robert. *The Rights of Government Employees.* New York: Avon Books, 1978.

Peres, Richard. *Dealing with Employment Discrimination.* New York: McGraw-Hill Book Company, 1978.

Pomroy, Martha. *What Every Woman Needs to Know about the Law.* Garden City, NY: Doubleday & Company, 1980.

Rather, Lillian. *Franchising—Today's Legal and Business Problems.* New York: Practicing Law Institute, 1970.

Ross, H. Lawrence. *Settled Out of Court.* New York: Aldine Publishing Company, 1980.

Ross, Martin J. *Handbook of Everyday Law.* Greenwich, CT: Fawcett Publications, Inc., 1967.

Sack, Steven Mitchell and Howard Jay Steinberg. *The Salesperson's Legal Guide.* Englewood Cliffs, NJ: Prentice-Hall, Inc., 1981.

Walker, Glen. *Credit Where Credit Is Due.* New York: Holt, Rinehart, & Winston, 1979.

Warner, Ralph. *Everybody's Guide to Small Claims Court.* Reading, MA: Addison-Wesley Publishing Co., 1980.

INDEX

A

Absences from work, 21
Accidents, 208–231
  children and, 226
  color photographs after, 210,
    213
  on common carriers, 229–230
  with consumer products, 219–
    221
  damage documentation for,
    213–215
  diary for, 215–216
  doctor visits after, 210–212
  early settlement of claims for,
    215
  at home, 224–226
  insurance companies and, 211–
    212
  insurance company detectives
    and, 215
  lawyers and, 213, 230–231
  on-the-job, 227–229
  proving liability for, 216–230
  requesting help after, 212–213
  witnesses to, 219, 223, 227
  (*See also* Automobile accidents;
    Injuries; Insurance compa-
    nies; Shopping-related acci-
    dents)
Advances, 27–28

Advertising, false and misleading:
  for computers, 194, 205
  for employment positions, 15–17
  for franchises, 149–150
Age discrimination, 53–56
  in hiring, 9
  in promotion, transfer and firing decisions, 12–13
Age Discrimination in Employment Act, 53, 106
American Arbitration Association, 288, 290, 292
  regional offices of, 301–302
Arbitration, 286–303
  advantages of, 289–290
  appeal of, 297–298
  arbitrators chosen for, 289–290, 292
  arrangements needed for, 299–300
  behavior and dress for, 300
  decisions reported in, 296–297
  Demand for, 291–292
  disadvantages of, 290–291
  enforcement of, 300
  evidence rules for, 288
  fact organization for, 298–299
  hearing procedure for, 295
  lawyers for, 290–291, 298
  mediation vs., 300–301
  mutual written agreement needed for, 287–288
  opponent's case in, 299
  practice for, 300
  pre-hearing conferences in, 295
  state laws on, 303
  steps to hearing, summarized, 291–295
  submission agreement for, 288–289
  witness interviews for, 299
Arbitration Act, 289

Arrest records, employer's questions about, 10
Audits, of tax returns, 122, 124–133
  appeals process for, 130–133
  conduct at, 129
  criminal investigation and, 129
  items increasing probability of, 124–125
  notification of, 126–127
  preparation for, 127–128
  probability of, 124–126
  records and, 128
  types of, 126–127
Automobile accidents, 221–224
  with commercial vehicles, 223
  helping injured in, 222
  incriminating remarks in, 222
  information exchanged at, 222–223
  no-fault insurance and, 224
  police called for, 222
  remaining at scene in, 221
  seat belts and, 224
  site inspection for, 223
  Small Claims Court and, 275–276
  traffic obstruction from, 221
  witnesses to, 223
Automobiles (see Car repairs; Lemons; Used cars)

B

Benefits, employment, termination and, 97, 104–107
Better Business Bureau (BBB), 16, 17, 166
Bonuses, 25–27
  contract provisions for, 26
  gratuitous, 26
  pre-hiring discussion of, 19
  prorated, 19, 26
  termination and, 104

Building contractors, 165–174
  common illegal practices of, 167–168
  contracts with, 168–169
  formal complaints against, 172–174
  after job completion, 171–174
  during job, 169–171
  on-the-job accidents and, 226, 228
  licensing of, 166
  references from, 167
  releases from, 171
  written estimates from, 167
Business Arbitration: What You Need to Know (Coulson), 298–300

C

Car repairs, 183–184
  description of problem for, 183–184
  parts retrieval in, 184
  recommendations for, 183
  specialty shops for, 184
  written estimates for, 184
Career counselors (*see* Employment agencies, career counselors, and search firms)
Citizenship, employer's questions about, 9
Civil Liberties Union, 13
Civil Rights Act, 60
Civil service employment:
  arrest record and, 11
  fingerprinting in, 33
  residency requirements for, 33
Claims Court, 131–133
Collection agencies, 305–317
  credit rating and, 305
  debt verification and, 310–311
  fees of, 305, 309
  getting rid of, 312–313
  location attempts by, 309–310

nationwide impact of, 306
ornamented letters from, 308
remedies for abuses by, 313–314
steps summarized for, 315–316
suits against, 306, 313–314
tactics of, 306
(*See also* Fair Debt Collection Practices Act)
Commissions:
  advances on, 27–28
  pre-hiring discussion of, 19
Common carriers, accidents on, 229–230
Computer software:
  custom vs. packaged, 197
  legal points in purchase of, 197–199
  liability for, 199
  payment for, 198
  restrictions on, 198–199
  revisions of, 198
  service bureaus and, 203–204
  specifications and functions of, 198
Computers, 193–206
  consultants for, 196
  delivery dates for, 201
  desirable features of, 200
  disclaimer clauses for, 201, 206
  geographic restrictions on, 200
  hardware in, 199–201
  installation clauses and, 200
  misrepresentation of, 194, 205
  negotiating prices for, 206
  operating manuals for, 197
  payment for, 200, 206
  preliminary investigation of, 195–197
  salespeople for, 196
  security in, 203, 206
  shipping of, 200–201
  training for, 201
  (*See also* Service bureaus)

Consumer products, accidents
   with, 219–221
Contracts:
   with building contractors, 168–
      169
   for computers, 200–201, 205–206
   for computer software, 198–199
   disclaimers in, 201, 206
   with service bureaus, 203–204
   for used-car purchases, 179
   (*See also* Employment contracts)
Coulson, Robert, 298–300
Council of Better Business Bureaus, 16
Covenants not to compete, 22–24
Credit checks:
   of employers, 6, 16
   of job applicants, 12
Criminal convictions, employer's
   questions about, 10, 11

D

Defamation, lie detector tests and,
   36
Direct Mail Marketing Association,
   178
Disciplinary proceedings, em-
   ployee representation at, 4
Disclaimers, 201, 206
District Court, 131–133
Doctors, post-accident visits to,
   210–222

E

Employees:
   access to records by, 4, 50
   federal laws in support of, 116–
      117
   files on, 50, 100
   interrogations of, 49–50
   lie detector tests administered
      to, 35–46
   privacy rights of, 35–51
   searches of, 46–48
   termination of (*see* Termination
      of employment)
   unions and, 51–52
   wiretapping and eavesdropping
      of, 51
Employer-employee relationship:
   discipline in, 4
   fixed term for, 29–30
   hiring phase in, 5–34
   legal trends in, 4, 22, 34–35
   letter agreement as basis of, 30–
      33
   pre-hiring discussion about, 18–
      20
   sex harassment in, 4
   steps summarized for, 94–95
   Workmen's Compensation and,
      227–229
   (*See also* Employment discrimi-
      nation; Termination of em-
      ployment)
Employers:
   credit checks conducted by,
      12
   employee's pre-hiring investiga-
      tion of, 6–7, 16
   inspecting records of, 6–7, 27
Employment agencies, career
      counselors, and search firms,
      186–192
   agreements with, 187–188
   differences among, 186–187
   New York law on, 189
   prepayment to, 188–189
Employment contracts, 21–25
   absence of, 22, 29–33
   advances covered in, 27–28
   firings and, 98
   negotiation of, 18–20
   restrictive covenants in, 22–24,
      114
   term of, 28–29

Employment discrimination, 52–68
  age as basis for, 9, 12, 13, 53–56
  EEOC complaints and, 62–65
  handicaps as basis for, 10, 11–
    12, 61
  lawyer's role in, 15
  pre-employment inquiries and,
    7–15
  race as basis for, 9, 60–61
  religion as basis for, 61–62
  sex as basis for, 56–60
  by small employers, 63
Equal Employment Opportunity
    Act, 52, 60, 90
Equal Employment Opportunity
    Commission (EEOC), 9–10,
    13, 15, 46, 52–55, 61–68, 87,
    98
  complaints filed with, 62–65
  offices of, 65–68
Equal Pay Act, 56

F

Fair Credit Reporting Act, 12
Fair Debt Collection Practices Act,
    306–314
  exceptions to, 307–308
  restricted activities under, 308–
    309
  small debts and, 313
Federal Trade Commission (FTC),
    153
  on debt collection, 305, 310, 314,
    316–317
  job misrepresentation and, 16,
    17
  mail fraud and, 177
Fingerprinting, as condition of
    employment, 33
Fixed employment terms, 29–30
Franchises, 149–154
  analysis of deal for, 151–153
  investigation of, 150–151

  misleading advertisements for,
    149–150
  professional advice on, 153
  remedies for fraud with, 153–
    154
Fringe benefits, pre-hiring discus-
    sion of, 19

G

Guaranteed earnings claims, 16
*Guide to Record Retention Require-
    ments,* 139

H

Handicap discrimination, 10, 11–
    12, 61
Hiring, 5–34
  discussing employment terms
    in, 18–20
  illegal inquiries in, 7–15
  investigating employers prior
    to, 6–7, 16
  job misrepresentation in, 15–17
Home improvements, 165–174
  dissatisfaction with, 170–174
  (*See also* Building contractors)
Homeowners' insurance, 225
Human Rights Commission, 13

I

Ideas, protection of, 20, 23, 91–94
  sample agreement for, 92–93
Injuries, 210–231
  assets of injurer and, 230
  claim settlement for, 252–253
  discussion of, 213
  faking of, 211
  from faulty products, 219–221
  insurance company medical
    examinations of, 216
  liability for, 216–230

Injuries (*cont.*):
  on-the-job, 227–229
  proof of, 210–213
Insurance adjusters, 211–213
Insurance companies, 211–212
  detectives hired by, 215
  medical examinations by, 216
Internal Revenue Service (IRS),
    122–138
  appeals process and, 130–133
  delinquent accounts and, 138
  informants paid by, 138
  installment payments to, 138
  manuals used by, 127–128
  Notice of Deficiency (ninety-day
    letter) from, 130
  private letter rulings from, 133
  Special Agents of, 129
  tax shelters and, 145–146
  (*See also* Audits, of tax returns;
    Tax deductions; Taxes; Tax
    returns
Inventions, employer's vs. em-
    ployee's rights to, 20, 23, 91–
    94
Investments:
  "Ten Commandments" for, 148
  (*See also* Real estate purchases;
    Tax shelters)

J

Job applicants:
  illegal inquiries of, 7–15
  potential employer investigated
    by, 6–7
Job misrepresentation, 15–17
  legal protection against, 17
Job relocation:
  post-employment inquiries and,
    12–13
  pre-hiring discussion about,
    19

L

Lawyers, 232–258
  accident claims and, 213, 230–
    231
  accident settlements and, 230
  advertising by, 236
  appeals and, 255–257
  arbitration and, 290–291, 298
  associates and, 242
  availability of, 250
  bar associations and, 236
  case appraisal by, 237–241
  change of, 253–255
  choice of, 235–236
  for collection agency abuses, 314
  conflicts of interest and, 251
  correspondence copies from,
    249
  employment contracts examined
    by, 24, 25
  employment scheme victims
    represented by, 17
  evaluation of, 241–243
  frequent causes of disputes
    with, 233
  funds handled by, 251–252
  initial interview with, 236–252
  job discrimination advice sought
    from, 15
  lie detector use challenged by,
    45
  malpractice by, 254
  need for, 231, 234
  opinion letters from, 238–241
  practical training of, 242
  procrastination by, 250–251
  product liability cases and, 221
  for real estate purchases, 159
  recommendations for, 235–236
  reputation of, 242
  settlements and, 252–253
  specialty areas of, 235
  steps summarized for, 257–258

Lawyers (*cont.*):
  valuable ideas and, 94
  at Workers' Compensation hear-
    ings, 227–228
Lawyers' fees, 243–250
  for arbitration, 289
  arrangements compared, 248
  billing of, 249
  contingency, 246–248
  deductibility of, 249–250
  documentation of, 249–250
  flat, 244
  flat, plus time, 244–245
  hourly rate for, 245–246
  payment of, 248–249
  retainer agreements for, 244–
    245, 247–248, 251, 256
Legal Aid, 17
Lemons (defective new automo-
    biles), 184–185
Letters (sample):
  as agreement on employment
    terms, 30–33
  to building contractors, 170–171
  to collection agency, 311–313
  to commence used-car abuse
    investigation, 182
  of complaint, against building
    contractors, 173–174
  of complaint, against collection
    agency, 316–317
  of complaint, against employment
    agency, 191–192
  of complaint, against real estate
    brokers, 164–165
  demand, 265, 277–278
  to employment agency, 190–191
  for idea protection, 93–94
  on illegal hiring practices, 14–15
  against inaccurate references,
    106
  on lawyer fee arrangements,
    244–245, 247–248, 256
  on lie detector test results, 44

for mail fraud, 176–177
  of opinion, from lawyers, 238–
    241
  to real estate brokers, 162–163
  to request discharge informa-
    tion, 99
  of resignation, 113
  of severance agreements, 107–
    111
  on sex harassment, 59–60
  on smoke-free environment, 88–
    91
  to used-car dealers, 180–181
Lie detector tests, 35–46
  in collective bargaining agree-
    ments, 43
  examining results of, 43–44
  misinterpretation and error in,
    43
  state regulation of, 36–42
Limitation of liability clauses, 201,
    206

M

Mail fraud, 174–178
  unordered merchandise and,
    177
  unsolicited mail as, 178
Mail order transactions, 175–177
Marital status, employer's ques-
    tions about, 10, 12–13
Maternity leave, 97–98
Mediation, 300–301
Medical conditions, discrimination
    based on, 10, 11–12, 61
Merit Board, 87
Merit raises, 19
Mitigation of damages, 22, 111

N

National Association of Realtors
    (NAR), 161–165

National Labor Relations Act, 51
National origin, employer's questions about, 9
New York State, employment agency abuses illegal in, 189
No-fault insurance, 224

O

Occupational Safety and Health Act, 69–70
Occupational Safety and Health Administration (OSHA), 69–86, 90
   regional offices of, 71–86
Opinion letters, 238–241

P

Personnel records, access to, 4, 50
Physical examinations, pre-employment, 11, 19
Post-termination benefits, 98, 100, 103–107
Postal Service, U.S.:
   Inspection Service of, 176–177
   job misrepresentation and, 17
Power of attorney, 129
Pre-employment inquiries, illegal, 7–15
   confronting employer about, 13
   formal challenges to, 13–15
Privacy Act, 12
Products liability, 219–221
Progress payment schedules, 198
Promotions:
   post-employment inquiries and, 12–13
   pre-hiring discussion of, 19

R

Racial discrimination, 9, 60–61
Raises, 19

Real estate brokers, 159–165
   apartments and, 165
   complaints against, 163–165
   interviews of, 162
   NAR and, 161–162
   salespeople vs., 163
Real estate purchases, 154–165
   binders for, 160–161
   developer investigated for, 157–158
   documentation for, 156–157
   "free inducement offers" for, 156
   land investigation for, 158–159, 163
   promotions and advertisements for, 154–156
   Property Report for, 157
   "rush game" for, 156
Rehabilitation Act, 61
Relatives, employer's questions about, 9
Religion, employer's questions about, 10, 11
Religious discrimination, 61–62
Residence statutes, 33
Rest periods, 21
Restrictive covenants, 22–24

S

Safety and health in workplace, 20, 68–91
   (See also Workers' Compensation)
Salary:
   advances as, 27
   pre-hiring discussion of, 18, 19
Search firms (see Employment agencies, career counselors, and search firms)
Service bureaus, 201–204
   advantages and disadvantages of, 202
   fees of, 204

Service bureaus (*cont.*):
  function of, 201–204
  important points for, 202–203
  record retention and recovery
      in, 203
  software rights and, 203–204
Service letter statutes, 99–100
Settlement of claims, 215, 230,
      252–253, 266, 273
Severance pay, 104
Sex discrimination, 56–60
Sex harassment, 4, 58–60
Shopping-related accidents, 216–
      219
  area inspected for, 219
  cause documented for, 218–219
  proof of liability for, 217
  reporting of, 219
  slip and fall as, 217–219
  witnesses of, 219
Small Claims Court, 114, 259–285
  affidavits, statements and tele-
      phone testimony in, 269
  appeal of decisions in, 272–273
  for assault and battery cases,
      283–284
  automobile accident cases in,
      275–276
  for bailment cases, 279–280
  car repairs and, 184
  claim estimates for, 263–264
  claim validity and, 262–263, 274
  for consumer product pur-
      chases, 276–278
  continuance requests in, 267–268
  corporate defendant name in,
      264–265
  counterclaims in, 266, 273
  default judgments in, 267, 271
  defendant strategies in, 273
  demand letters and, 265, 277–
      278
  denial by defendant in, 266–
      267, 273

documents needed for, 270
effectiveness of, 261
employment agencies and, 192
filing claims in, 264–266
for goods sold and delivered
      cases, 282
for improper work, labor, or
      service, 278–279
for insurance policy cases, 281
judgment collection in, 272
judgments in, 271–272
legal advice for, 269
for loan cases, 283
money limit in, 262
moving party duties in, 267–
      268
names for, 261
organization of facts for, 269
possible uses of, 260
procedural points for, 272–273
selection of, 263
settlement offers and, 266, 273
steps summarized for, 284–285
subpoenas in, 268–269
summonses served in, 265–266
trial in, 269–271
used-car abuses and, 181, 183
witnesses in, 268–269
for wrongful taking cases, 279–
      280
Smoke-free environments, 68, 87–
      91
State laws:
  on advances, 27
  on arbitration, 303
  on collection agencies, 314
  on franchises, 153
  on hired-at-will employment, 22
  on "lemons" (defective new
      automobiles), 184–185
  on lie detector tests, 36–42
  on pre-employment inquiries,
      13
Subrogation, 228–229, 231

T

Tax Court, 131–133
Tax deductions:
    for auto use, 134
    for business gifts, 134–135
    for convention and seminar
        expenses, 136–137
    for meals and entertainment,
        137–138
    for parties, 135
    for travel expenses, 136
    (See also Audits, of tax returns;
        Tax shelters)
Tax Equity and Fiscal Responsibil-
    ity Act, 132
Tax returns, 122–126
    filing extensions for, 122–123
    IRS review of, 123–124
    (See also Audits, of tax returns)
Tax shelters, 144–147
    appropriateness of, 147
    business risk of, 145–146
    IRS and, 145–146
    losses from, 147
    operation of, 144–145
    professional advice needed for,
        146–147
    prospectus for, 146–147
    reputable sponsors and general
        partners for, 146
    tax risk of, 146
Taxes, 122–142
    appeals process for, 130–133
    court action concerning, 130–
        133
    record retention times for, 138–
        142
    (See also Audits, of tax returns;
        Internal Revenue Service;
        Tax deductions; Tax re-
        turns)
Termination of employment, 29–
    30, 95–116
    for absence, 97

    for cause, 29–30
    contracts and, 98
    cover story for, 105–106
    to deny benefits, 97
    firing as, 98–112
    fixed employment term and, 29
    job search following, 111–112
    for maternity leave, 97–98
    post-employment inquiries and,
        12–13
    resignation as, 112–115
    response to, 98–103
    settlement deals and, 98, 100,
        103–107
    steps summarized for, 116
    unfair discharge as, 95–98
Time clock regulations, 21

U

Unemployment benefits, 111
    lie detector tests and, 46
Uniform Deceptive Trade Practices
    Act, 17
Unions, 51–52
Used cars, 178–183
    bought from private individuals,
        183
    contracts for, 179
    dealers and salespeople for,
        178–182
    inspection of, 178
    mechanical problems with, 180

W

Wages (see Salary)
Waivers, for lie detector use, 43
Warranties, 205
Whistleblowing, 96
Workers' Compensation, 86–87,
    91, 97, 227–229
    documentation for, 227
    home accidents and, 225
    independent contractors and,
        228

About the Author

Steven Mitchell Sack is a practicing lawyer, author, lecturer, and disseminator of the law in a variety of media.

Mr. Sack is a Phi Beta Kappa graduate of Boston College Law School. He is a member of the American Bar Association, New York County Lawyers' Association, and is admitted to practice before the United States Tax Court.

In addition to conducting a private law practice in New York City, Mr. Sack serves as General Counsel for many business organizations and companies, and serves as a commercial arbitrator for the American Arbitration Association.

He is the co-author of *The Salesperson's Legal Guide*, he creates legal training films and newsletters, and conducts nationwide corporate seminars with the American Management Association. Mr. Sack lives in Manhattan and teaches family law to college students in his spare time.